Ocean Warrior

MY BATTLE TO END THE ILLEGAL SLAUGHTER ON THE HIGH SEAS

Paul Watson

KEY PORTER BOOKS

*To Lisa, the true love of my life, whose wisdom has inspired me
with the passion and the desire to fight for the living earth.*

Canadian Cataloguing in Publication Data

Watson, Paul
    Ocean warrior: my battle to end the slaughter on the high seas

ISBN 1-55013-569-4 (hardcover)
ISBN 1-55013-599-6 (paperback)

1. Watson, Paul. 2. Wildlife conservation.
3. Marine mammals. 4. Marine fishes.
5. Fisheries. 6. Conservationists — British
Columbia — Biography. I. Title.

QL31.W3A3 1994   333.95'9   C94-931240-1

The publisher acknowledges the financial assistance of the Department of
Communications, the Canada Council and the Ontario Arts Council.

Key Porter Books Limited
70 The Esplanade
Toronto, Ontario
Canada M5E 1R2

In Canada, to contact Captain Paul Watson for information on joining his crew,
or becoming a Sea Shepherd Supporter, please write to: The Sea Shepherd
Conservation Society, P.O. Box 48446, Vancouver, B.C., V7X 1A2.

In the United States, to contact Captain Paul Watson for information on joining
his crew, or becoming a Sea Shepherd Supporter, please write to: The Sea Shepherd
Conservation Society, P.O. Box 628, Venice, California, 90294.

Typesetting: MacTrix DTP
Design: Peter Maher
Printed and bound in Canada

96 97 98 99 6 5 4 3 2 1

Contents

Whom when I asked from what place he came,
And how he hight, himselfe he did ycleepe,
The Shepheard of the Ocean by Name,
And said he came far from the main-sea deepe.

Edmund Spenser
Colin Clouts Come Home Againe

Foreword

The last three decades of this century have witnessed the eruption of the most significant internal conflict ever to engage the human species. It is not the struggle between capitalism and communism or between any other set of "isms." It is not the contest between affluent societies and impoverished ones. It is not the conflict between warmongers and peaceniks.

It is the conflict between those who possess the means and the will to exploit the living world to destruction and those who are banding together in a desperate, last-ditch attempt to prevent the New Juggernaut from trashing our small planet.

If the right side wins, this combat may become known to future generations as the Crusade that Saved the Earth. If the wrong side wins — there will *be* no future generations.

The struggle is an unequal one. The big battalions belong to and are commanded by some of the most powerful individuals and cabals history has ever recorded. Their battle cry is "Progress!" Their arsenals are supplied by Commerce and Industry. Their most fearsome weapon is Technology. Science is their supportive theology. Politics is their handmaiden.

They are now effectively the masters of our species. They believe they can and will become masters of the planet, if not the universe. They purport to believe their dominance is benign. "What's good for General Motors is good for the world" is a thesis to which they give vigorous support.

Because it is so dominant, and because it also controls most means of communication, this master class is all too well known to us. However, we know all too little about the forces that oppose it. These are so new and present such a confused and kaleidoscopic set of images that we bemusedly lump them into one amorphous aggregation which we vaguely refer to as the Environmental Movement.

This is not good enough. If we, the opposition, are to become united and effective in defence of animate creation, we need to know who *our* warriors are; what forces they command; what principles they espouse; and how they plan to prevent the living fabric which clothes this earth from being ripped asunder.

Amongst those who have taken it upon themselves to defend the living world against the forces which are well on their way to destroying it, one man stands out head and shoulders above the rest. Paul Watson comes close to being unique. This is a matter of relief to many so-called environmentalists who do not share Watson's dedication, or his courage, or the abilities which currently make him the most active defender of life on earth. It is, however, a matter of deep distress to those who comprehend the truly dire situation which now obtains. Ten thousand Paul Watsons would not be too many to do the job that must be done. But since there is but one, we must be as supportive of him as if life on earth depended on the crusade he represents . . . as it very well may do!

I have watched Paul's progress for almost two decades — watched with growing admiration (and not a little envy) as he committed himself heart, soul and body to the defence of the living planet.

His cause has been my cause for a great many years.

Almost all young children have a natural affinity for other animals, an attitude which seems to be endemic in young creatures of whatever species. I was no exception. As a child I fearlessly and happily consorted with frogs, snakes, chickens, squirrels and whatever else came my way.

When I was a boy growing up on the Saskatchewan prairies, that feeling of affinity persisted — but it became perverted. Under my father's tutelage I was taught to be a hunter; taught that "communion with nature" could be achieved over the barrel of a gun; taught that killing wild animals for sport establishes a mystic bond, "an ancient pact" between them and us.

I learned first how to handle a BB gun, then a .22 rifle and finally a shotgun. With these I killed "vermin" — sparrows, gophers, crows and hawks. Having served that bloody apprenticeship, I began killing "game" — prairie chicken, ruffed grouse, and ducks. By the time I was fourteen, I had been fully indoctrinated with the sportsman's view of wildlife as objects to be exploited for pleasure.

Then I experienced a revelation.

On a November day in 1935, my father and I were crouched in a muddy pit at the edge of a prairie slough, waiting for daybreak.

The dawn, when it came at last, was grey and sombre. The sky lightened so imperceptibly that we could hardly detect the coming of the morning. We strained our eyes into swirling snow squalls. We flexed numb fingers in our shooting gloves.

And then the dawn was pierced by the sonorous cries of seemingly endless flocks of geese that came drifting, wraithlike, overhead. They were flying low that day. Snow Geese, startlingly white of breast, with jet-black wingtips, beat past while flocks of piebald wavies kept station on their flanks. An immense V of Canadas came close behind. As the rush of air through their great pinions sounded in our ears, we jumped up and fired. The sound of the shots seemed puny, and was lost at once in that immensity of wind and wings.

One goose fell, appearing gigantic in the tenuous light as it spiralled sharply down. It struck the water a hundred yards from shore and I saw that it had only been winged. It swam off into the growing storm, its neck outstretched, calling . . . calling . . . calling after the fast-disappearing flock.

Driving home to Saskatoon that night I felt a sick repugnance for what we had done, but what was of far greater import, I was experiencing a poignant but indefinable sense of loss. I felt, although I could not then have expressed it in words, as if I had glimpsed another and quite magical world — a world of oneness — and had been denied entry into it through my own stupidity.

I never hunted for sport again.

During the years that followed, I tried to find my way back to that moment when I first sensed a magical unity with other living beings, but I chose the wrong path. I set out to become a biologist. I did not realize that biology — the scientific study of life — would have been more accurately defined in those days as necrology — the study of death. For the pursuit of biological knowledge then entailed (and to a large extent still does) the *killing* of animals in order to study their physical mechanisms.

Until 1940 I spent much of my time "collecting" specimens for graduate biologists to study in their laboratories. It was all done using the most exemplary procedures, and for the highest possible purpose: the amassing of scientific knowledge. In my case, it mostly entailed killing birds and small mammals with traps and guns on a scale quite equal to the slaughter I had done as a sportsman.

After the Second World War, most of which I spent trying not to be killed by my fellow men (an experience which gave me considerable empathy with wild creatures), I tried to continue as a biologist, but the scales were falling from my eyes. In 1947 I went to the Arctic charged with studying caribou and wolves for the federal government. I was equipped with a small arsenal of guns, traps and ampoules of cyanide. My instructions required me to use these to collect as many wolves as I could find, together with several score caribou, and then to dissect them all in order to ascertain their food habits, growth rates, rates of sexual development, parasitology and other recondite matters of the flesh.

I was unable to adhere to these instructions because I experienced a second revelation shortly after my arrival in the North, this time under the tutelage of a man who was attuned to the living world as we can never be — an Inuit of an older time.

On an evening when the sun hovered above the horizon's lip I sat beside this man who was not of my race and watched a spectacle so overwhelming that I had no words for it.

Below us, on the undulating darkness of the tundra plains, the caribou were moving, a tide of life flowing out of the dim south to engulf the world, submerging it so that it seemed to sink beneath a living sea. The very air was heavy with the breath of life. There was a sound as of the earth breathing and moving. It was as if the inanimate crust of rock below us had been imbued with the essential spark.

The man beside me stretched his hands out to that living flood. He was no longer with me. He had gone from me into that all-embracing torrent. There was an ecstasy upon him as if his spirit had found union with the amorphous entity which was sweeping across his land.

Darkness had come full across the barrens. The shadows still held the faint murmur of ten thousand vital pulses beating with indomitable power on every side. Although it was too dark to see, I knew he had turned towards me. He spoke, and his words might have been an echo of the divided voice of the visitation I had witnessed.

"*Tuktu-mie!* This is the world's heart's blood."

During the rest of that Arctic sojourn I abandoned the blinkers of science and struggled instead to fathom the nature of the interspecies empathy and understanding which existed between the Inuit and the other creatures of the barrenlands. I strove to leap over, or crawl under (it hardly mattered which), the barriers my own kind has erected between us and our non-human fellows. By the end of my second year in the land I had come to realize just how far modern men have distanced themselves from the world that gave us birth. And I remembered reading one of Rudyard Kipling's stories in which Baloo, a wise old bear, tells the human child, Mowgli (who has been adopted in the jungle world by wolves), "We be of one blood, ye and I." I had felt that this was true when I read it at the age of eight or nine. Now I know it to be true, and I became more and more anxious to bridge the abyss that yawned between.

When the 1960s began I was living in the remote Newfoundland outport of Burgeo. And there I had still another revelation.

During the early spring of 1967 a 70-foot female fin whale became trapped in a saltwater lagoon close to the settlement. By the time I heard about her presence she had become the target of a dozen or so rifle-wielding sportsmen shooting steel-jacketed bullets into her.

Not all those who knew about the whale wanted her dead. In fact as the days went on it began to appear that not only would she be permitted to survive but eventually she would be returned to her own aquatic world.

Meantime I spent days with her, in a small dory accompanied by a fisherman friend. Once she surfaced 50 feet from the dory, thrusting her forebody out of the calm waters. The gigantic head appeared to rear directly over us, like a living cliff. This might have been a moment of terror, but I felt no fear, even when she altered course so that one Cyclopean orb looked directly at us. She had deliberately emerged from her own element as far as she could in order to see us in ours, and although her purpose was inscrutable, I knew it was not inimical.

She submerged, and, a few seconds later, I heard her voice — a throbbing, sonorous moan with unearthly overtones almost more felt than heard. It was a voice not of our world.

When the whale had gone, my fisherman friend turned and looked at me with an anxious and questioning gaze.

"That whale . . . sure, she spoke to we! I t'inks she *spoke* to we!"

I nodded, for I believed then, and always will, that she had purposefully tried to span the abyss between our species, if only to acknowledge that she knew we were on her side. So long as I live I shall hear the echoes of that haunting voice, and they will continue to remind me that life *itself* — not *human* life — is the ultimate miracle upon this earth, and that all of life reaches out to all of life.

In the end we could not save her. The bullet wounds, which in my ignorance I had thought might have meant no more to her than flea bites, gave rise to massive and virulent infections from which, one night, she died.

That evening I climbed to the lonely summit of a cliff overlooking the place where she lay dead. I sat there for a long time, locked in the confines of my mind and savouring the bitter taste of defeat. Then, slowly, I became conscious of the eternal sounding of the sea and my thoughts drifted away from myself and the world of man and his machines, turning outward to the world of whales.

It was full dark by then, and there was no one to know that I was weeping, not for the whale alone, but because the fragile link between her kind and mine was gone.

I wept because I knew that this fleeting opportunity to bridge, no matter how tenuously, the gulf that is increasingly isolating mankind from the totality of life had perished in a welter of human stupidity and ignorance — some part of which was mine.

The death of the fin whale radically changed my life. I had now to accept and learn to live with the bleak knowledge that I was a member of the most lethal, murderous and unnatural species ever to run riot on earth, which left me no choice but to become a full-fledged member of the conspiracy to save the planet.

Since 1967, I have served the cause as propagandist and preacher. In those roles I have written several books and scores of shorter pieces in defence of nature and in explanation of man's true place in nature. I have been a spokesman for the other beings who have no voice in how we treat them. My efforts have not been entirely ignored. I have been sued by Canada's largest "conservation" organization, a consortium of hunters and fishermen calling itself the Canadian Wildlife Federation. I have even been denied entry to the ultimate citadel of the Masters — the United States of America — because some of the environmental causes I have espoused are considered subversive there.

In 1984 I made what I think may be my most useful contribution, a book called *Sea of Slaughter*. It details five centuries of human destruction of life on the Atlantic seaboard. Its epilogue sums up what I believe to be the truth about the works of modern man, and the future of life on earth.

I sit at the window of my home beside the Atlantic Ocean. This task is almost done. Having led me through so many dark and bloody chronicles, this book comes to its end. The question with which it began is answered.

The living world is dying in our time.

I look out over the unquiet waters of the bay, south to the convergence of sea and sky beyond which the North Atlantic heaves against the eastern seaboard of the continent. And in my mind's eye I see it as it was before our coming.

Pod after pod of spouting whales, the great ones together with the lesser kinds, surge through waters everywhere a-ripple with living tides of fishes. Wheeling multitudes of gannets, kittiwakes and others such becloud the sky. The stony finger marking the end of the long beach below me is clustered with resting seals. The beach itself flickers with a restless drift of shorebirds as thick as blowing sand. In the bight of the bay, whose bottom is a metropolis of clams, mussels and lobsters, a concourse of massive heads emerges amongst floating islands of elder ducks. The walrus' tusks gleam like lambent flames . . . and then the vision fails.

And I behold the world as it is now. In all that vast expanse of sea and sky and fringing land, one gull soars in lonely flight — a single, drifting mote of life upon an enormous and an empty stage.

When our forebears commenced their exploitation of this continent they believed its animate resources were infinite and inexhaustible. The vulnerability of the living fabric which clothed the New World — the intricacy and fragility of its all-too-finite parts — was beyond their comprehension. So it can at least be said in their defence that they were mostly ignorant of the inevitable results of their dreadful depredations.

We who are alive today can claim no such exculpation for our biocidal actions and their dire consequences. Modern man now has every opportunity to be aware of the complexity and inter-relationships of the living world. If ignorance is to serve now as an excuse, then it can only be wilful, murderous ignorance.

The hideous results of five centuries of death-dealing on this continent are not to be gainsaid, but there are at least some indications that we may at last be developing the will, and the conscience, to look beyond our own immediate gratifications and desires. Belatedly, some part of mankind is trying to rejoin the community of living beings from which we have for so long a time been alienating ourselves — and of which we have for so long a time been the mortal enemy.

Evidence of such a return to sanity is not yet to be looked for in the attitudes and actions of the exploiters who dominate the human world. Rather, the emerging signs of sanity are seen in individuals who, revolted by the frightful excesses to which we have subjected animate creation, are beginning to reject the killer beast which man has become.

Banding together under the leadership of men like Paul Watson, they are challenging the self-granted licence of the vested interests to continue plundering and savaging the living world for policy, profit or pleasure. Although they are being furiously opposed by the old order, they may be slowly gaining ground.

It is to this new-found resolution to reassert our indivisibility with life, to recognize the obligations incumbent upon us as the most powerful and deadly species ever to exist, and to begin making amends for the havoc we have wrought, that my own hopes for a revival and continuance of life on earth now turn. If we persevere in this new way we may succeed in making man humane . . . at last.

FARLEY MOWAT

Preface

Margaret Mead, the anthropologist, once told me that I should never underestimate the power of the individual. "There has never been any positive social change initiated by governments or institutions," she said. "All progressive change has to come about because of the actions of individuals or small groups of individuals. Never believe that an individual does not have the power to change the world."

I intend to change the world. I believe, with Margaret Mead, that any single person can make a difference if he allows his passion to be expressed through action. My passion is the living Earth, especially her oceans. I am a conservationist, a protector of species and ecological systems, and a defender of the rights of nature.

I was raised by the sea in eastern Canada and, at an early age, ran off to be a sailor. I learned my trade on the decks of Scandinavian merchant vessels in a hundred exotic ports. In 1971, I sailed with a small group of activists to defend the environment from nuclear testing by the United States Atomic Energy Commission. We sailed with two ships, *Greenpeace* and *Greenpeace Too*. Although we didn't physically stop the detonation, we did publicize the issue and, in doing so, we created a new approach to solving problems. We created the Greenpeace Foundation, the first media-savvy environmental organization.

In 1973, my education as a warrior began when I served as a medic with the American Indian Movement during the occupation of Wounded Knee. We held the territory against the military might of the United States for 70 days, despite heavy gunfire and many casualties.

In 1977, after leading many Greenpeace campaigns, I left the Greenpeace Foundation. My experience with Greenpeace underscored Margaret Mead's belief that established institutions were not to be relied upon to bring about change. When Greenpeace was a collective of dedicated individuals it was an effective organization. Unfortunately, the collective became an institution and then a bureaucracy, and now it's part of the problem. I am critical of Greenpeace for reasons that will be clear to readers of this book. Sometimes I feel a bit like Dr. Frankenstein, having helped to create a green monster that is now totally out of control. Greenpeace exists now only to perpetuate itself.

I now give my energy and leadership to the Sea Shepherd Conservation Society, an organization dedicated to channeling the zeal of concerned individuals into direct-action campaigns that challenge those who illegally exploit marine wildlife.

For more than 20 years I have tried to make the world a little better for those who will inherit it. I have fought for the rights of indigenous peoples in North and South America. I have tracked elephant poachers in East Africa, saved wolves in the Yukon, defended bison in Montana, crusaded for the rain forests in Brazil and saved tens of thousands of trees in British Columbia. I have been both a strategist and a tactician for the environmental movement.

I have made friends and enemies. I cherish both. My enemies are a challenge, my friends a source of strength.

To some I am a hero. To others I am a pirate, a villain, even a terrorist. The qualities that make me appear heroic to some also make me appear piratical to others. All heroes have enemies; the greater the hero, the greater, stronger and more numerous the enemies. I look forward to cultivating many more enemies in my career on behalf of the Earth.

I am not alone. Lisa Distefano, my wife, is another who has shown courage and resolve in the fight for ecological justice. Many people who have gone to sea with me have also been champions of the whales, dolphins and other citizens of the ocean. I think of engineers Peter Woof, Carroll Vogel, Myra Finkelstein and Jeremy Coon; officers Neil Sanderson, Peter Brown, Rod Coronado and Susana Rodriguez Pastor; supporters Cleveland Amory, Edward Abbey, Steve Wynn, Pridim Singh, Susan Bloom, Lavinia Currier, Robert Hunter and Farley Mowat. There are many others.

In this book, I have tried to explain what motivates people like us to serve and protect the natural world. At the same time, I have tried to show the political, social and philosophical opposition that serious environmental activists encounter.

This book documents the oceanic campaigns I have led since 1979. Campaigns to protect terrestrial ecosystems and land species are not included. My history with Greenpeace has been documented in other books by other people and in my book (written with Warren Rogers) *Sea Shepherd*, published in 1982. I have also not included an account of my campaigns to protect the seals off Labrador and in the Gulf of St. Lawrence, a story worth a book of its own. This book is devoted to my campaigns on behalf of whales, dolphins and the victims of pelagic drift nets. It is a story of action in a cause to protect life and serve the Earth.

My campaigns and those of the Sea Shepherd Conservation Society have been less widely publicized than those of other groups, especially Greenpeace. This is at least partly because we have always devoted our resources to action rather than self-promotion. I hope to persuade readers of this book of something already known to the pirate whalers of Norway, the dolphin killers of Japan, the outlaw drift-netters of Taiwan and the pilot whale killers of the Faroe Islands: that the Sea Shepherd Conservation Society is the most aggressive, no-nonsense and determined conservation organization in the world.

1
Moby's Revenge

What I've dared, I've willed; and what I've willed, I'll do.

Captain Ahab

The crew quickly packed their bags and scurried down the gangway to the dock. I had given them only 10 minutes to make their decision: either stay with the ship and ram the whaler or pack your bags and leave. I had expected to lose a few but not this many. Thirteen of them stood on the pier. Chief engineer Peter Woof and third engineer Jerry Doran threw them their bags. Peter I never had any doubts about. Jerry was a welcome surprise.

Some of the crew on the pier were angry. Michael Louis, the carpenter, shouted to Peter, "Wake up man, he's a nut-case. We can't attack that ship. It's illegal. It's —"

"Shut up, you wanker." Peter was quick to anger. "You ain't doing anything, mate, you or any of the rest of you, so just shut the fuck up."

Alex Pacheco entered the wheelhouse. He was clearly upset. "Order me to stay, Paul, and I'll stay."

"I can't do that, Alex. It has to be your decision."

1

"But what will happen to us?"

"I can't say you won't be injured or even killed. There is a serious possibility of injury. Those bastards are armed. But I can guarantee you one thing. You'll go to jail here in Portugal, of that I am certain. We can't outrun the Portuguese Navy, and two of their ships are just over there."

"Are you ready to die? I don't know if I am."

I hadn't really thought of dying, but Alex's question drove the reality of the situation home. I felt my throat go dry. I looked at him. He was confused. He wanted to strike this blow but he was young, only 18. This was his first confrontation and I was taking him straight into hell.

"Alex, we've got it covered. I need a spokesperson on the dock who won't call us crazy if we don't make it. You know why we're doing this. Tell them. But damn it, Alex, we've got to shove off before the Portuguese notice, before that bastard captain escapes. We've chased her across the Atlantic. She's the target. We've got to take her out and we've got to do it now."

"I need time to think, Captain."

"There isn't any time. Alex, grab your stuff and leave the ship. Take some pictures."

"I don't know . . ."

"Alex, I will not order you to stay but I'm asking that you get on the dock."

He turned to leave. I stopped him. "Alex."

"Yes, Captain."

"Take care of yourself."

He smiled. "Good luck, Captain."

I leaned out the port-side window, ignoring the taunts of some of the crew. "Peter, start the engines. Jerry, make ready to let the lines go. We're out of here."

Peter looked up with a broad smile across his bushy-bearded face. "Aye, aye, Captain."

"Away the lines, Jerry."

I signalled slow astern on the telegraph. The engine started with a loud whine. Immediately her direct drive kicked into gear. The *Sea Shepherd* slowly backed away from the dock.

My throat still felt dry. I grabbed a bottle of warm beer and took a swig. It helped.

I was where I had placed myself. I had vowed to ram that outlaw whaler and ram her I would.

"Forget about yourself," I muttered to myself. "Think of the whales, think of the objectives, the goal." I picked up the VHF transmitter. "*Sierra, Sierra.*"

A thickly accented voice responded. "This is the *Sierra*."

"Goddamn you, you whale-killing son of a bitch, your career is going to end today."

"Who is this? What you want, eh?"

"Look outside and clear your decks. I've got you, you bastard. Prepare to be rammed. Repeat, I intend to ram you."

Captain Arvid Nordengen rushed out of the wheelhouse. I could see him, his mouth open in amazement. A seaman ran up beside him with a rifle. We were only 550 yards (500 m) away and coming straight at him at full speed. Dead in the water, he could do nothing. He was a sitting duck and completely at our mercy.

Peter rushed into the wheelhouse, panting from the exertion of running up from the bowels of the engine room.

"This I've got to see, mate. Jesus Christ, we're almost on her already. Where are you going to hit her?"

"A warning blow across the bow; let's take off her goddamn harpoon."

With one hand on the wheel, I snapped off a few pictures with my camera. We were looking into the horrified faces of a couple of dozen filthy-looking crew, all of whom were stunned into immobility.

"Here we go, boys!"

The ice-strengthened, concrete-reinforced bow of our 779-ton North Sea trawler connected with the bow of the 650-ton *Sierra*. We struck her just behind the gunner's platform and we kept on going. I heard the scream of twisted metal and I saw the whaler heel over to her starboard side, but the *Sea Shepherd* kept going like nothing had been in her way.

Within seconds, the bow of the whaler was to our stern and I was pulling the wheel hard to starboard to come around her for a second run. Looking back from the starboard side of the wheelhouse, I saw *Sierra* crew members pouring out of hatches like disturbed termites. The first strike had served its purpose. We had their full and undivided attention.

Peter dashed below to increase the speed to the maximum. The *Sea Shepherd* executed a 180-degree turn around the stern of the whaler and came full on at a slight angle towards her forward port side. I saw the man on the bridge with the rifle. He brought it to bear on me. I ignored him and pulled the wheel sharply to port.

We hardly felt the impact. From the wheelhouse I could see that we were practically on top of the whaler, pushing her far over to starboard as we ripped into her refrigerated cargo hold, exposing the whale meat in her frigid gut. We had torn a 7- by 10-foot (2- by 3-m) hole in the *Sierra*.

It all happened quickly but, strangely, everything seemed to be happening in slow motion. My ship pivoted off the whaler and our 1,600-horsepower engines drove full ahead. We slammed starboard-side into the weaker frame of the whaler, staving in about 45 feet (14 m) of her port-side hull and snapping her support beams. For a moment, the two ships came together and the space between myself and Captain Nordengen narrowed to only a few yards. He stood on his port bridge wing and I saw a mixture of terror, anger, hate and confusion in his bloodshot eyes.

He screamed something indecipherable at me in Norwegian.

I bellowed back, "This is for the whales, asshole."

The *Sea Shepherd* then lurched ahead, leaving the dazed whalers in our wake. I pulled the wheel hard over to port to hit her a third time from the other side.

Jerry ran up to the bridge "He's started his engines."

By the time I pulled her around, the *Sierra* had hustled away in the direction of the Portuguese naval ships. We set off in pursuit, but it quickly became obvious that we would not catch her before she reached the protection of the military. She was listing heavily to port, however, a sign that she was taking on water.

"Jerry, run down below and tell Peter we're heading out to sea, bound for England." I turned the ship around and headed out of the harbour, setting a course north.

Peter and Jerry came running up to the wheelhouse.

"We did it guys, we bloody well did!"

Peter was more sober. "We didn't sink her, goddamn it."

"We did what we could. It's not like we have a lot of experience ramming ships. But we did damage her. We sure as hell caused some damage."

Jerry suddenly looked worried. "Do you think we'll get away with this?"

Peter answered, "Looks good so far, mate."

We had struck the *Sierra*, the most notorious and despicable pirate whaler of them all. It felt good; it felt damn good. All three of us were elated, deliriously so. We broke out three more bottles of warm beer and Peter led us in a toast as we began our run for freedom.

"One of the bastards down. Let's get the rest!"

It was a beautiful day. The sun was hot, the waters were smooth and the forecast was promising. We should be able to make Britain in a few days. Most important, we should be able to reach Spanish waters in a few hours, getting us clear of Portuguese jurisdiction. In the lull after the ramming, it almost seemed possible that we would get away with it.

A full hour passed, and then a second. Our chances of escaping looked better all the time. Another hour passed and we were into the fourth, and the impossible outcome was becoming probable. And then, just eight miles (13 km) from Spanish territorial waters, a Portuguese destroyer came up on our stern, seemingly from nowhere.

"Jesus, look at that mother," yelled Jerry, turning a little pale. "Do they still torture prisoners here?"

"Just Yanks, I think," answered Peter, as he hustled off back to his engine room.

Jerry came running into the wheelhouse. "Paul, look, put me in a large box and toss me off with a load of galley garbage. I'll swim to shore. Christ, I don't need to get tortured."

"Jerry, calm down. We're 20 miles [32 km] off shore."

"I can swim. Better 20 miles than the torture chamber."

"No one's going to torture you. Besides, that there destroyer will cut you into little pieces with her props if you jump off now."

"So, what do we do?"

"Nothing. We wait to see what they intend to do. Run down and tell Peter to give us more speed. Maybe we can still make Spanish waters."

With little hesitation, Jerry turned and raced down to the engine room five decks below.

It didn't take long for the Portuguese to take action. The destroyer's captain brought his ship up a hundred yards off our starboard side.

The radio crackled. "*Sea Shepherd, Sea Shepherd*, please stop your engines."

Peter re-entered the wheelhouse, appearing angry and agitated.

"That son of a bitch tried to stab me."

"What are you talking about?"

"Doran. He told me to go faster. I told him we were going as fast as we could. He said you ordered me to go faster. I told him to fuck off and he pulled out a pocket knife and accused me of mutiny. I told him he wouldn't be able to stab me through my life jacket, so he put his knife away. The guy's bonkers."

"Nah, he just watches too much television."

Jerry returned to the wheelhouse. He looked a little sheepish. We had to decide what to do — either to stop or make a run for it. Peter wanted to go for it. "Damn the torpedoes. Full ahead, I say." I thought it best to stall for time.

"*Sea Shepherd, Sea Shepherd*. Do you copy us? Stop your engines. You are ordered to acknowledge." The Portuguese captain was running up flags signalling the same message, which meant we couldn't claim later that we hadn't been listening to the radio.

I picked up the transmitter reluctantly. "This is the *Sea Shepherd*. We are on our way to Great Britain. I suggest you let us proceed. I would not like to involve Portugal in this affair. We will voluntarily turn ourselves over to British authorities."

The Portuguese captain hesitated for a few moments and then said softly, "You want I should fire my guns?"

"No," I replied, "that won't be necessary. Hold on one minute and we'll give you an answer." I turned to Peter and Jerry. "Well?" Both of them shrugged and said they had no suggestions. I picked up the radio transmitter again.

"This is the *Sea Shepherd*. We'll return to Leixões harbour."

I turned the ship about and the Portuguese followed close behind for the four-hour trip back to port.

We arrived about a half-hour before sunset. A pilot boarded and guided us down a long channel in the harbour. We coasted slowly past the *Sierra*. The whaler was still listing some 30 degrees. Some of her crew stood on the deck and on the bridge. A couple of them had climbed the mast to see us pass. They screamed obscenities at us and threatened to kill us. We smiled, waved back and bowed to them.

The pilot placed us in a berth at the opposite end of the channel from the stricken whaler. He then shook my hand and departed. There were no police, no soldiers, nobody.

Some time later David Sellers, my former first officer, recently discharged, stepped on board with a German gentleman who introduced himself as Axel Wolter, our agent. David explained that he had taken the liberty of hiring us an agent to help us with the bureaucracy. The agent explained that the authorities really didn't know what to do about us. It was obvious that a crime had been committed, but technically the *Sierra* did not exist, because trading whale meat to the Japanese was illegal and therefore the whale meat that had regularly been offloaded at Portuguese docks and reloaded onto Japanese reefer ships did not officially exist either. This meant, of course, that the *Sea Shepherd* could not have actually rammed a vessel that did not exist.

I queried the agent further. "Did they not complain to the authorities?"

No, they had not.

"Then why in hell did they chase us down and order us back?"

The agent laughed. "They saw you ram the ship twice and they saw you leave. Obviously a crime was committed but they haven't quite figured out what it is. They told me to request that you stay around your ship until further notice. They also told me to request that you stay away from the *Sierra*. They don't want any more injuries."

"What do you mean, more injuries? Did we hurt anybody?"

"You did not, but *they* did."

David Sellers explained, "That idiot Richard Morrison got himself hit over the head by a two-by-four."

"What?"

"Remember the other day when he was arguing that violence was not the answer and that we should try to talk with the *Sierra*'s crew."

"Yeah, so?"

"Well, the silly bastard went over to the *Sierra* when she came limping alongside the dock to apologize for your actions. He walked up the gangplank and identified himself as a *Sea Shepherd* crew member, and they promptly brained him with a board. He's in the hospital in Oporto with a fractured skull, still unconscious."

Peter had little sympathy. "What an idiot."

"David, do you think they'll come after us tonight?" I asked.

"No, I don't think so. The police have warned them that they will arrest any of them if they come within a half a mile of this ship. They also said that they will arrest any of us if we go near *their* ship."

"Where's the crew?"

"I put them up in a cheap hotel in Oporto about 20 miles from here. Except for Morrison and his girlfriend Diane, the rest of the crew seemed to be excited. Al Indelicato told me that he would have been with you if he had known you'd get away with it."

"So would they all, but we haven't gotten away with it, yet. Let's see what tomorrow brings."

At the hotel, a message was waiting for me from David McTaggart, the new chairman of Greenpeace International. He was in town and wanted to meet with me. A taxi took me across town and dropped me off in front of a large expensive hotel. The receptionist called a bellhop to escort me to the pool, where I found David lounging, drink in hand, his eyes obscured by reflecting sunglasses.

I had known McTaggart for years — since 1972, when Greenpeace had chartered his boat to sail a protest voyage against atmospheric nuclear testing in the South Pacific. Since then, he had taken over the organization completely.

In the course of our conversation, McTaggart proposed that Sea Shepherd become a supplier of information to Greenpeace. His idea was that Sea Shepherd volunteers would take risks for the sake of the cause that his people wouldn't consider. He also seemed to think that Greenpeace would do a better a job of getting that information out to the public.

I reminded McTaggart that I had asked him a year ago to work with us and he had refused. I pointed out that I had led and participated in more Greenpeace campaigns than he had, that I was a Greenpeace director years earlier when he was smuggling watches into New Zealand. I saw no reason now to put my organization at his beck and call.

"Play my game or don't play at all," said McTaggart. "You have a nothing group, no name, no money — nothing. I'll let you work with us, but first you demonstrate to me that you deserve our support."

I got up from where I had been sitting on the edge of a lounge chair.

"David," I said quietly, "I may have a nothing group without any money. But we stopped the *Sierra*; Greenpeace didn't. We are the only group to take a ship in to confront the sealers in the icepacks, not Greenpeace. We don't need to curry any favours from you."

McTaggart laughed. "Suit yourself, but you'll be sorry. I'll have Sea Shepherd black-listed within this movement. Our money guarantees us respect. That respect gives us the credibility to denounce you. Think about it."

"I don't need to think about it, David. Screw you."

I returned to the hotel on the other side of town, leaving McTaggart sipping a drink by the poolside.

2
The Pirate Whalers

Those who profess to favour freedom and yet depreciate agitation
are men who want crops without plowing up the ground.
They want rain without thunder and lightning. They want the ocean
without the awful roar of its waters. Power concedes nothing without
a demand. It never did, and it never will.

Frederick Douglass (August 4, 1857)

Hunting down the *Sierra* was something I was born to do. If I had done nothing else with my life, I felt the ramming of this one ship would stand as a sufficiently worthwhile achievement.

Before the hunt, I had studied her thoroughly. A British conservationist named Nick Carter had taken it upon himself in 1974 to investigate unregulated whaling. His research was extremely revealing. He had traced the movements of suspect ships through insurance companies and bills of lading in numerous ports, tracked down rumours and interviewed former crew members. His painstaking work revealed a conspiracy of illegal whaling on a global scale.

Carter's detective work focused on a fast whale-catcher boat formerly of the Dutch Antarctic whaling fleet. She had been reconstructed with a freezer compartment and a stern slipway that made her a self-sufficient hunter-killer/factory-freezer ship. Operated since 1968 under different names, different flags and different owners, all the while working her way back and forth across the Atlantic, both north and south of the equator, she hunted without control and without rest. By 1979, it was estimated that her whale kills exceeded 25,000 individuals.

She moved like a wraith in and out of African and southern European ports. Since 1968, she had changed her name three times. The *Robert W. Winke* became the MV *Run* and then the *Sierra*. She changed her flag as if it were a shirt, from Dutch to Bahamian to Sierra Leonean to Somalian to Cypriot. From her Dutch roots she shifted her ownership papers to Norway and then to shadow companies in Liechtenstein, the Bahamas, South Africa, Panama and Cyprus.

Carter's research demonstrated that the ship had violated the whale conservation and fishing regulations of dozens of nations. Her owners had been brought before the courts in the Bahamas and in South Africa. She was forbidden to enter British-controlled ports. A Nigerian Coast Guard patrol boat had caught her with two dead whales inside their three-mile (5-km) territorial zone. The *Sierra* cut the whales loose and ran for the open sea after turning her harpoon cannon on the Nigerians and threatening to fire. She had been twice run aground and had left a trail of unpaid fines in her wake.

Her crew were a collection of scupper rats and low-life scum drawn from a score of international ports. Tough, rough, ignorant savages who would do anything for money, they hailed from Norway, the coast of Africa, India, the Cape Verde Islands and Portugal. Included in this crew of ruffians were four Japanese employees of the Taiyo Fishing Company.

She had even had a mutiny. Knud Hansen, her burly bearded Norwegian captain, had been shot in 1974 by first mate Arvid Nordengen, also a Norwegian. Left for dead on a dock in Moçâmedes, Angola, Hansen watched as the *Sierra* left him marooned and destitute as she resumed her duties under a commander more ruthless than Hansen himself. Nordengen continued the *Sierra*'s modus operandi of harpooning every whale he encountered, regardless of species, size, sex, age or nursing status. He killed without discrimination and observed no season, jurisdictions or rules, dispatching the whales cruelly with cold harpoons and using the explosive heads only as a last resort.

The outlaw whaler operated with shocking efficiency. Her Japanese meat inspectors simply selected the prime tail meat, and the rest of the whale — more than 80 per cent of its mass — was cut loose for the sharks. And she made money: her running costs were small compared to her profits. But she could never make enough to satisfy her owners.

Nick Carter publicized his investigations in 1975, when I was serving as first mate during the first Greenpeace anti-whaling campaign. The story was then further investigated by the *Argus*, a newspaper in Cape Town, South Africa. A friend of mine in Durban, Peter Rorvik, sent me a copy of the article. The newspaper had interviewed Andrew Maurice Behr, the director of the Sierra Fishing Company in South Africa. Behr defended his company and the *Sierra*. According to him, the International Whaling Commission (IWC) was of no significance. Whales were, according to Behr, "endangered anyway. The world would soon be rid of them, so why not make a profit from them before they disappear." Behr went on to say, "People come first and I'm providing jobs for people."

In 1978, the *Observer* revealed that the *Sierra* was owned by Forrentningsbanken, a Norwegian bank. The bank denied ownership. Within a week of the denial, registered ownership shifted to a company called Beacon-Sierra Ltd. in Vaduz, Liechtenstein. The Japan Whaling Commission pleaded ignorance of any activity by the *Sierra*, but further investigations led to the discovery of cargo manifest papers from Spain and Portugal that identified the Taiyo Fishing Company of Japan as the primary purchaser of the outlaw whaler's catch.

Still, the International Whaling Commission took little action. South Africa banned the *Sierra* from her waters. The whaler responded by conducting her operations with even more secrecy. She never used her radio and never announced her destination when leaving port. She was a ghost ship, seldom seen and seldom heard from, but she continued to spill the blood of the whales.

As I followed her grisly career, I vowed to myself that I would hunt her down and destroy her.

In 1977, I had begged Greenpeace to give me the *Ohana Kai*, which they were going to sell for scrap. Ross Thornwood and I offered them a dollar for the ship so that we could take her out and ram either the *Dalyni Vostok*, the Russian factory ship, or the *Sierra*. We called our plan Operation Asshole and the objective was to run the ex–U.S. Navy submarine chaser straight up the stern slipway of a whaler, jamming her in so tightly that she would incapacitate the target vessel.

Greenpeace said the plan was too violent and voted us down. I wrote off letters to every group I knew. The only answer I received was from Cleveland Amory, the founder and president of the Fund for Animals, based in New York City. I met with him in 1978 and told him that I would like to fly the Fund's banner into battle with the sealers and whalers. Cleveland asked me what I needed. I answered that I needed a ship. He sent me off to Europe to look for one. In October 1978, I located a 200-foot (60-m) British-registered Yorkshire side trawler, the *Westella*.

The *Westella* was surveyed and passed as a sound and solid vessel. The Fund for Animals sent over £60,000, a bill of sale was drawn up and the transaction was completed. On December 5, 1978, three days after my twenty-eighth birthday, the *Westella*, now renamed the *Sea Shepherd*, became the first ship in history dedicated exclusively to the enforcement of international marine wildlife conservation law. The whales now had a navy.

The Royal Society for the Prevention of Cruelty to Animals (RSPCA), thanks to the support of wildlife director Dr. William Jordan, pitched in an additional £24,000 to prepare and fuel the ship. In early January 1979, I sailed her across the North Atlantic to Boston. In March, Cleveland Amory led a joint Fund for Animals and RSPCA expedition to the Canadian seal hunt, where the *Sea Shepherd* became the first ship to enter the Canadian ice fields to protect seals and not to slaughter them.

After the seal campaign, I took the ship back to Boston, then down to Bermuda, where we were given a free dock by the British Royal Navy and permission to use their extensive facilities. I painted the entire vessel battleship grey after the Royal Navy donated hundreds of gallons of paint to us. After our success with the seal campaign, I was focusing all my energy on convincing Cleveland Amory to support my plan to hunt down and intercept the most notorious pirate whaler of them all. I now had the means to hunt down the *Sierra*.

Cleveland flew down to Bermuda to discuss the plan. At first, he wanted me to sail to the Bering Sea to protect fur seals in July, when they would begin to fall under the brutal clubs of the Aleuts. It was a good idea, but the cost of moving the ship that great a distance by way of the Panama Canal was incredibly high. The *Sierra* was closer, more accessible and less expensive, the plight of the whales more critical. Cleveland was wary of the risk involved and concerned for our safety. I could tell, however, that the old bear would come around. It's his nature to be stubborn, but he hated that bloody whaler as much as I did.

I could understand his dilemma. At 63, Cleveland Amory, president of the Fund for Animals, renowned author and social commentator, was not often asked to sponsor a sea battle. Protecting animals was one thing; waging war on their behalf was a different matter altogether.

"I want her stopped dead, Cleveland. She's out there in this ocean somewhere, killing every whale she sees. Her harpoon is most likely hot as we speak. I want her bad."

He shook his head slowly. "Well, I don't know, it sounds pretty tough to me. It's too damn dangerous. I like the idea but, well I . . ."

"Look, Cleveland, let me try. If it doesn't work, I'll sell the ship in Spain. I can find her, goddamn it, I know I can."

"Perhaps you can," he said. "But the Atlantic is a big ocean. It's a hell of a lot of money to commit to a remote chance of stopping her. I don't know if I can gamble the Fund's money to take a chance like this."

"Let me work on it then, I'll keep you posted on the plans. Give me time to obtain more data on her. Don't make a decision yet, but don't reject the idea either. Give me a month to come up with something."

He agreed to give me time. Time for me to organize some sort of strategy and for him to consider the implications.

I knew I had some support within the Fund for Animals. Lewis Regenstein, the vice-president of the Fund, had already told me that he would support an attack on the whaler. "I'd like to give you a few torpedoes, Paul. Sink the bitch if you can," he had said. But how? The thought of tackling the *Sierra* intimidated and overwhelmed me. Where was she? Where would I look? What would I do for a crew? What would I do when I found her? What would I do if I could not find her? Hell, I had absolutely no idea where to start looking, or how to begin.

The *Sea Shepherd* could do the job, of that I was certain. She was larger, heavier and, I hoped, as fast as the *Sierra*. If I could find the whaler, I was confident that the *Sea Shepherd* could destroy her. The problem would be in the hunting, not the killing.

I remembered that Don White, the president of Greenpeace Hawaii, had been interested in shutting down the operations of the *Sierra*. Don once told me that destroying the *Sierra* was the priority goal of the anti-whaling movement. Two years before, while surfing together at Makapu Beach on Oahu, he told me he was ready to hire some Vietnam vets as mercenaries to sink her.

Our phone was located at what we called our Bermuda office. It was a small red British call box just outside the walls of the colonial prison. I walked down to the booth and placed a call to Honolulu.

"Hello, Don, Paul Watson here. I'm calling from Bermuda. What would you say to chasing down the *Sierra*? I've got the ship to do it. I just need a good volunteer crew and all the information you've got."

Don's response was far from enthusiastic. "It's impossible to find her. I don't know if I can help you very much."

"Look, Don," I said. "Two years ago, you told me that you wanted her more than anything, more than the Russians or the Japanese. All I'm asking for . . . hell! I'm just giving you an opportunity to join the crew and shut the bastards down."

Sheepishly Don replied, "I'd like to, man, but we've got this walkathon planned. I can't get away."

"Screw your bleeding walkathon! This is the *Sierra*. Here's your chance to help make a fantasy come true. We can get her."

"Paul, Paul," he said patiently. "It's fine to dream but maybe you should step back into reality. We could never find her."

"What about information?" I asked. "Greenpeace has a file on her. You've been keeping track of her movements. Steer me in the right direction."

"John Frizell has all that in San Francisco. Why don't you give him a call?"

"Okay, I'll do that. What about anyone else? Have you got anybody that might be interested in going?"

"I'll ask around, see what I can do," he answered. "I wouldn't count on it. It's kind of busy around here."

I asked him if Greenpeace had any active plans for the summer. He said they were working on something but that everybody's energies were tied up in the power struggle between Greenpeace Canada and Greenpeace USA and the emerging Greenpeace International under David McTaggart.

Putting the receiver down, I paused for thought. Frizell should be more helpful. After all, I had brought him into Greenpeace and nominated him as a director. I picked up the phone and called him.

"Hey, John, Don White said you may have some information on the *Sierra*?"

"What kind of information?" he asked.

Feeling a little more hopeful I said, "I need to know where she's been sighted, where the best chance of finding her would be and how fast she is."

Smugly he replied, "We may have something on that. What do you want it for?"

"I want to hunt her down, John. I want to take the *Sea Shepherd* out after her."

"Sounds a bit wishful to me. You'll never catch her in your ship. She's faster."

"How fast?" I asked.

"Faster than you," he replied.

"Hell, John, you don't even know how fast we go. Gimme a break, will ya. How fast is she?"

"How fast are you?" he countered.

"We do 18 knots, John," I lied.

"She's much faster than that," he responded without hesitation.

"Sure she is, but do you know where she is?"

"Perhaps, but that's classified Greenpeace information and the *Sea Shepherd* is not a Greenpeace ship."

I hung up on the bastard. Clearly, Greenpeace would be no friend to me.

All I could determine was that the *Sierra* was somewhere in the Atlantic between the Bay of Biscay in the north and halfway down the African coast in the south, and somewhere east of the Azores or the Cape Verde Islands. I told Cleveland that I had the co-ordinates worked out to a "few" miles of ocean off the coast of Portugal or Morocco. What finally won him over, however, was the offer from the Royal Navy to sell us their fuel at very low prices.

While in Bermuda, we were supported with great enthusiasm by Anselm Genders, the Anglican Bishop of Bermuda. He introduced us to Governor Ramsbottom and to the senior officers of the naval base. We found great sympathy for our mission from these well-placed people. This resulted in contributions of food, equipment and supplies in addition to the paint, fuel and services provided by the Royal Navy.

We left for Boston for final preparations and hopes of recruiting a crew. Having been refused co-operation from Greenpeace in the Pacific, I ventured to approach Greenpeace in Boston.

Arriving at the Greenpeace office in Boston, I was again disappointed. They had plenty of volunteers, but told me they could not spare anybody because they were working on a walkathon to raise money to save the whales.

"How are you going to save the whales?" I asked.

"We're going to buy a ship to chase the whaling ships," they replied.

"I have a ship. I've got the means to chase down the *Sierra*. All I need are a few dedicated volunteers. Why can't you ask a few of your volunteers if they would like to sail with us."

They dismissed me curtly: "Your ship is not a Greenpeace ship."

Al Indelicato, a Greenpeace office volunteer, overheard my request, however, and appeared on the dock the next day. And the Fund for Animals supplied a few people, including Alex Pacheco. The rest I recruited by running a classified ad in the *Boston Globe* and the *Boston Herald American*. This brought me a slew of drifters, adventurers and people looking for a free passage to Europe. I rejected three out of four and built the crew up to 21 plus myself. Finally, on July 3, 1979, we let go our lines and pulled away from the dock and Boston harbour. We were at last ready to begin the hunt.

It was almost too late. Since 1976, the *Sierra* had been joined by other pirate whalers. The wholesale massacre of the North and South Atlantic had begun. I remember thinking of the buffalo on the Great Plains. I had always wished there had been champions for the buffalo back then. The Plains Indians had indeed tried, but what had been needed were buffalo defenders with the technology to have made a difference. I had often fantasized about riding over the hills with a Sherman tank, an armoured shepherd blowing the buffalo hunters to hell and taking on the U.S. Army if they tried to intervene. Now I had the opportunity to do for future generations what I wished some of our forefathers had done for us.

What was needed was a mechanical Moby Dick, and the *Sea Shepherd* could certainly duplicate the tactics of that great whale, which had rammed the Nantucket whaler *Essex*, sending her and her despicable crew to a watery grave.

In 1978, the sister ship of the *Sierra*, called the *Tonna*, a vessel commanded by the Norwegian captain Kristhof Vesprhein, met a similar fate. On June 27, 1978, the *Tonna* set out from the Canary Islands, leaving the *Sierra* in port, where she was completing repairs. A month later she was on her way back with her hold packed with 460 tons of whale meat. She was low in the water and still some 200 miles (320 km) away from Portugal when she came upon a 70-foot (21-m) fin whale. Her greedy captain could not resist the prize. He ran the whale down and sent a harpoon into her back.

This was no helpless small whale but a powerful leviathan. The whale fought back, whipping the laden whaler about in rising swells. The crew worked furiously to winch the whale in and up the stern slipway, heedless of the rising seas. And then suddenly, when the 60-ton animal was halfway up the slipway, a large swell rose up and set the *Tonna* hard over to port. The whale's massive body slid to port and crashed into the bulkhead. The overburdened whaler keeled over, the rails went beneath the seas and the decks were awash with swirling sea water. Mountains of water cascaded across the decks and poured in torrents through the open hatchways and portholes, quickly flooding the engine room. Fuse boxes exploded. The generators seized and the main engine was immobilized. Without power, the winch was stopped. Now the crew could neither tow the whale in nor release it.

The ship was at the mercy of the dying whale. As the whale slid slowly back into the sea, the vast weight of sliding blubber slammed the 200-foot (60-m) ship back and forth, submerging her decks. The *Tonna* took on more and more water. Forty-one of her 42 crew dashed for their life jackets and the lifeboats, every man for himself. Only Captain Vesprhein refused to abandon his ship. He stayed on the bridge.

At last the whaler rolled over and the dying fin whale pulled the *Tonna*, her captain, and 460 tons of frozen whale meat down to a cold grave. That was the last those pirates saw of their captain as the blue waters closed over the pirate ship silently and forever.

When I heard the news report I cheered the whale and celebrated the death of the pirate whaling captain. The next whaler would be mine.

The *Sea Shepherd* set sail for the Azores on July 3, 1979. Our arrival there gave us an opportunity to take on water and fresh supplies. It also gave me the opportunity to make some inquiries about the *Sierra*. What I learned gave me some hope. The ship was apparently operating off the coast of Portugal.

The night before our planned early-morning departure, I swam across the harbour by myself and with a hacksaw and a small hatchet, I stove in the bottoms of half a dozen whale boats. Perhaps, I thought, this might slow down the locals in their so-called traditional hunting of sperm whales.

In the Azores, I kicked off some troublemakers. They had disobeyed my direct orders about getting drunk on shore. One of them fell from the pier and almost drowned. In a drunken stupor, he blamed me for his mishap and began beating on my door in the early hours of the morning. He was a Vietnam veteran and I didn't take any chances. I opened the door with a sword in hand and promptly marched him and the other drunk down the gangplank at sword point and marooned them on the dock. We left them there and continued east. All I knew about the *Sierra* was that she was in the area bordered in the north by the Atlantic coast of Spain and in the south by Morocco, and anywhere within 500 miles (800 km) of that coastline — in other words, in an area of some thousands of square miles. I never allowed myself to entertain the notion that I might not find her. I was certain I would, though I can't explain why.

Two days east of the Azores, we spotted hundreds of loggerhead turtles. I stopped the ship rather than risk hurting any turtles. We spent almost six hours swimming with and riding passing turtles, most of which seemed to tolerate our intrusion into their lives. When the turtles had passed, we resumed our course towards the east. I went to bed to dream of leading a cavalry charge against the *Sierra* while riding on the back of one of hundreds of turtles.

The next day at noon our lookout sighted a ship. I kept my eyes glued to it as we approached. Within a half-hour, it was obvious that she was a whaler. I hardly dared to hope. It must be a Spanish whaler, I thought; it couldn't possibly be the *Sierra*, not this easily found. It was July 15. We had left Boston only 12 days before . . . no, it couldn't be.

As we came closer, however, a chill rose up the back of my neck. I made out the whaler's slipway, and then a large *S* on her stack. There could be no doubt.

"My God," I shouted, "it's her. It's the *Sierra*!"

Peter Woof ran up to the bridge. "Is it really her?" he asked incredulously.

"It's the *Sierra*," I answered. "It's definitely her."

Peter, overjoyed, shouted, "Well, let's do her in!"

"I can't, Peter. The seas are too rough. We can't control a ramming here."

"I suppose you're right," he agreed, "but we can't let her get away. I'll give the engines everything we've got."

The *Sierra* had changed course. She was running full speed to the east towards Portugal some 200 miles (320 km) away. I ached to hit her now, to destroy her now, forcing back every desire within me to unleash all my anger and the power of my ship against her. "We have to do this right," I muttered to myself.

We matched her speed and it quickly became obvious to her captain that he could not outrun us. He decided to seek help in the port of Leixões.

The sun rose on the morning of July 16 to reveal both the *Sea Shepherd* and the *Sierra* drifting less than a mile offshore. I would have to act soon or she would escape.

3
McLuhan's
Warriors

Societies have always been shaped more by the nature of the media by which men communicate than by the content of the communication.

Marshall McLuhan (*The Medium Is the Message*)

Axel Wolter arrived early the morning after the ramming. He sat down and Jerry rustled up some coffee.

"The Port Captain would like you to meet with him at 10:00," he said seriously.

A few hours later I walked down to the Port Control Office, arriving a few minutes before 10:00. It was a white stone, one-storey building with a large ship's anchor propped up in the front courtyard. I waited in the foyer for an hour before being ushered in by a uniformed sailor. A handsome man in a well-tailored uniform rose from behind the desk.

"I am pleased to meet you, Captain Watson. You have been getting much publicity for your little affair yesterday — surprisingly, mostly sympathetic, especially from the Portuguese press. Look at this headline. It translates as "British Ship Rams Cypriot Pirate.""

Smiling, I said, "I think that's a fair statement."

"This is very well and good, but you have broken the law."

"What law have I broken?" I asked.

"I believe that the charge should be gross criminal negligence in the operation of a ship."

"That is not an appropriate charge," I responded.

"And why not?"

"I was not negligent. I hit that ship exactly where I intended to hit her. The ramming was deliberate."

The Port Captain laughed. "You have a point there. Besides, I do have a problem. The owners of the *Sierra*, whoever they are, have not come forward to lay a complaint."

Relieved, I asked, "Then there are no charges?"

"Not exactly, we may be laying charges against you for causing a navigational hazard. Meanwhile, I must request that you and your two companions turn over your passports and remain in port."

"For how long?"

"I cannot say. This matter could take months to resolve."

"Sir, I need to leave temporarily to publicize this incident. We need to get a message out to the world that pirate whaling must end. I could return in two weeks."

"Captain Watson, I am personally very much in sympathy with your actions. Unfortunately, I must answer to my superiors and they are adamant that you remain in Portugal until this is resolved."

I stood up. "Very well, Captain. Call for me when you need me. I'll deliver the passports later today."

"That won't be necessary. I'm sending an officer back with you to collect them, and you will need to give him your ship's registry also."

I left the office and walked back to the ship, escorted by the assigned naval officer. A Portuguese television crew had arrived. I sent Peter to get the registry and to retrieve the passports.

He returned to the deck a few moments later.

"Sorry, Paul. Jerry won't give up his passport."

The officer looked at me for a moment and reached for his radio.

"One moment, sir." I turned to Peter. "Peter, please tell Mr. Doran to give you his passport or else he will be arrested immediately and most likely tortured."

Peter returned a few minutes later with the passport and I politely handed all the documents to the officer.

After the interview with the local television station, I called Cleveland Amory in New York. He wanted me to come to the States as quickly as possible. He had arranged for an interview on *Good Morning America* and with *Parade* and *People* magazines. Could I make it? Damn right I could. I assured him that I would be in New York in two days.

Peter, Jerry and I met in the bar of the hotel in Oporto. Most of the crew were preparing to return home. A couple of them came over to join us at the table. I waved them away. Except for David Sellers, Paul Pezwick and Alex Pacheco, we didn't want them. Alex and David were loyal. Pezwick was also, but he was involved with Gail Lima. She wanted to leave and convinced him to leave with her — just another case of hormones winning out over duty. He'd be back.

I ordered three beers. "Well, boys, I need to split. There isn't any point in ramming a whaler if you can't tell the world that you did so. In a media culture, a thing just doesn't happen unless the media covers it. We need to send a message loud and clear that whaling isn't going to be tolerated any longer."

"That's fine for you, mate, but what do you expect us to do?" Peter said as he twirled his finger in the foam of his beer. Jerry just sat there quietly.

"I expect you to do what you think you should do. They may get around to arresting us or they may not. They may seize the ship. I don't know. I do know that we won't be accomplishing much sitting on our asses around here. I can leave without a passport; a seaman's book is all I need to return to the States. But I don't know what the two of you can do."

Peter smiled and said, "Hell, don't worry about us. We can get out of here on our own. Do what you have to do. Give 'em hell."

I left Peter and Jerry to have a farewell drink with a few of the crew. Crossing the street, I saw a taxi slowing down to discharge a passenger. I ran to the car just as the back door opened and a burly man stepped out in the street in front of me.

"How do you do?" He said with a wide smile. His accent was thickly Norwegian.

"Do I know you?" I asked, little alarms going off in my mind.

"Knut Hustvedt, first mate and harpooner on the *Sierra*."

He reached out a ham-sized right hand and shook hands with me.

"I am very pleased to meet you," he said. "Very pleased."

"I'm not so sure I'm pleased to meet you."

He smiled again. "I understand."

I got in the taxi and began to shut the door, muttering a quick goodbye as I did so. The cab drove off back to Leixões. I turned and looked out the rear window. He stood on the street, looking at me and waved goodbye. It was really quite strange, I thought, strange and curious. I would have expected him to take a swing at me, not to shake my hand.

Back at the ship, I packed my bags, called Axel Wolter the agent and requested that he watch the ship until the authorities had resolved the legal quandary. I told him to apologize to the Port Captain on our behalf but I had things that I needed to do in the States. The agent dropped me off at Oporto airport, where I bought a ticket to Lisbon and then caught a flight to New York. The U.S. Immigration officer gave no more than a quick glance at my passport-like Canadian seaman's book and signalled me through.

Meanwhile, Jerry had hitchhiked a ride to the Rio Mino on the Portuguese–Spanish border. That night, placing his clothing and money in a plastic bag, he swam across the river to Spain. He joked later that he was probably the first Yankee wetback to enter Spain in such a manner. He managed to get himself to Madrid, where he obtained a new passport from the United States embassy.

Peter simply hopped on a bicycle that he bought in Oporto and cycled north over the mountains into Spain and on over the Pyrenees to France. He whistled happily as he rode on to Calais and hopped a ferry to Dover. His heavy Aussie accent convinced the British to let him in after he told them his passport had been stolen in Paris. Three weeks after leaving Portugal, Peter got off his bike and knocked on David Sellers' door in Inverness, Scotland, to ask for a cup of tea.

During this time, I made the rounds of the media in New York. Cleveland took me to dinner at the Harvard Club and booked me onto dozens of television and radio programs. *People* magazine made me break an antique harpoon over my knee. Overall, the reception by the media was overwhelmingly positive, until I went on to my native Canada.

In Vancouver, a media inquisition began. Who did I think I was? Who made me judge and jury? What gave me the right to take the law into my own hands? Jack Webster, the curmudgeonly Scot who reigned as king of the West Coast media, took me down to Kitsilano Beach. Thrusting a microphone into my face, he opened the interview with a hostile question.

"You're nothing but a pirate yourself, Watson. Who appointed you as executioner?"

"Jack, sometimes it takes a pirate to stop a pirate. Call me a pirate if you like, but remember, it was a pirate that stopped piracy in the Caribbean in the seventeenth century. The Royal Navy couldn't do it. Henry Morgan, a pirate himself, was the man who tamed the Spanish Main. The fact is that the *Sierra* is an outlaw and nobody was doing anything to bring her to justice. We got tired of the talk and decided to take action."

Webster looked me over, his voice sternly judgmental. "So you're an outlaw, you admit it. How do you justify acting like a common criminal?"

"I don't have to justify anything. Ramming that whaler was one of the most satisfying things I've ever done in my life."

"So you have no remorse, no regrets?"

"Absolutely none. I did what had to be done, didn't hurt anybody and saved the lives of many whales. Whales would be dying right now from the harpoons of that pirate, if not for us. No, I have no regrets."

Jack wasn't going to let me off easy. "You haven't accomplished anything permanent. The whalers will collect insurance, repair their ship and they'll be back killing whales. You got yourself a bit of publicity, but admit it, you haven't accomplished very much in the long run."

"The *Sierra* will not collect insurance. It was a deliberate act of war. Their underwriters have already declared that deliberate sabotage is not covered under their policy. It will cost a million dollars to repair that whaler, and that is something they understand. We cost them. And I'll hit them again and again if need be."

"How will you do that without a ship? Your ship has been seized. What will you chase them with now?"

"I'll get my ship back and I'll ram the *Sierra* again."

Jack got the last word. "Not if saner minds prevail. You can't just take the law into your own hands. That's why we have law and courts and judges. This kind of action verges on anarchy and is a threat to the foundations of our society. I'm sorry, Paul Watson, but you're wrong." The camera clicked off. Jack Webster smiled and added, "Off the record, I like your style."

Annoyed, I asked, "If you like my style then why did you just haul me over the coals?"

"That's television, my boy, that's television. I can't be agreeing with you on the air. It's a good piece. It'll make them think, piss some of them off and have others screaming curses at me. It's the nature of the beast."

I was continuing to experience in practice what my academic background had taught me in theory. I had been a communications major at Simon Fraser University at the time Professor Marshall McLuhan was winning rave reviews as a media theorist. Survival in a media culture meant developing the skills to understand and manipulate media to achieve strategic objectives. The issue of whaling is purely academic unless high drama is introduced to make it newsworthy. Ramming the *Sierra* was dramatic. The hint of romance and piracy or the possibility of violence guaranteed coverage and thus presented an opportunity to educate the public through the media.

Knut Hustvedt, the harpooner on the *Sierra* whom I had briefly met on the street in Oporto, appeared on an NBC television program called *Amazing Animals*, where he was interviewed by Priscilla Presley. Surprisingly, Hustvedt defended my actions against his ship. Priscilla Presley asked him what he thought about the *Sea Shepherd* ramming his ship. In his thick Nordic accent, Hustvedt said matter-of-factly, "It was the only way we could have been stopped."

Pushing him, Presley asked, "But how did you feel about it? The *Sea Shepherd* used violence to stop you, to take your livelihood away from you. Didn't that make you angry."

In a calm voice, the big Norwegian answered, "At first it did, but it also made me think about what I was doing. To me, whales were just big fish. We killed them and made money. I never thought about them as intelligent creatures. When I saw people willing to take such risks to protect them, I began to think about what I was doing. I will never kill a whale again. And if the Sea Shepherd people would like, I would volunteer for their crew to stop other whalers."

We had been criticized by mainstream groups for being radical. They had told me that education, not confrontation, was the solution. It appeared to me that we were, in fact, a highly effective educational organization. Instead of preaching to the converted we had publicized whaling through confrontation, making it a dramatic news story and bringing it into the homes of hundreds of millions of people. Most important, we had managed to educate a whaler and motivate him to change his way of life. It's all well and good to preach the save-the-whales message to 300 million North Americans: they aren't killing whales. But to teach a whaler to save whales, to make him lay down the harpoon and become a saver of whales — in my book, that's an educational achievement.

In early November, I boarded a plane bound for Portugal to work on the release of the *Sea Shepherd*. I was greeted by some very bad news. Axel Wolter told me that the court had decided to turn the ship over to the *Sierra*'s owners as compensation for the damage they had suffered.

"They can't do that," I said. "There hasn't even been a court hearing."

Axel sighed. "Well, they did it. They will release the ship to you, however, for a payment of US$750,000."

"That's ridiculous, I only paid US$120,000 for it."

"I'm sorry, Paul, but that's the ruling of the judge."

"How can he have done that without a hearing, without listening to our side of the story."

"I believe the judge was given some motivation for his decision."

"What? A bribe?"

Axel shrugged. "I didn't say that, but call it what you like."

Further inquiries with some of the reporters I had met a few months before suggested that the judge had taken US$60,000 from Richard Shepherd, business manager for Andrew Behr, the listed owner of the ship.

The *Sierra*, meanwhile, had been towed to Lisbon for repairs. I took a train south and found it at a dock. A team of welders were hard at work repairing the hull. I took some photographs and met with the American consul. He was shocked when I told him that the whaler was in Lisbon. He had been told by Portuguese authorities that the ship had left the country.

I returned to England and called Peter Woof, who was still in Scotland, and requested that he return to Portugal to help steal our ship back. We recruited a small crew of volunteers, including Peter's girlfriend from Australia, Lins Masterton.

On December 29, 1979, we arrived in Oporto and made our way to Leixões harbour. The port was quiet because of the Christmas holidays. The plan was to break into our own ship, get the engines started and then escape, and this time there would be no stopping for the Portuguese Navy.

Once inside, we were disappointed. The ship had been looted. The fuel had been pumped off. Many of the pumps and most of the navigational equipment were missing. It quickly became obvious that our plan to escape with the ship was impracticable.

Except for Peter, Lins and me, the rest of the crew left. The three of us sat around in the cold, lonely mess room, drinking tea to keep warm and discussing our next move. Peter was infuriated that the Portuguese had robbed us. He wanted some sort of revenge.

I told them, "It's my concern that this ship will be converted to whaling operations."

Lins interrupted, "We can't allow that."

Peter perked up. "No, we can't. We'll have to destroy her."

I offered a suggestion. "Should we burn her?"

Peter responded sharply, "No, much too messy. We should scuttle her."

"Can you do that?" I asked.

"Of course I can. Simple monkey-wrenching actually."

Lins cleared her throat, "Isn't that illegal, I mean, to sink her?"

"Well," said Peter, "technically yes, which means . . ."

". . . we should plan our escape," I finished.

On the evening of December 31, Peter, Lins and I groped our way with flashlights to the bottom of the engine room. Peter lifted some deck plates to reveal the sea valve. I held the light as he began disconnecting the bolts on the valve with a monkey wrench.

A few minutes later, Peter warned me to stand back. A loud thump was followed by the roar of harbour water rushing in. A geyser shot some 15 feet (5 m) into the air. We stared at the torrent in amazement and then headed for the ladder to the topside decks. As we left the engine room, the water was already lapping at our ankles.

We left the ship at a walk so as not to arouse suspicion and headed towards the road, where we caught a cab for Oporto. Lins and Peter went straight to the train station and caught the next train to Madrid. I booked a hotel room in Oporto and went to bed. Fireworks and drunken parties marking the arrival of the new year made it difficult to sleep.

Early in the morning, I took a cab back to Leixões. As we approached the harbour, I could see the bow of the *Sea Shepherd* pointed at an angle to the sky, like a missile ready to be fired over the horizon. Her aft section was completely submerged to the midship area. She was still sinking and there was no preventing it. I could see hundreds of people gathering at the port gates to stare in fascination as the ship slowly sank. Closer to the ship, a few dozen soldiers, all dressed in black, many of them armed with machine guns, scurried about.

I calmly requested the cabdriver to take me back to Oporto. He dropped me off at the train station. A quick look at the schedule told me that the next train would be leaving in an hour, headed to Lisbon. I bought a ticket and walked out to the platform. The train was in the station being cleaned. Looking about to see that no one would see me, I stepped on board and hid myself in one of the baggage compartments.

I was lucky that I had taken that precaution. Some 20 minutes later, a truck-load of soldiers pulled up and immediately set up checkpoints. They proceeded to check the identification papers of every passenger before boarding. They examined every passport and document carefully and looked every passenger over thoughtfully before letting them proceed. At last satisfied, they signalled the conductor to leave. The train slowly chugged out of the station. Ten minutes later, I walked back to the dining car and ordered breakfast.

I arrived in Lisbon in the early evening and took a cab to the airport. Checking the departure board, I saw three flights scheduled for the rest of the evening. I had just missed the 1930 British Caledonia flight to London. The other two flights were headed for Rio in Brazil in an hour or Johannesburg in South Africa in three hours. There were heavily armed Portuguese soldiers in black all over the airport. I hadn't seen them at this airport before so I assumed that I was the reason for their presence. They were checking passengers on the flight to Brazil.

Thinking that I would have to lay low for a bit and try again in a few days, I made my way over to the British Caledonia desk and asked for a schedule for London. To my surprise, the airline rep told me that I could still board the 1930 flight if I wanted.

"I thought it had left already."

"No, it's been delayed for a minor mechanical check. It's on the runway now, but I could run you out there if you like?"

"Sure thing," I said.

He took my credit card, issued me a ticket and then escorted me through a security door to a British Caledonia van.

"Excuse the backdoor treatment. The army is looking for some terrorist, probably some Arab or Iranian. This Ayatollah thing is getting to be a real aggravation. Anyway, if we went through the regular departure area, they'd just hassle us and you might miss the plane."

"Thank you, that's thoughtful," I said a bit nervously.

Arriving at the plane, I climbed the boarding stairs and a very pretty flight attendant in red highland tartan escorted me to a seat.

"Did you enjoy your stay in Portugal, sir?"

"Not really. I'm actually quite happy to be leaving."

She look concerned. "Did you have any trouble during your stay?"

"Oh." I smiled. "Just the usual. Nothing too exciting, I'm afraid."

"Then I hope your stay in Britain will be more exciting."

"It could be, especially if I had the pleasure of your company for dinner in London."

"I'd love to, but this flight terminates in Edinburgh, I'm afraid, where I live."

"Then I'll just have to carry on with you to Edinburgh."

She laughed. "That would be nice, but you're not serious?"

"Of course I am. I've never been to Edinburgh. Why not?"

She smiled again, "Why not? I'll show you around."

I sat back and looked through the window as the lights of Lisbon slowly disappeared beneath the clouds. I realized just how tired I was. I could use a few days of R and R, I thought to myself, and besides, I had an exceptionally pretty tour guide to take my mind off the whale wars, if only for a while.

4

Underwater
Demolition
Team

The *Sierra*'s repairs continued in Lisbon. In another month she would be ready to resume her grisly career. The *Cape Fisher*, the last remaining pirate whaler in Andrew Behr's fleet, had changed her name and flag and had been sighted in the Canary Islands. In Spain, the legal whaling operations of the Juan Masso Whaling Company had just become illegal after they blatantly violated their fin whale kill quota. Without any enforcement agency to stop them, the Spanish whalers were continuing to kill.

The media coverage and the public response to our attack on the *Sierra* demonstrated that we had seized the moral high ground in this battle with the whalers. We had to keep that advantage and escalate the war. Aggression against the whalers appeared to be socially acceptable. However, public opinion could turn quickly against us if a whaler were injured or killed. Our objective was to destroy the whaling ships without injuring any of their crew.

A few months before, while in Washington, D.C., in late September 1979, I had received a secretive call from a man with a British accent. He requested a meeting. I agreed to meet him in the garden dining room of the Tudor House Hotel, where I was staying. When we met, he gave me his name but I agreed to keep his identity confidential. He said he represented a small group of concerned professionals who had the means and the skills to help the whales.

"What kind of professionals?" I asked.

He answered cautiously. "We have the funding and the technical skills to finish off what you started. What we need is whatever you can tell us about the *Sierra* — how thick the hull, the layout of the ship and anything relevant to our plan."

"And what are your plans?"

"To sink her before she has the chance to resume the killing."

I smiled. "You have my complete support for that plan."

He looked at me, hesitated for a moment and then said, "I cannot give you names and I'll be your only contact. I do need to know how you feel about using explosives."

"Explosives!" I responded. "What kind of explosives? It won't help the whales to have someone killed."

"I agree. Small limpet charges, sufficient to breach the hull with little risk of injury if applied in the appropriate place."

I was still sceptical. "Do these people you're involved with know what they're doing?"

"I should think so. The ordnance is American and the personnel are military based in Europe. I won't tell you whose military. I'm simply the contact between the money and the action, with another middleman between me and the money. I can't tell you who's paying for it, although from the contact there was an indication that you may know the person. However, the source is no longer important to our plans."

I did have an idea of who it might be, but he was right, it was not that important.

"Of course, if anything happens, I'll be the prime suspect."

"We are aware of that. We'll make sure you have an alibi. I'll need your schedule for the next six months."

"No problem." I mentally reviewed where I would be. "I do have a trial date in the Gaspé region of Quebec in early February."

"Good." He seemed satisfied. "I'll keep in touch. Here's my contact number in London. Call me there only if you are in the U.K."

In late January, I had my hands full preparing for my trial in Quebec. I had been arrested in March 1979 for the crime of protecting seals in the Gulf of St. Lawrence. I had been charged along with seven members of my crew with breaking the Seal Protection Act, first, by witnessing a seal hunt without permission of the government and, second, by interfering with the killing of seals by spraying an organic, indelible dye on the living seals to destroy the commercial value of their pelts.

On the morning of February 6, I had been dozing through a monotonous monologue by the crown prosecutor when the bailiff tapped me on the shoulder and motioned me to leave the courtroom. I followed him into the foyer of the Percé courthouse. A Mounted Police officer was holding the receiver of a pay phone.

"There's a call for you."

"Thanks. Hello."

"Is this Paul Watson?"

"Yes, it is."

"Mr. Watson, this is Randy Stanfield of External Affairs. We just wanted to make sure of your whereabouts."

"I'm here, in Percé, in the courthouse. Why?"

"How about Peter Woof?"

"He's here with me, not on trial but keeping us company."

"That's quite convenient, isn't it?"

"I don't know. Why would you think so?"

He laughed. "The *Sierra* was sunk with a limpet mine this morning in Lisbon. You wouldn't know anything about this, would you?"

A little chill ran up my spine. I was thrilled but cautious. "I may know something about it. After all, it's well known that I've tried to sink it once before. The vessel is a pirate, which makes me curious as to why the federal government is even concerned."

Stanfield answered, "Our interest is restricted to the investigation of possible criminal actions by Canadians in Portugal. It's obvious that you were not directly involved. However, the Portuguese authorities and some media received a report from a woman shortly after the explosion. She said that the *Sea Shepherd* was now avenged. We would like to know if any Canadians were involved."

Without hesitation, I answered truthfully, "I can assure you, Mr. Stanfield, that not a single Canadian was involved. Do you know if anybody was hurt?"

"No. There were no injuries, but you do know who did it?"

"I don't know names, but I know of the action. The *Sierra* was a pirate and she deserved sinking. The operation was perfectly executed, no injuries and one less whaling ship in the world. So, does the government wish to charge me with anything?"

"No, I don't think so. You seem to have a perfect alibi. However, the Portuguese government may wish to charge you."

"Well, I'm sure that Canada will assist them if they do."

I walked back into the courtroom with a smile on my face, waved to the judge and sat down. The judge scowled back.

The *Sierra* had been sunk with one well-placed limpet mine in the early-morning hours as she lay berthed at a dock in Lisbon. A security guard on the dock had not even heard the explosion. The vessel just began to settle lower in the water and then turned on her side and came to rest on the bottom. There she lay, half submerged, for many months afterward. I could only imagine how frustrated her investors must have been. After a million dollars in repairs, the denial of my ship as compensation and now on the eve of her return to whaling, her sordid career was ended forever. The *Sierra* was at long last dead.

A few months later, I sent my friend Jet Johnson to the Canary Islands. As a captain for American Airlines, he could fly for a fraction of the regular fare. His job was to post 500 Spanish-language reward posters around the harbours. The Sea Shepherd Conservation Society would pay US$25,000 to any person who sank the pirate whaler *Astrid*, formerly the *Cape Fisher*.

I flew to London to meet with my limpeteer contact. He said that they had targeted the *Astrid* and the whaling fleet of Juan Masso in Vigo, Spain. A few weeks later, on April 28, 1980, the Spanish whalers *Ibsa I* and *Ibsa II* were sunk with limpets in Vigo harbour. Unfortunately, the two mines on the remaining two vessels in Masso's fleet failed to detonate. This disappointment was quickly forgotten, however, with the realization that we had indeed destroyed 50 per cent of the illegal fleet. Besides, with only two ships, Masso would now have a difficult time overstepping his IWC-allotted quota.

Meanwhile, in the Canary Islands, the covert owners of the *Astrid* began to realize that things were far too hot in the pirate whaling business in the Atlantic. The reward signs were everywhere and had been reported in the local press. It was a big temptation to their underpaid crew. Two weeks after the reward was posted, the owners announced the sale of the *Astrid* to a Korean fishing company to be converted to a fish packer.

In less than a year, Sea Shepherd and our mysterious allies had shut down every single pirate whaling operation in the North Atlantic. We had achieved in one year what 10 years of rhetoric and game playing between nations had failed to do. It felt good. It felt damn good. I felt that I had actually achieved something of value, a legacy. Hundreds of whales would live because we had taken action. Tens of thousands of whales would be born over the next century and beyond because we had thrown a wrench in the works. We had put our bodies on the line and said emphatically and aggressively: No! Stop the killing, stop the madness. And we had backed up our words with force. The force of a steel saviour rammed into the side of a steel killer, the explosive force of a well-placed limpet and the media force of a well-placed sound bite.

Greenpeacers called me a terrorist. Some members of the media called me a fanatic. Others called me a hero. The mainstream environmental movement accused me of setting the cause of whale protection back a decade. It meant nothing to me. The bastards would talk and condemn and argue and debate until the last whale was killed. For all of their self-righteous blather, they had saved nothing. The knowledge that we had made a difference made Peter, Jerry, Jet, myself and our friends in covert operations completely immune to the squawking of the hypocrites who made their living from selling misery, doom, gloom and the spectre of extinction.

The International Whaling Commission met in Brighton, England, in June 1980. I attended as an NGO delegate for the Fund for Animals. I met with a very mixed reception.

Lyle Watson, one of my favourite writers, who was representing the Seychelles as its whaling commissioner, came over to congratulate me for the ramming of the *Sierra*. He laughed when he introduced himself to me and said, "The Japanese think it was I who rammed the whaler because of our shared surname."

I answered with a compliment. "I think you've been causing them considerable damage on your own."

"I would like to think so," he answered.

Sir Peter Scott, whose father, Captain Robert Falcon Scott, had always been a hero to me, came over to express his approval of our actions.

The Greenpeace delegates avoided me like the plague.

Allan Thornton, whom I had introduced to Greenpeace in 1975, walked towards me in the lobby.

"Hey, Allan, how are you?"

He didn't look at me. In fact, he looked right through me, as if I didn't exist, and walked past me. I was shocked. Nobody had ever done anything like that to me before. It very soon became evident, however, that Thornton's behaviour was official Greenpeace policy. The other Greenpeace delegates all acted the same way.

Michael M'Gonigle was the only exception. He was a Greenpeace lawyer from Vancouver whom I had known from earlier days. He bought me a beer in the hotel lounge. We had just begun talking when another Greenpeacer, John Frizell, walked over to the table, ignored me and spoke directly to M'Gonigle.

"Michael, David doesn't approve of who you keep company with."

M'Gonigle shrugged. "Is that so? Tell McTaggart he can kiss my ass."

Frizell left, presumably to report this act of insubordination to his boss. M'Gonigle just shook his head.

I called a press conference to announce our involvement with the sinking of the Spanish ships. At the same time, I announced a $25,000 reward for the sinking of any whaling ship in Taiwan. The Greenpeace crowd immediately denounced the reward and boringly accused me again of being a terrorist.

That afternoon, as I was walking through the lobby of the hotel, Michael M'Gonigle walked up beside me. Quietly he said, "Do you see those three men coming down the stairs? The one on the right is the Spanish whaling commissioner and the one in the middle is Juan Masso."

I walked over to the trio of men. They were dressed in expensive grey business suits. Approaching the man in the middle, I extended my hand, which he automatically took and shook.

"Señor Masso?" I asked.

"Si."

"My name is Paul Watson. We sank your ships, you bastard." I smiled and walked away, leaving a stunned whaling boss in my wake.

I don't know how much our reward offer had to do with the decision, but shortly after the IWC meeting, the Taiwanese announced that they were shutting down the operations of the five illegal whalers in their nation. This gave me the time to look for a ship to replace the *Sea Shepherd*. I had negotiated movie rights with Warner Brothers over the *Sierra* ramming story. Producer Tony Bill had met with me to explore the potential for a story suitable for an action-adventure film. The upfront option money was the ticket needed to secure a new ship.

I went back to Kingston-upon-Hull where I had purchased the *Sea Shepherd* and found a nearly identical trawler named the *St. Giles*. This was a good sign, St. Giles being the Scottish patron saint of animals. I purchased the ship from a

Yorkshire fishing company for £37,000 and moved it around the top of Britain to Greenock on the Clyde, near Glasgow. The 657-ton trawler was renamed *Sea Shepherd II*. I recruited a crew and put them to work refitting and painting our new ship. When the refit was complete, we'd set out for Alexandria, Virginia, the first leg of the long haul to Siberia and a campaign to expose illegal whaling by the Soviet Union.

5

Ostroga

When this ship becomes a democracy,
you'll be the first to know.

Captain James T. Kirk, to a crew member
on the starship *Enterprise*

Standing at the wheel, rolling with the 657-ton trawler, I sensed the arrival of the dawn over my shoulder. A pale blue light infused the windows of the wheelhouse and then faded, as though the sun had some hesitation about rising. I heard only the throb of the main engine, the hiss of water spraying up and over the deck. The crew, except for the watch, were asleep. The helmsmen were down in the galley having a mug-up. I had relieved them, relishing the opportunity to take the wheel once again as in my deck crew days. It was an opportunity to be alone, to reflect on our present situation. I felt empty and fatalistic. My head was clear and free of fear. A twinge of apprehension still knotted in my gut, but it was easily controlled.

The flock of puffins skimming the water as they crossed the bow seemed so perfect. My ship, this beautiful rust-adorned veteran of the North Atlantic fishing fleets, was a lover of cold water. She heaved and bucked and flung herself forward. She seemed to me to be laughing, mocking those of my crew whose courage was faltering on the threshold of confrontation.

A reddish glow beckoned on the horizon as the sun rose to our stern and cast its fiery net over Bering Strait. A soft spray of golden light trembled across the *Sea Shepherd II*'s dewy poop deck and reflected glassily on the grease-smeared gunnels. The gunnels had been greased deliberately to make them difficult to grip, in the event that unfriendly forces attempted to board. A 10-foot-high (3-m) fence of barbed wire circled the outer reaches of the deck, similarly intended to make boarding difficult. The barricade gave the ship a bleak, sinister aspect, a foretaste perhaps of capture and imprisonment.

The barbed wire and grease would be of little use against guns, if guns were used, but it did give the crew a slight sense of security. It was a signal, too, that I had no intention of submitting peacefully to arrest. I'd done that before, in Portugal, and lost my ship. This time there would be no submission. They'd have to take us by force. There was a chance that my crew would be injured or worse, killed or captured and imprisoned in the notorious Soviet Gulag. The possibilities weighed heavily upon me. True, they were volunteers, but it would be my decisions that decided their fate. Most of them were not fully aware of the risks, of the possible consequences. I pondered the risks and mentally reviewed the skills and capabilities of each crew member, but I had already decided that I was prepared to accept full responsibility for the consequences of this campaign.

We were approaching the International Date Line at the point where the line suddenly bends to the west to enclose the Aleutian Islands. Just a few miles ahead of us it was Sunday, although we were still in Saturday. Politics, however, defined more than time in this region. To cross the dateline was to step through the looking glass and enter that part of the Earth that inhabited another dimension of time and consciousness. We would step from the Western Bloc reality into the sphere of Solzhenitsyn's inferno. Directly before us across a few miles of frigid water lay the treeless, marshy plain of Siberia, with its grim legacy of Tatars crushing the Siberian aboriginal tribes and being crushed in turn by Ivan the Terrible.

Beyond those cold shores, however, lay mystery and the last refuge in Eurasia of the wild citizens of the north — the Siberian tiger, the wolf, the polar bear and the Marco Polo sheep.

Now that we were only a few miles from our objective, the horrible reality struck me like a mailed fist in the gut. We were on the point of launching an unarmed invasion of the Soviet Empire. It was the thought of prison — a long, long time in prison, perhaps a lifetime — that was worst to contemplate. My only taste of prison, in Canada, had left me aware of just what a torture confinement is. I understood how animals must feel in captivity. Even death could be easier to accept than prison.

The Russian language teased me with the irony of our situation. *Ostrog*, the word for jail, derived from the original name of the forts built to maintain Ivan's terrible grip once he had wrested the land from the Tatars. *Ostrog(a)*, the Russian word for harpoon, the symbol of death for the whale, the symbol of fate for my crew, my ship and myself.

My thoughts were interrupted when I glimpsed a pair of ivory scimitars reflecting the brilliant glare of the rising sun: the tusks of a walrus. I watched as he rolled and dove. Beyond him, I could make out the bleak dark outline of the American island of Little Diomede two miles (3 km) to the north of us, partially obscured by a rising mist. A little farther to the west, Big Diomede, bleaker still, the most easterly outpost of the Soviet Empire.

I remembered a former Greenpeace shipmate, Yuri Korotva, a Czech, who had actually been locked away in a Siberian coal mine for a long time before escaping, one of the few to do so and survive. He'd made the mistake, as a student in the Prague Spring of 1968, of lifting his voice publicly against the Empire. He found out in a remote camp in Siberia what at least one department of hell was like. Even going insane wouldn't have helped him there. The guards beat prisoners so savagely they came back to functioning "normalcy." They believed in Pavlov, not Jung or Freud, those guards. In a Siberian prison camp, hope was unknown.

Yet this night before crossing into the gravitational pull of the dying moon of Marxism, I had slept soundly. Some of the crew had been agitating to turn the ship around, now that the existential moment loomed close on the literal horizon. The 'tween-deck lawyers were nothing more than a nuisance. I knew the solution to whining and sniveling. I had gone to my cabin, locked the door, climbed into my bunk and slept until 0340 hours, just as the twelve-to-four watch had spotted Fairway Rock, the signpost pointing the way to Siberia.

With my watch returned, I warmed my hands around a steaming mug of sage tea and fiddled with the radio. I tried to raise the American station on Little Diomede to notify them of our position. There was no answer. Apparently, the eternal vigil is not eternal and the watch for the enemy across the Strait is a nine-to-five affair. I would have felt better if they had answered.

We had left behind the halibut boats and the crabbers. Their voices still jabbered on various frequencies. A couple of times, through the crackle of static, we had heard Japanese voices calling to one another. The last conversation I picked up was between a fisherman and his wife: "*Zzzzt* . . . love you, darling . . .

weeeet, zit, zweet . . . hear me, over?" Now the only sound in the wheelhouse was random twitterings from far away in space. The radio voices had died. It felt as if we, too, were dwindling out of range, sinking into an enormous void. And indeed, the security of Fortress America was well to the stern.

We had come all the way from Scotland by way of Panama to reach the Bering Sea — a journey of 15,000 miles (24,000 km). As with all voyagers who went one step farther than the others, we had met with ridicule, apathy and hostility along the way. There had been plenty of times when the *Sea Shepherd*'s hull had felt like Sisyphus's rock, and the ocean a long upward climb. It took $40,000 just to fill her tanks. We had been threatened by Soviet agents, hamstrung by Canadian bureaucrats and spurned by fellow environmentalists. So there should have been no small thrill of triumph when, against all odds, I took my beloved ship over the edge of the earth. But all I felt was a "click" of awareness at 0413 hours, and a certain dryness in the throat when we crossed the 1867 Convention Line dividing Russian and American territorial waters. I wondered if Soviet satellites had picked us up yet. Were gunships on their way to intercept? Would they send MiGs?

"That's it," said Marc Busch, my second mate. "We're in." He was shivering slightly, but then he was just coming off one of his frequent fasts and was always complaining about being cold. I swear he'd die of hypothermia in the tropics. But Marc was a good man and, overly skinny or not, he was a good navigator. He and first mate Neil Sanderson had helped me get this far. It was my job alone to get the job done and to get us out again, hopefully intact and without injuries or worse.

We had come to the coast of Siberia to uphold the law, international law — to be specific, the regulations set forth by the International Whaling Commission (IWC). I had good reason to believe that the Soviets were violating Clause 13B of the IWC regulations governing aboriginal whaling. By international agreement, the Russians were authorized to "take" (a euphemism for kill) 179 California grey whales for the subsistence of the aboriginal peoples along the Siberian coast. Aside from the fact that 179 whales provides an excessive quantity of meat for a native population of fewer than 3,000, there was also the historical fact that prior to 1957 the average number of whales utilized annually by the Siberian natives was 41. In 1957, they quite suddenly needed nearly 200 whales a year to survive.

It had smelt somewhat fishy to me and I suspected that back in the mid-1950s, some enterprising, upwardly mobile young Communist had set up a mink, sable or fox farm collective and needed a cheap source of meat to feed Russia's manufactured need and desire for fur coats. Some members of the IWC's

Scientific Committee had similar suspicions, but they were unable to obtain confirmation for the simple reason that the Soviet Union would not allow any official observers into the area. At the annual meetings of the IWC, the Russians maintained that the hunt was aboriginal. Each year they refused permission to observe and each year they requested and received the quota they desired.

So, I thought, if the Russians won't allow observers in, then we would simply go to Siberia uninvited. Thus was born the plan to invade the Siberian coast of the Soviet Union with my small, motley band of conservation-oriented brigands.

By 0630 hours, we were three miles (5 km) off the coast of Siberia. I changed course and headed south along a shoreline of grey-green tundra littered with patches of dirty snow. Even though it was summer, we could feel winter in the wind, the taste of an Ice Age that had never entirely passed. The ground, I knew, freezes to a depth of 600 feet (200 m) on that bitter plain stretching all the way to the Ural Mountains far to the west. Over that awesome expanse lies the still-preserved frozen corpses of prehistoric mammoths and woolly rhinoceroses, resting side by side with more recently slain slaves of the Czar or, later still, of the New Order. There was an odd elation to do with the astonishing fact that we hadn't been jumped or blasted yet. It was like tiptoeing along the spine of a hibernating bear. We scanned the shore through binoculars, we monitored the radar and the radio. Nothing. The coast was as deserted as it was undefended.

At 0800 hours, the whales came.

Although there were clouds beached like kelp on the horizon, the sky directly above was a bottomless blue, so astonishingly lovely and mysterious that it might have been a gigantic lens opening onto another dimension. The crew had gathered on deck, their hysteria forgotten. It's impossible to be mean-spirited in the presence of whales!

I saw a trail of white mist beyond the port stern, as if a wave had broken over a rock. But there was no land there. A hint of darkness in the water, then it was gone with only a crystal spray drifting in its wake. The water made smacking sounds against the hull. The engine chug-chugged calmly along. To begin with, all my crew had loved whales, almost worshipped them, with a fierce, passionate love equal in intensity to the hatred of Captain Ahab for Moby Dick. They saw in whales not the blind, destroying power of nature, but the sacred quality of the living world. Yet few of my crew had actually ever encountered Leviathan in his element. It was a moment — one's first encounter with a cetacean — that I had often seen change people's lives. It changes their view of themselves in the world. One whale can do that.

And now not one but hundreds had appeared. Hundreds! It was a spectacle the likes of which I, who had sailed every ocean, had never witnessed before. This spot was for whales what the mythical elephants' graveyard was to that terrestrial leviathan. It was the summer gathering place of that incredible and still mysterious species of *Eschrichtius robustus gibbosus*, more commonly known as the California grey whale.

The anxiety of the crew eased visibly. The whales surfaced. Their backs poured — it is the only word — upward, like animated asphalt roadways. Turning. Turning like great wheels, like mandalas, until it seemed that they had completed a circle and were, after all, mythological serpents devouring themselves. But then, the slow-motion crash, hundreds of minor waves, the tail emerging like a catapult, sunlight glistening in the water on their flanks — flesh I knew to be as warm as human flesh and every bit as sensitive to pain and pleasure. Barnacle-crusted as they were, with mighty 3,000-pound (1.5-tonne) tongues locked behind the baleen comb they use to dredge the sea bottom. (I have seen them mating and mothering in the warmer waters off Baja, California, have had them come right up to me, so close I could touch them. I could easily believe their singing to be a form of prayer.) They came up out of the sea, their clear Siamese cat's eyes the size of saucers looking at us unblinkingly. We were witnessing the gathering of the whales at the terminus of their long northward migration. And we were awed.

These greys were the same whales that had begun life in a warm Mexican lagoon. They had migrated past the beaches of Malibu in southern California, had paraded their calves past the magnificent harp of the Golden Gate bridge, had swum past the pale dunes of the Oregon coast, and moved like half-hidden wraiths through the fog-shrouded straits of British Columbia. Witnessed only by the occasional fisherman, they had proceeded in an ancient trek past the volcanoed portal of Unimak Pass into Bering's sea. Now they were here, moving along the barrens of Siberia. Here in this place, many would die, obscene craters opened in their sensitive flesh by the cold steel of *ostroga*.

Roughly 18,000 greys survive today, a miracle of biological resurrection. Yankee whalers had slaughtered them for a century until there were barely a couple of hundred left. In 1910, while the Czarist Empire shuddered in its death throes, a moratorium on the killing of the grey whale was called. In the Atlantic, the grey — there once called the "Scrag" whale — was not so lucky. It's now extinct.

To have these hundreds of whales emerging around the *Sea Shepherd* like a crowd of well-wishers was all the more poignant because we had seen for ourselves how end-of-the-world lonely the gulfs and straits of the North Pacific had become. South of the Aleutian Islands there had once existed a massive two-lane whale highway, a migratory path followed by fins and blues and humpbacks as well as greys. They were the largest Earthlings, kings of the sea. But the sea now was empty: only the swells, a rare albatross, gulls, a few puffins, an occasional shearwater and here and there a few porpoise and dolphin; not a single plume of spray had we seen until now. Our journey until this moment had presented us with only the "great shroud of the sea," as Herman Melville called it, a grave-yard. Moving in their age-old procession, the largest Earthlings had been ambushed and massacred. It was as though a plague had spread across the water.

The Aleutian chain is dotted with abandoned whaling stations, oil vats knocked down by the fierce williwaws — hurricane-force winds — wooden sheds collapsed like deck tables, roof beams bare as a skeleton's ribs, machinery mellowed in rust and pockets of loam, tall grain leaping out of sockets, flowers sprouting between the spokes of overturned wheels, lichen clinging in patterns to the walls of engines. The equipment has begun to flake away like shale. The wind plays through those tubes and pipes not yet filled with soil or ground seashell. And bones everywhere. Bones of dried pulp, surfaces pitted with tiny holes. Ribs stick up through the daisies and snowdrops and horsetails like old picket fences. Vertebrae the size of toilet bowls lay half buried in moss and this-tles. Jawbones thrust out of the soil like torn sheets of grey plywood, like the leftovers from some long-ago giant's meal. The horror of what has happened here cannot be fully appreciated. There is nothing to indicate that those gargantuan ribcages, spines and skulls had been torn from a whale at all. If you didn't know that the ruins had once been whaling stations, you would assume you had stum-bled across the bones of a vanished race of prehuman titans wiped out in a for-gotten time of genocide.

A double tragedy had happened here in this desolate earthquake-racked, cloud-impacted netherland, as alive with volcanoes and rip-tides as it must have been at the beginning of time. The Aleutian Islands, some 1,200 of them, had formed the land bridge (or so goes accepted theory) across which the Asians had migrated to the Americas, in a kind of unfinished parenthesis to the infi-nitely older polar wanderings of the whales. Ah, but! An old Indian looked at me scornfully once when I asked him about this. A land bridge? An ancient exodus from Asia? "Look carefully at the footprints," he said. "They point the other way." The Hopi state flatly that their homeland was the world from which all civilization ranged afield.

Whichever way humanity marched across the gloomy, moss-enfolded stepping-stones of the Aleutian archipelago, the unlucky ones were those who clung to the islands, moving no farther: the Aleut people. Here, because the Japanese current warms the foggy air, it was possible for a civilization, a kind of northern Polynesia, to arise. And to thrive for a while. Empires within empires grew and fell. Great chieftains struggled for control. Political alliances coalesced, came apart, changed into bitter antagonisms. Then the ships of the Czar arrived. Cannons laid waste to human flesh, as they later would, with barbs and explosives attached, to the flesh of whales. But even before the whales, the Aleuts perished. At the Bay of Women on Unalaska Island, the Russian invaders killed every male, old or young, leaving only the women, some of whom were pregnant; otherwise there would be no pure Aleuts left in the world. As it is, only a fragment of the Aleut race remains, huddled in little government-built villages — comfortable concentration camps where alcoholism, suicide and despair are the rule.

It is easy to suspect that a curse hangs over Bering's sea; in the last few days, along the Alaskan coast, we had seen the immense, bloated bodies of headless walruses lying like dirty brown sandbags on the tide flats, killed and decapitated for their ivory tusks. Indian children poked at the carcasses with sticks while sandfleas and flies buzzed around the festering flesh excitedly. Even the sea gave no sanctuary from the horror. First one, then two, then three and then more headless walrus carcasses buoyed by putrid gases floated by on the swells.

Ivory, the white gold that has caused so much misery — to elephants, to walrus and to man. To slaughter grand and beautiful creatures like these tuskers, whether terrestrial or marine, solely to obtain a few teeth indicates that we have not evolved so very much since the days when our forebears lived in caves and sought to prove their superiority by adorning themselves with teeth and claws. Could our lack of these natural weapons have caused us to be so jealous that we coveted them? Can personal adornment justify such senseless slaughter? And yet, Native Aleuts and Inuit, people who have touched the earth, participate in the slaughter. The rifle triggers are pulled by aboriginal fingers to satisfy the ivory lust of people who will never see the source of their treasure. The aboriginal hunter barters a part of his soul with every spent bullet.

As if the destruction of Native culture were not tragedy enough, the Aleutians have been the site of mechanized, modern slaughter. Ten thousand soldiers of Imperial Japan died for their emperor when they made a futile grab for a military toehold on the North American landmass in 1942. Later, in the 1950s and 1960s, and into the first two years of the 1970s, the same Aleutian chain would tremble as the guts of Amchitka Island were ripped repeatedly by the radioactive detonations of underground nuclear tests. Shock waves from the explosions killed sea otters and seals by the thousands. It was while sailing in protest against the Atomic Energy Commission tests in 1971 that I saw the Aleutians for the first time.

When I listen to the winds in the Bering Sea, I seem to hear the sighs of the natural spirits yearning for peace and praying that the pain be relieved. Whales and Aleut Indians. The Bay of Women and crumbling whaling stations. Abandoned nuclear test sites and mountainsides littered with spent shell casings and skulls. Vanished ancient societies. Vanished species. Here, somehow, by the strange alchemy of modern geopolitics, East met West with no buffer, the Canadian shield that stood between the Soviet Union and the United States gone. From Alaska to Siberia was a journey by sea of a single night. In Nome, just a day ago, a distraught schoolteacher had screamed at me: "If you go in there, you'll start World War Three!" Visions of apocalypse were close to the surface of consciousness, and in such a corner of the universe, why not? If not a final apocalypse, holocaust had come often enough.

It felt like a tightrope walk, this journey southward along the Chukotski Peninsula. Either the satellites had not spotted us or the Soviet defence apparatus was cumbersome, perhaps even rusty. Had we been commandos intent on nothing more than slipping ashore and fading into the cold sponge of the land, we could have done so a dozen times and still have turned the ship back to safety. The whales gradually moved away to concentrate on their main business of sucking up mollusks, crustaceans and worms. And we kept going in search of a whaling ship or a functioning whaling station.

It didn't take long. Out of the sterile tundra and scabs of snow, a town emerged. Depending on which chart or atlas you consulted, it was called either Loren or Lorino. At 1300 hours, after an entire morning of cruising unmolested in Russian waters, I asked Peter Woof to throttle down the engines. We stopped precisely 2.2 miles (3.6 km) off shore and scanned the land with binoculars.

A whaling station, yes. In design, they had changed little over the centuries. The difference was a coat of paint, now peeling, and evidence of winches. There were signs of human activity but no indication that anyone had yet noticed us, or if they had, that they took us for anything other than one of their own ships.

We watched closely from our vantage point at sea. The station was on the beach; up on the bluff, a town, and beside the town — there they were! Long sheds that could be used only for housing animals. A fur farm! I was sure of it!

"Okay," I said, "we're sending in a shore party. Get the Zodiac ready!"

The thought crossed my mind that if this situation had any parallel, it would have to be a gang of burglars trying to break into the biggest prison in the world. I was about to lead my crew in an illegal landing in the Union of Soviet Socialist Republics. The charge, if we were captured, would probably be espionage. The punishment . . . well, I didn't want to think about it. But I *was* apprehensive. Very.

Was it a foolish idea? It was, according to one nameless bureaucrat of the U.S. State Department who had told Eleanor Randolph, a Washington, D.C., correspondent for the *Los Angeles Times*, what he thought about my plan. "If he antagonizes the Russians up there, he might just disappear under an iceberg."

John Frizell, a director of Greenpeace, commented that, "of all of Watson's stupid campaigns, this is the most stupid and useless yet." Greenpeace was consistent in their condemnation of the expedition, hounding us in the press and accusing us of being violent and terroristic. In Vancouver, Greenpeace Canada president Patrick Moore said on a talk show, "Watson is more stupid than I thought if he thinks he can take on the Russians and win."

The plan to invade Russia was, of course, somewhat unorthodox, and for this reason I did have a few problems with fund-raising. We were starting from Alexandria, Virginia, having brought the ship over from Glasgow, Scotland. To voyage south to Panama then north to Siberia we needed a minimum of $50,000. Diesel fuel was expensive.

Naturally, Greenpeace would not support us. The Whale Protection Fund were uninterested. Friends of Animals hung up on me before I could explain the plan. Defenders of Wildlife, the Animal Protection Institute, the Humane Society of the United States — all turned me down flat.

Friends of the Earth came forward with $500. Thanks to Lewis Regenstein, the Fund for Animals threw in $5,000. This was explained in Washington, D.C., environmental circles as understandable since Lew was considered about as crazy as me. He was, however, vice-president of the Fund for Animals, a former intelligence officer for the CIA, born and raised in Atlanta, Georgia, and author of two renowned books: *Politics of Extinction* and *America the Poisoned*. He is a daring, crazy, eccentric, conservative, radical, animal-loving environmentalist — my kind of a guy. He was one of the few established eco-types to stand up for us when we hunted down and rammed the *Sierra*. He was a supporter of deeds, not words, and his support was much appreciated now.

We were fortunate in having a berth donated by the U.S. Coast Guard at the

Ford Plant dock. This was thanks to Leslie Fillebrown, who utilized her feminine charms to our great advantage by flirting with the Coast Guard commander. It was a convenient location from which we had a beautiful view upriver to the marble Congressional dome.

The Alexandria Yacht Club came to our aid with (6,800 l) 1,500 gallons of diesel fuel that had been lying about in some abandoned fuel tanks for the past decade. In order to get it, the crew had to form a bucket brigade a quarter of a mile long between the Yacht Club and the ship.

Our $5,000 gift from the Fund for Animals was matched by a very generous contribution from a D.C. schoolteacher, Suzanna Bryan. We received small donations of money and food from hundreds of schoolchildren, but even with a little more than $10,000 in the ship's safe, we were a long way short of our target. We needed twice that amount before we could head out to sea. Thus was born Operation Tom Sawyer.

The solution would be to recruit a crew willing to pay $1,000 each for the opportunity to work hard, get dirty, and risk life, limb and freedom in an invasion of Siberia. A few days, $14,000 and 14 new crew members later, the *Sea Shepherd* was fueled, provisioned and ready to leave for the Pacific. Possession of $1,000 doesn't make one a great sailor, or even a good sailor or any kind of sailor at all, but it did provide the ship with adequate manpower and the cash to go to sea.

All of this frantic fund-raising activity had not gone unnoticed. Feature articles in the *Washington Post* and *Star*, the *Baltimore Sun* and the *New York Times* tipped off the Soviets, who quite naturally decided it was in their interest to check us out. Our first confrontation with the Russians actually took place on a government dock in Alexandria, Virginia, months before reaching Siberia.

We were scheduled to depart the next day. The preparations had been completed and we were taking it easy. It was a warm June night. A full moon illuminated the ivory profile of the Capitol dome. The moonbeams danced across the Potomac, and the ripples and wavelets converted themselves into a myriad strobe lights.

It was not all that unusual to see people photographing our ship. However, two men in dark glasses carrying super-sophisticated camera gear and taking pictures at midnight was a trifle out of the ordinary, and for curiosity's sake, my first mate, Neil Sanderson, decided to ask the photographer just what he was doing.

The photographer answered gruffly, "Taking a picture of the Woodrow Wilson Bridge there, if you don't mind."

Neil replied sarcastically, "No, I don't mind, but the bridge is behind you and you would probably get a better shot by turning your camera 180 degrees."

The photographer countered that he was with "Starbuck Productions" and what he was doing was none of Neil's or anyone else's business. Neil, being under the impression that having your picture taken was indeed your business, countered by taking a picture of the photographer. The response was immediate. Instead of looking into a camera, he found himself staring down the barrel of a rather large and rather ugly .45 revolver, behind which stood a rather large and rather ugly individual with a finger gently caressing the trigger.

"Would you please point that thing someplace else. I don't like guns. They tend to be dangerous."

Neil's polite plea made no impression on the man with the gun.

"Give me that goddamn film or I'll show you just how dangerous it can be."

At that moment, a government security guard walked around the corner. Seeing the man with the gun, the guard fumbled for his revolver. The man with the gun lowered his pistol and flashed a badge at the security guard that identified himself as a U.S. Agriculture agent. That was all he would say. The guard was satisfied with the flash of the badge and apologized to the man with the gun, who promptly left with his comrade and Neil's film in a nearby car, which sped away into the night.

What the Department of Agriculture wanted with us was a mystery. The next day, I had the badge number checked out and found that there was no record of any agent with that number or description, nor did they have any reason for one of their agents to be checking us out.

With all the publicity, and then the secret-agent melodrama, we hardly expected to enjoy clear sailing in Soviet waters. But nothing and no one hindered our invasion of Siberia.

6

Passage to Siberia

The next morning, our worries about the presumed Soviet agents were put aside. We sailed with the tide. We cracked a few timbers on the dock and scared the hell out of a few wary marina yachtsmen, but otherwise had a pleasant departure with scores of well-wishers waving from the quay. A send-off party had been organized by Alexandria artist Nancy Reinke. She had arranged for bluegrass musician Bill Pounds to provide his band for our departure ceremony. Bill had honoured us by writing a song especially for our ship. We could hear their song as we began to get under way.

Ballad of the Sea Shepherd

The pirate whaler Sierra, *her anchor weighed,*
harpoons were ready for to kill.
She sailed out from the Portuguese shore

to the realm of the whale.
But the whales they had a friend that day,
came sailing o'r the bounding main.
Yea, a friend that tried to save them
from the harpoon's blow.
Sea Shepherd *was her name.*

(chorus) *But the times are tough*
   The seas are rough
   So let's all lend a hand
   Till the hunter is the hunted
   all on the salt sea.
   And whales are befriended by man.

On the Shepherd's *deck,*
her captain stood,
Paul Watson was his name.
He chased the Sierra *back to her port*
and he told her she was fair game.
Then the Shepherd, *she rammed the* Sierra's *bow.*
Well, she hurt that whaler full sore.
Stove in her side and disabled that ship
so she'd hunt the whales no more.

(chorus)

The wrecked whaler, it was a sad, sad sight.
I know it grieved some people full sore.
But the losing of just one great sperm whale
would grieve us about ten times more.
The captain and crew are ready to sail once again.
Going to take this ship from our shores.
Sailing to the land of ice and snow
where the whale fishes blow
to shepherd them once again.

(chorus)

I blew the ship's whistle to signal the operator of the Woodrow Wilson Bridge to open up for us. It was a beautiful, exhilarating, wonderful day which boded well for our journey. The brown, lazy waters of the Potomac carried us past Mount Vernon and into Chesapeake Bay. Within hours we were once again on the beautiful free oceanic highway heading south in the direction of Panama.

Our journey south was calm and, for the most part, uneventful. We were buzzed by U.S. fighter planes in the vicinity of Cuba and again when we drifted close to an island south of Cuba that had sensitive military significance for the Americans. When we had approached the historic site of Christopher Columbus's first landfall, Neil turned to me and said, "Just think, I'm seeing in our radar what Columbus saw in his radar in 1492." Neil had a weird sense of humour but he was usually pretty serious. A graduate student of mathematics, an excellent navigator, a master radio operator, a former radio announcer and a vegetarian from Winnipeg, Manitoba, he was in truth my most reliable and most qualified officer. He was a no-nonsense watch officer and I took a great deal of secret pleasure in the fact that some of the crew referred to him as Lieutenant Bligh. He was the kind of man that the *Sea Shepherd* needed.

Neil kept the deck crew in line. It was a job I was happy to delegate. Our second mate, Marc Busch, was an Australian. Although a competent officer, he was also one of the boys, far too well-liked to be able to keep the rabble in line; but he had many redeeming qualities. Our third mate was a French-Canadian economist named Bobby David, a man of dry wit and great intelligence. Fortunately, I still had Peter Woof in charge of the engines. I would have had second thoughts about this campaign if not for Peter. Another veteran of past campaigns was Paul Pezwick.

These four had ample opportunity to train the new crew, some of whom turned out to be quick learners. One landlubber was promoted immediately to bosun. Ben White, a tree surgeon from Virginia, was a good man with a rope, a dedicated conservationist and a man with a foundation in Native activism similar to my own experiences at Wounded Knee. Ben had helped in the American Indian Movement occupation of the Bureau of Indian Affairs building in Washington, D.C., in 1972. Afterwards he had served as an apprentice to Rolling Thunder, a holy man in Nevada.

We had volunteers from around the globe. Ethan Milrod from New York City and Kai Nernheim from West Germany were assigned to the engine room. "Chauffeur Bob" Osborn came from Georgia, and his credentials as a limo driver won him the position of official Zodiac driver. Iain MacDonald had been with us since Scotland and remained our radio operator despite his incomprehensible Glaswegian accent. Eddie Unterman was the last to join the crew. He had ridden down to Alexandria from Philadelphia after reading about us in the newspapers. He quit his job as a stockbroker to join the ship.

We had six women members of the crew when we left Virginia. Four of the six were redheads, which was sort of appropriate for a voyage to Russia. They included Lins Masterton, a musician from Australia and girlfriend of the chief engineer, which automatically gave her an engine-room position. Marly Jones from England and Sue Weidman from Virginia joined the deck crew. Odene Cusask from Pennsylvania became chief cook, with Leslie Fillebrown from Virginia as second cook. The sixth woman was Denise Dowdall from California, who continued as part of the engine crew, where she had been since joining us in Scotland.

I had only a few malcontents, cowards, malingers, mattress lovers and wimps, but that was par for the course on any crew and, fortunately, they were not in any position to cause trouble.

One problem that quickly developed was that of shipboard romances. It had always been my belief that romance on a ship was a source of trouble, especially since most ships' crews have more men than women. Such relationships cause jealousy, hard feelings and fights. Of course, my experience was gained on the decks of Scandinavian merchant ships where I had seen men stabbed and scarred in petty fights over women. I supported women crew members in principle, but I remained prejudiced against "friggin' in the riggin'" in the belief that it could only lead to trouble.

Despite the ban on such relationships, it was not long before the dreaded affairs began. The first started between Denise Dowdall and Iain MacDonald. I took to getting on their case at every opportunity, lecturing them for neglect of duties and exploding when I caught them in romantic interludes on the bow with a night-time switch of the searchlight beacon.

Despite my annoyance, Lins Masterton told me she thought the whole affair entertaining. "It's sort of like a super-slushy movie full of mooning and spooning and Hollywood and languid dreamy-eyed painting of hatch covers, and then there was that bea-u-tee-ful necking scene on the foremast."

"Great, Lins, just great. It's a damn lucky thing the two of them didn't end up in a bloody heap on the deck. If they weren't such good workers, I would maroon them together on one of these islands. This is not the *Love Boat*. This is serious business, or leastwise it's supposed to be."

But what the hell, we would soon be in Panama. The trick now was to survive shore leave in Cristobal, make it through the locks intact and then head north to Los Angeles. If we could make it to California, I knew we would make it to Siberia.

Panama was sighted early on the morning of June 24. By 0400 hours, we were behind the breakwater and braced to encounter the chaotic bureaucracy of the Panama Canal Commission. We were cleared quickly and ordered to stand by for instructions later in the morning. Bobby David left with the pilot and the Canal agent. He would take a bus from Panama City to Mexico City, then fly to Vancouver to prepare for our arrival there. We would need a dock and provisions and he would have to prepare for the bureaucracy. Vancouver would be our final stop before leaving for the Bering Sea.

I went ashore to arrange our transit through the Canal. Between the yacht club and the town, I ran a gauntlet of Customs and Immigration officials, a full-scale riot by dock strikers, a barrage of tear-gas canisters fired by the Panamanian troops advancing towards the strikers in front of me and a horde of beggars, street merchants and prostitutes. I felt fortunate to reach the Commission's office intact.

Transiting the Canal meant taking on reams of paperwork in search of solutions to the bureaucratic problems facing us. Before we could transit, we would have to hire a welding boat to weld on some closed chocks. And to top this off, I found that the transit fee would be based on measurements of our ship by local officials. It would be at least two days before we could transit.

That first night in Cristobal was an experience for most of my greener crew members. Against my advice most of them left the yacht club bar and headed for the waterfront saloons. I found them in the first shady place I looked, surrounded by a bevy of Colombian whores. Having sated their visual appetites, and lacking the means to indulge further, it was a simple matter to get them all back to the yacht basin and onto the ship without incident.

The next day we managed to get the welding done. Luckily the harbour welding boat had a sympathetic skipper and crew who closed our chocks for half the normal price. Ethan Millrod deserved full credit for this. He convinced the skipper and crew to accept Sea Shepherd T-shirts in lieu of half the fee. Ethan pulled T-shirts off the backs of crew members to provide for the welding crew.

With the American pilot on board we hoisted anchor and headed into the channel bound for the Gatun locks and the Pacific.

The passage through the locks and Lake Gatun was uneventful. The crew saw little of the interior of Panama, as the passage was completed during the night. Morning found the ship steaming northward along the Panamanian coast. Except for the fact that the Mexicans do not keep up the batteries in their lighthouses, we encountered few problems on our passage north to Los Angeles. We had one close call off the coast of Baja. Our radar had broken down, the lighthouse we were looking for apparently was out of order and we were wrapped in dense fog only a short way off shore. The chart indicated sand bars in the general vicinity. Neil got us out of that mess with his newfound ability to navigate by sea lion. He simply kept the barking of the sea lions on the starboard side and thus avoided the rocks until we were able to regain the safety of the sea.

We were also treated to a spectacular sight off the Baja coast when a humpback whale breached, rocketing skyward only 20 feet (7 m) before our bow. The whale descended to the port side and drifted past us, leaving a crew stricken dumb by the sight.

Arriving in Los Angeles, we took on a pilot and proceeded to a berth at San Pedro.

In Los Angeles our ranks were increased by five more volunteers. The first was David Smith, a radio news director from KSSN radio in Portland, Oregon. Dave had raised $2,000 with a comedy fund-raising event. He now arrived to claim his berth. A big cigar-smoking Vietnam veteran, he was not happy to learn of the no-smoking rule.

The second volunteer was Patrick Wall. Originally from Newfoundland, Patrick was a disillusioned Greenpeacer. He was bitter over his treatment by Greenpeace after he had returned from Iki island in Japan, where he had freed a few hundred captured dolphins and served three months in a Japanese prison. Returning to San Francisco a hero, he ran for the board of directors of the Greenpeace Foundation. He was not elected. He had been beaten by a paper-pusher.

Frankie Seymour, Vivienne Smith and Craig Simmons flew in from Australia, bringing our total compliment from Oz to six.

I was anxious to leave Los Angeles to push on north. I was tired of interviews and talking about what we intended to do. I just simply wanted the opportunity to do it. With a crew of 21, we left San Pedro after a week, a crowd of supporters cheering us off. In the background, a car from the Soviet consulate watched the send-off celebrations. The four beefy Slavic characters inside did not appear to be amused. We pointed them out to some members of the media. As the reporters approached, the four covered their faces and drove off.

We proceeded up the coast towards Canada. I looked forward to seeing Vancouver again. When we got there, our reception by the Canadian media was unenthusiastic and, after the excitement of the Los Angeles send-off, disheartening. I wasn't surprised by it, however: my countrymen are rarely stirred to action, especially when it comes to environmental or conservation issues.

On the positive side, Bobby David had done his part and had secured us a dock. Unfortunately the berth was short term — only two days. We would have to secure a new berth before the return of the tug whose space we were occupying. This would not be an easy task in a harbour owned and operated by a government that respected commercial dollars above noble causes.

I have had to learn to tolerate greedy, parasitical port authorities throughout the world. The docks are overrun with vermin eager to cheat honest sailors of their hard-earned money. I've dealt with wharf rats in the ports of three oceans. Give me the corrupt pilots of the Persian Gulf, the bribe-demanding harbourmasters of Portugal, the sleazy ship chandlers of Singapore and the thieving customs officials of Mexico, but Lord spare me from the money-grubbing, insensitive, selfish bureaucrats of the Canadian corps of federal swivel servants.

Canada Customs spearheaded the assault on our ship. They would allow us into the Port of Vancouver but they would not allow us to leave. They demanded to see papers we did not have, were not required to have and did not know even existed.

"Where's your load line certificate?"

"It's not required," I answered.

"Who said?" responded the Customs man.

"The British Board of Trade," I retorted. "This is not a cargo ship."

"You got that in writing, eh?"

"No, it never occurred to me since it's never been required before."

"Well, it's required now. I'd advise you to get it."

The Customs man continued, "Now, where's your steamboat inspection certificate?"

"My what? Never heard of it," I answered.

"Never heard of it, eh? Not only should you have heard of it, you should have it. There is absolutely no excuse for not having it."

In frustration I replied, "This isn't a steamboat."

"Oh, you got any proof?"

"Yes, would you like to see the diesel engines?"

"No, I would like to see your papers."

The interrogation went on and on. The ship had passed two recent U.S. Coast Guard inspections and our last Board of Trade inspection in the U.K. had taken place less than a year before. Obviously we were being dealt a heavy hand from the boys in Ottawa. Of course, the character standing before me attired in the Customs official's uniform didn't know anything about that. He was just doing his job — strictly routine, he said.

He left the ship but not before warning me that we would not be allowed to leave until we had satisfied all of his requirements.

Marc Busch came into my cabin after the Customs man had left. "It looks like the Russians have some pull with your government," he said.

"Looks like it, doesn't it. It's pretty interesting that we only get this bureaucratic hassle just before we embark on a campaign. Anyways, we will be leaving here in seven days with or without that federal idiot's approval."

"We can't leave without clearance!"

"Marc, we'll be leaving in seven days. During the next week we will have our hands full scrounging food, fuel and money. I'll put Bobby onto this problem."

The first day in Vancouver found me signing up three additional members of the crew. Two reporters would be joining us. Eric Schwartz flew up from Los Angeles. He was freelancing for United Press International and *Omni* magazine. Arriving from New York was John Chenery, an Aussie reporter from the New York bureau of the *Sydney Morning Herald*.

A day later, another new crew member signed aboard. His name was Stephen Maxwell, a cameraman from New York. I suspected he was an amateur as a cinematographer. But Ron Precious, the only cameraman I did have confidence in, could not come. And there was another $1,000 to consider. The addition of the new crew members brought in another $3,000 for fuel. Considering we needed $20,000 for fuel, we had quite a problem on our hands if we were to depart within a week.

Meanwhile, I thought I might stir up the media by protesting our harassment by the feds. I issued a press release stating that the government of Canada was siding with the Russians to prevent our ship from reaching Siberia. This statement had the desired effect, putting the authorities on the defensive. They denied harassment of course, continuing to argue that their actions were purely routine.

"Why," they asked, "would the government help the Russians?"

In answer, I put a few questions of my own to the media. "Why did Canada vote to support Soviet whaling operations at the 1980 meeting of the International Whaling Commission? Why would a non-whaling nation, where the public opinion polls indicated there was overwhelming support to end whaling, support whaling? We don't know why, but we do know that Canada's official stand is pro–Soviet whaling."

Customs retaliated by telling the press that our safety inspection papers had expired. This was a lie. Not only were our papers valid, but they had not even asked to see them. I defended our position by sending photocopies of our valid safety inspection certificates to the media. The government then came up with new reasons for harassing us. The next day they told the press that the *Sea Shepherd* was not properly registered.

Vancouver radio talk show host Rafe Mair took up our cause. He demanded answers from the Canadian government and when these answers were not given, he accused the Canadian government of being puppets to the Russians.

The Customs people were becoming embarrassed. In desperation they passed the ball to the Federal Port Authority.

When our two days of docking at Riv-Tow expired, we let go the lines and allowed a harbour tug to pull us from the dock to a new berth that Bobby David had located for us. The pilotage authority had refused to allow us to move under our own power unless we paid them $600 for the privilege. We thought that was an excessive amount to move a mile. Riv-Tow had volunteered a tug, which allowed us to avoid the fee. Unfortunately, just as we were preparing to dock at the new position, we were informed by the owner that he would not after all allow us to use his berth. He told us that he had been advised by Canada Customs that they would not appreciate the offer of his dock to the *Sea Shepherd*. This left us stranded in Vancouver harbour with no place to go. I called the harbour-master and informed him of the problem. He, of course, had already been advised of the situation. In fact, it soon became obvious that he was himself involved in the conspiracy.

"*Sea Shepherd, Sea Shepherd*, this is the harbourmaster. Please advise us of your intentions."

I picked up the VHF telephone and replied, "*You* tell us our intentions. It seems we've been successfully sabotaged by Customs. Where do we go?"

The harbourmaster answered, "I don't care where you go, but you better go somewhere. You're interfering with normal ship and seaplane traffic."

I responded angrily, "This ship is staying right here until you find us a dock."

"You can't do that. We're not responsible for locating berths for ships. Your agent should have made proper arrangements."

"My agent did make proper arrangements and the government screwed us over. We can stay here and we will stay in this position until the government finds us a berth."

Thus began a five-hour stand-off in Vancouver harbour. The television crews appeared on the nearest docks. I sent Neil Sanderson ashore to explain the situation to the media. Once again we were successful in turning government interference into an embarrassment for the authorities. The stand-off was interrupted after three hours when the harbourmaster informed me that he had located a dock in North Vancouver. What he didn't tell me was that the dock was in the middle of a coal-loading area with no public access. I told him that I wanted a dock on the Vancouver side and if I couldn't get that, then I would drop anchor and spend the rest of the week as a navigational hazard.

The confrontation ended when we were informed by Bobby David that he had obtained permission from the owners of the Terminal docks in East Vancouver to use their property. The Longshoremen's Union had also given us permission to tie up without having to pay them. The tug-boat crew were relieved to tow us there. They were anxious to get home for dinner. Needless to say, the harbourmaster and Canada Customs were not happy.

With a new dock providing some measure of security, we were able to gather the needed provisions. We picked up donations of produce, rice, flour and other supplies from around the city. Behind us at the new dock was a large Swedish-built, Hong Kong–registered freighter. Her British officers generously allowed us the use of their machine shop for some much-needed repair work. Later in the evening, under the dark starless sky, one of the British mates lowered a stock of paint to us from their bow — 50 gallons (230 l) in all, with a 60-fathom nylon line thrown in. All that remained was to secure enough fuel for the voyage. The problem here was that it is impossible to get a contribution, a discount or even credit from an oil company. The best I could do with fund-raising was to borrow another $3,000 from the bank to supplement the $7,000 in hand — enough for half the fuel we needed. We also required about $2,000 worth of engine lube oil.

I called Shell Oil and ordered the lube oil and $20,000 worth of fuel. I gave the head office a cheque for $10,000 and told them that I was expecting the balance to be ready later in the day. I told them I would give the cheque to the driver of the truck. They were not too happy about the arrangement, but since they had already scheduled the fueling, they agreed. Later in the afternoon, after the office had closed and the fuel had been loaded, I handed the driver an envelope that he assumed was the cheque but was actually a letter in which I regretted that I had been unable to obtain the money from a bank transfer and I would pay the bill upon our return from the Bering Sea. We had done the impossible: we had convinced the Shell Oil Company to grant us credit, albeit against their will.

Fueled, provisioned and with a crew ready to go, we had only one problem remaining: how to deal with the government.

I decided that the best way to proceed was to take a high-profile, aggressive stand. I announced to the media that the ship would be leaving on Monday, July 18, at noon, with or without government clearance.

Meanwhile, Ben White brought up a man in flowing green robes to the bridge to talk with me. He described himself as Scion Davies, a devotee of Wicca, or Witchcraft. He wanted to bless our mission.

About an hour later, Bobby came into my cabin to inform me that a rather strange-looking person was burning incense on the deck while chanting and dancing around some chalked symbols.

"Oh, that's just some witch or warlock or something."

Bobby was mystified. "What's he doing on the ship?"

"I believe he's blessing the ship. It can't hurt."

"I didn't know you were superstitious."

"All sailors should be superstitious, Bobby. You never know who's got the truth market cornered."

The priest of Wicca left after talking Ben White into climbing the foremast to tie a witch's broom to the top. He told us that the collection of twigs he called a broom would protect us from storms and capture by the Russians. I had no argument with that. The broom stayed despite a few strangely serious protests from Leslie Fillebrown, a devout southern Baptist. She was horrified that I would sanction such a blasphemous service. I told her that we never turned down an offer of help, either material or immaterial. You just never knew.

Early Monday morning, Bobby David left for the Customs office to make a final attempt to have the ship cleared for departure. I called the pilot and the crew took care of their last-minute personal affairs.

With noon fast approaching and a crowd of media and well-wishers gathering, I positioned a few crew members with fire hoses on the fore and aft decks of the ship. Their orders were to turn the hoses on any official who attempted to board the ship to prevent our departure.

The pilot arrived but notified me that he would not take us out without clearance. Bobby returned and informed the media that Customs was still denying us clearance. A few police officers were gathering and a small Coast Guard vessel was lurking about.

At the stroke of noon, I ordered the crew to cut the lines and we proceeded towards the harbour mouth without a pilot, without clearance, and despite the promise of the Customs Department that we would not be allowed to leave.

The authorities had not expected such blatant defiance. They had been hoping to intimidate me with the presence of uniformed officers and the refusals of clearance.

I called the harbourmaster. "Vancouver Traffic, this is the *Sea Shepherd II*. Please be advised that we are bound outward under the Lion's Gate. ETA to the bridge will be 15 minutes."

The harbourmaster replied angrily, "*Sea Shepherd II*, this is Vancouver Traffic. Please be advised that you do not have clearance to leave. Repeat, you do not have clearance."

I picked up the mike for the VHF and calmly said, "Vancouver Traffic. This is the *Sea Shepherd II*. I repeat, ETA to the bridge is 15 minutes. We do not seem to be able to copy you. This is the *Sea Shepherd II* outward bound for the Bering Sea and Siberia. So long, Vancouver Traffic. Thank you for your co-operation and for your hospitality. My crew and I are very grateful for all the assistance you provided. *Sea Shepherd II* out." With that, I cradled the mike, turned down the volume and stepped out on the bridge wing to say a final goodbye to my family and friends.

We were followed by an entourage of small boats carrying reporters and supporters. From one boat, my year-old daughter waved goodbye. She was quite obviously enjoying the excitement. For my part, as I waved back, I wondered very seriously if I would ever see my Lilliolani again. Leaving her behind was my single great regret and my only source of worry. The Coast Guard vessel followed but made no attempt to interfere. We set course towards Victoria to round the southern tip of Vancouver Island for the voyage north to Unimak Pass, the entrance to the Bering Sea.

Bobby David left the dock with us but we put him ashore near Victoria. He would stay behind to take care of our business in Vancouver before flying to Nome to join us just prior to our departure for Siberia.

We transported Bobby to shore at sunset after passing Victoria. He jumped from the inflatable and waved goodbye. What we did not know was that we had accidentally deposited Bobby on military property. When we met again in Nome, he said he had spent hours looking for a way to sneak off the base undetected. He was successful, which doesn't say much for security at the Canadian Forces base at Esquimalt. Or it may say something about Bobby's abilities at espionage work.

The plan for Siberia was simple. I told the crew that we would enter Soviet waters, search for and possibly disable the Soviet whaling vessel believed to be in the area, and look for evidence of illegal whaling activities. Oh yes, the plan also involved getting away with the evidence and returnig home. Piece of cake really, if you're a devotee of spy and action novels or if you are young, naïve and searching for adventure. Unfortunately, most of my crew fell into one or both of these categories and I was unable to convince them of the dangers involved. But then, they still had until Nome to come to their senses and withdraw.

They may have been naïve, but that didn't make them happy campers. By the time we had crossed the Gulf of Alaska, I had had my fill of petty complaints. Half the crew seemed to be under the impression that their contribution of a thousand bucks had earned them a berth on the *QE II*. If it was not the water shortage, it was the fact that we had run out of salad vegetables or, worse yet, the reporters had run out of brandy and vodka. It was always something. I told the complainers that if they couldn't adapt to life on the *Sea Shepherd II*, I didn't think that they would be able to cope in a Siberian labour camp.

Tensions eased when we sighted the *Agunalaksh* — an Aleut word meaning "the shores where the sea breaks its back," known by the white man as the Aleutian Islands.

We left the North Pacific behind as we passed through Unimak Pass, the gateway into the Bering Sea. The crew were awed by the scene, the mist rising off the sea and, to the east, the smoking peak of Shishaldin volcano. Even though I had been here before, I had forgotten the magic aura of the place. It was like entering Valhalla. I could well imagine Odin himself looking down upon us from his smouldering perch. I prayed silently for his help.

I have never been able to visit the waters of the Bering Sea without reflecting sadly upon the fate of that once-great inhabitant of these cold and ruthless waters. Steller's Sea Cow, the greatest of the Sirenians, was slaughtered and driven into extinction by man. With each visit into these lonely waters I have always taken time to pay homage to the memory of this forgotten gentle being. On the first night of our passage northward through the Bering Sea, I stood on the bow and looked across the moonlit waters towards the east. I let loose a scream of anguish to the elements as a demonstration of my feelings for losing a friend I never knew.

I spoke the words of a poem to myself that had taken life through the pen of my friend David Day, a poem called "The Siren Song," a tribute to the passing in 1768 of Steller's Sea Cow.

Some still nights
on the shores of Bering's Sea
you may imagine them

Huge as the hull
of an overturned ship
Moaning in the rolling surf
Fountain of hot blood pulsing
Furnace of the deep heart
Wave-worn giants, idle lovers
on the swell of the sea
Bigger than elephants
Skin like the bark of an ancient oak
Snorting like horses
Pawing the kelp meadows
with their tough hooves
like bulls in pasture
Tide riders, storm biders
Slow to lust as elephants
Passionate as whales
Beauty here in a thing not itself beautiful
As delight in the play of light
on a mountain or a great rock
Yet something vastly alive
As these once were alive
Some still nights
on the shores of Bering's sea
you may imagine them
the great breath-song
through the sighing night

My voice sank into the sonic black hole created by the chill wind. I could only turn away in frustration at being born too late to have made a difference, my will to strive even harder for other creatures of the sea rekindled on the embers of frustration.

I was able to distract the crew from their gripes by embarking on some fun and games with the Japanese. The area was polluted by the presence of Japanese trawlers. Most of these vessels dabbled in a little bootleg fishing in U.S. territorial waters. Our navy-grey hull with the rainbow bow stripe resembled a Coast Guard cutter from a distance. Each time we spotted a trawler, we would change course and run in its direction. By the time we passed each trawler, we would see a dozen or so very angry but smiling, waving fishermen standing nonchalantly beside their dripping trawl nets.

These Japanese trawlermen were the greatest threat to marine mammals in the Bering Sea. Each year, thousands of Dall's porpoise and fur seals become entangled in the nets and drown. Sometimes the nets are lost. Because they're made of indestructible nylon, these "ghost nets" continue to entangle and kill both mammals and fish forever. This slaughter of dolphins and seals is written off as an incidental kill. I would have liked to write off a few trawlers as incidental kills. Only the fact that I had focused my sights on the Russians kept me from moby dicking a couple of the fishing boats. We needed to stop at Nome without the possibility of being charged with attacking the Japanese. That kind of trouble could seriously jeopardize the mission. I made a mental note to target them in a future campaign.

We came upon the Pribilof Islands a day after entering the Bering Sea. I passed them with regret. I had hoped to put a crew ashore to interfere with the July slaughter of 30,000 fur seals. I missed doing so by only a week because of a delay in raising the needed funds. Once again I had nothing but curses and contempt for the large animal-welfare groups that could have helped but would not. I had asked the Seal Rescue Fund. They were part of the Centre for Environmental Education, which also ran the Whale Protection Fund, the Sea Turtle Rescue Fund among others. This group told me that they did not have a budget to deal with the Pribilof situation and that it was not really a priority. I accepted that answer back in May, but when our ship reached Los Angeles I was shown a full-page ad in the *Los Angeles Times* requesting donations from the public to help stop the killing of fur seals in the Pribilofs. I was angry indeed when I read that all you had to do to stop the slaughter was to send a contribution to the Seal Rescue Fund. The ad didn't say they would do anything specific so I guess that makes it legal, but I was becoming more and more cynical about these big-time eco-businesses. Only the Fund for Animals and Friends of the Earth had come through for us. For the rest, I could not fathom, and nobody could explain to me, just what it was they spent their money on.

The fur seals are killed every year by the Aleut Indians. It is not an aboriginal right. The Aleuts had originally been brought to the uninhabited islands of St. Paul and St. George as slaves by the Russians. Their task was to slaughter seals to provide seal coats for the fashionable friends of the Czar in St. Petersburg. With the purchase of Alaska from the Russians, the United States acquired the islands and while the Aleuts were no longer officially "slaves," they were encouraged to continue the same line of work in return for meagre pay.

The United States had signed a treaty with the Russians, the Japanese and the British to regulate the "seal harvest." This treaty did eliminate the pelagic killing of seals but set up a program where the Aleuts would become federal civil servants charged with the task of seeing that Canada and Japan received 10,000 free pelts each for investing nothing but a promise to refrain from exterminating the seals at sea. This may have been a good idea at the time, but that was in 1911. Seventy years later, Canada and Japan were still splitting their bloody ransom money, the Aleuts are still slaving away bashing in the skulls of seals for wages, and the seals are still dying — all of this at an annual cost to the American taxpayer of $4 million. To be exact, the 1978 kill had cost $4,613,300. The sale of these sealskins brought in $684,036, and that was before the Canadians and the Japanese grabbed their share of the booty.

This hunt continues because the killing of seals is controlled by a bureaucracy called the Pribilof Island Program, a project of National Marine Fisheries, which is in turn a branch of the National Oceanic and Atmospheric Administration, which comes under the auspices of the U.S. Department of Commerce. It has not percolated down through the bureaucracy that the need to protect fur seals from the barbarian hordes of Japanese and Canadians no longer exists. A ransom was justified in 1911 when the territorial limit was only three miles (5 km). The 200-mile (330-km) limit of today means the U.S. taxpayer does not need to continue paying blood-money.

But any bureaucrat worth his tax of salt will be quick to invent a reason for his continued existence when the original reason is no longer valid. National Marine Fisheries stated that the hunt would have to continue regardless of the treaty for the simple reason that seals eat fish and the fish population of the Bering Sea would be doomed to extinction if the seals had anything to say about it. To protect the fish, the hunt would have to continue and the taxpayers would just have to sacrifice their dollars for the good of the environment.

Sounds pretty good until you look into the facts. You have to hand it to a Washington bureaucrat who has the brains to discover that seals consume fish. The fact that seals consume less than 2 per cent of the entire Bering Sea renewable fish population and that their role as a predator is actually beneficial, well, we don't want to confuse the issue.

Two of my previous crew had witnessed the Pribilof hunt in 1979. Keith Krueger and David MacKenney had studied and filmed the kill with the assistance of a Fund for Animals film crew. The cameraman was my friend Ronald

Precious, and his partner Michael Chechik was the soundman. From their accounts and the film footage, I had worked out a plan to interfere with the killing. Now, thanks to those with the eco-bucks, we were too late and the seals had died. It was with great sadness that I watched the Pribilofs fade away to our stern.

We arrived off Nome in the early hours of the morning of Thursday, August 6. We would have to anchor out nearly a mile. Nome is not noted as a deep-water port. The town had been named by mistake: about a hundred years ago, a map-maker had misread an old naval chart. The navy man who had first sighted the place had written down "? Name," because he was not sure whether or not the place had been named. The map-maker interpreted this as Cape Nome.

You would think from looking at it that the town, too, had been built by mistake. It sure as hell was an unlikely place to set up housekeeping. The village was built right on the beach along a treeless, barren, mosquito-infested coastline exposed to the full brunt of all that the Bering Sea could throw at it, including floods, high waves, ice, storms and the constant biting winds that swept unhindered across the Bering Sea from Siberia. There were no roads into the place and only an unreliable air service in and out.

But there was a reason for the existence of the town. There was no mistake about the gold. There had been plenty of it in the past and enough remained to justify the continued life of the place.

There sure as hell was no place like Nome. We had to wait until nine for somebody to respond to us on the radio. There didn't seem to be a Port Authority and the only radio connection we could find was with the airport. They didn't know much about ships. I told the airport operator that I needed to clear Customs and Immigration. He told me that he would track down a State Police officer to give me a call.

About an hour later, I received a call. "Calling the *Sea Surfer*, come in *Sea Surfer*."

I picked up the phone. "This is the *Sea Shepherd II*, repeat *Sea Shepherd II*."

"Yeah, hello *Sea Surfer*, this is the State Police. What's your pleasure?"

The officer did not appear to have heard my correction. I told him I needed to clear Customs so that we could come ashore for provisions.

"Well, what you waiting out there for? If you want to come ashore then for damn sakes come ashore."

I tried to explain that the ship was a British-registered vessel and that the crew included many non-Americans. We needed to clear our foreign nationals before they could legally enter the United States.

The officer was more than helpful. "Hell, you needn't worry about all that southern bureaucratic nonsense up here. The closest Customs officer is in Anchorage anyhow. Can the crap and come ashore."

So come ashore we did. To Dodge City north. The town was fabulous. The whole population seemed to exude a sense of freedom. Dirt streets, hitching posts, more than an adequate number of saloons and only one parking meter.

The parking meter had been placed by the Nome City Council in front of the offices of the *Nome Nugget*, the weekly voice of the North. It was there as a response to an anti–city council editorial penned by the editor/publisher of this frozen rag who answered to the name of Mark Furstenauw. It wasn't much of a parking meter, having been rammed a few times by the *Nome Nugget*'s truck.

I was very pleased to meet Mark and *Nugget* reporter Nancy McGuire. Having been a reporter for a weekly alternative newspaper myself, I had a keen interest in the profession and much admiration for anybody involved in putting out a newspaper in a place like Nome. After introducing myself to them, I told Mark and Nancy that we were just stopping off in Nome en route to invading Russia.

Mark looked at me and said, "Sounds like a stupid idea to me. What's in it for ya?"

"Nothing," I answered. "We know the Soviets are killing whales illegally and we want to do something about it."

"Still sounds sort of stupid to me, but what the hell do I know. I suppose you want a story on this in the *Nugget*."

I grinned and said, "We would indeed be honoured."

From the *Nome Nugget*, I took a walk over to the other newspaper. Yes, that's right; the metropolis of Nome supports two weekly newspapers. The other is called the *Bering Strait*.

Meanwhile, Bobby David had arrived and was in the process of relating his adventures to a few of the crew. I sat down, took a look at the price of beer on the menu and ordered a coffee. Damned if it wasn't near as expensive as the beer. Bobby was in the middle of his story about being put ashore on the Canadian Forces base at Esquimalt.

". . . then I waited until it was dark and made my way past the guards, the guard dogs, over a barbed-wire fence and onto the street."

Bobby stopped and Lins asked, "What happened then?"

"I hitched a ride into Victoria and caught a ferry to Vancouver."

Lins looked at him. "That's it?"

"Yeah, what did you expect?"

Obviously disappointed, Lins replied, "I expected an exciting story."

At this point, I interrupted and said, "Bobby, you should have gotten yourself shot or something, it would have made for a better story and poor Lins wouldn't be so disappointed."

Bobby had arrived in Nome before the ship and, having nothing to do, he decided to approach the Nome City Council for a contribution. I told him he had to be kidding. He said it couldn't hurt; they could only say no.

As a result there was hell to pay with the Natives. The local Inuit were not at all pleased to hear that the city council was considering giving a cash contribution to the Sea Shepherd Conservation Society. In fact, the local Native population was not all that happy to see us. They had a sneaking suspicion that we were up there to interfere with them and they wanted no part of us. It didn't help that the crew were buying T-shirts from the Native store and were wearing them about town. The T-shirts were a putdown of the movement to stop the killing of whales and they were not meant to be worn by environmentalist types. The T-shirts said: Save a Whale. Eat an Eskimo. I thought we should have a meeting with the local people to smooth things over and explain our position to them.

I approached the proprietor of the Bering Sea saloon. It was early in the afternoon and he was looking quite comfortable at the bar.

"Excuse me, sir, I'd like to know if we could have a meeting at your bar tonight to discuss our objectives with the local people."

Sitting there in his cowboy hat and hugging a beer, he didn't even turn around. Just mumbled, "People around here don't have much truck with eco-freak types. We just want to be left well enough alone, thank you. The answer is: no way, José."

"Look here," I argued, "we didn't come here to interfere with anybody. We're just stopping here on the way to Russia, where we intend to interfere with them."

Now he turned and smiled. "Well, why the hell didn't you say so in the first place? Sure you can use the place. Would you like a beer? Hey Judy, give the man a beer."

The barmaid put the beer on the counter.

"Thanks," I said.

"Hell, don't mention it. Just pay her the three bucks for it and tell me what all this nonsense is about going to see the Russkies."

The meeting wasn't much. Not much information was given or received. On the other hand, quite a bit of drinking took place, and with the crew and some of the locals getting sloshed together, a lot of latent hostility was dissipated.

The next day, we decided not to purchase any fuel in Nome. The price was practically double that in the south. We would instead refuel in Dutch Harbour on our return. As for provisions, we could not afford to take on much. Bread was three dollars a loaf, eggs three dollars a dozen and milk three dollars a quart. We were going to be breaking into the rice and beans soon, that was certain.

The prospect of eating rice and beans didn't bother me. The prospect of having to listen to the crew's whining and moaning did. Speaking of which, Nome did little to curtail the wimp brigade. The shower and bath set were upset with the street dust. The vegetarians were enraged at finding a butcher store that sold muk-tuk and seal meat.

Bob Osborn had discovered a more serious problem — the headless bodies of a number of walrus washed up on the beaches. I sent him back to photograph and measure the bodies. The walrus had been poached and the ivory tusks had been removed. Later, in a conversation with some reporters at the offices of the *Nome Nugget*, I found out that an estimated 8,000 walrus a year are killed illegally in Alaska. If we returned to the States from Siberia, I certainly intended to tackle this problem. For the moment, all that we could do was take pictures and ask questions.

Except for some of the staff of the *Nome Nugget*, I didn't find very many people concerned over the fate of the walrus. I *did* find quite a few people wanting to sell me raw ivory tusks. Sales usually took place in broad daylight on the main street. It was evident that the U.S. Department of Commerce was doing little to curtail the illegal ivory trade in Nome. Few people seemed to be concerned that the rotting walrus bodies might present a health problem. Bob Osborn had photographed Native children playing with and on the putrefying carcasses.

It was not surprising that the Nome City Council turned down Bobby's request for a contribution. Bobby and I met with some local Inuit leaders, but we were not very successful at finding common ground. One of the leaders, a man from the town of Gamble on St. Lawrence Island, told me that if we were against whaling, then we were the enemies of the Inuit. He felt that we had no right to interfere with the Russians either. "Once you stop them from killing whales then you will come after us. We do not want your people in our land."

He was quite obviously trying to pull some white liberal guilt bullshit on me and I was not in the mood for it.

"Let me see if I understand you correctly. You believe the whale must be hunted by your people, but do you hate this animal? Have you any respect for it at all?"

He answered that he did not hate the whale and that his people did indeed have great respect for the animal. He added, "But of course this is something that a white man would not understand."

"Maybe, maybe not." I said. "But I do know that if you are sincere about your respect for the whale then you are obligated to respect us, for we are protectors and defenders of whales. We act on behalf of the whale and in the interest of the whale. We receive no benefits for this. It is our spiritual responsibility and obligation and if you cannot understand this then you do not understand your own words, for those words are meaningless."

In response, they said that they would not support us but that they would not hinder us either.

I did not enjoy my position as an antagonist of the Inuit. I was fully acquainted with the Inuit arguments in favour of the whale hunt. I understood that it was a part of their culture, a test of manhood and a source of meat. Still, I would choose life over death, and the life of the whale meant more to me than a cultural right to kill. I could not buy their argument that the hunt was aboriginal. The last whale to be slain in the traditional manner was in 1888. After that, the killing was done with the weapons of the white man: guns and exploding harpoons. Today even more sophisticated tools are utilized, ranging from outboard-motor-powered metal boats to radios, power winches and high-powered rifles.

The hunt is not even an economic necessity any more. The Native communities had been experiencing unusual prosperity as a result of the pipeline boom, the construction boom, Beaufort Sea oil development projects and the Native Land Claims settlement. This prosperity has allowed many Inuit who could not previously afford it to outfit a whaling boat. Many of these new whalers have not served the traditional apprenticeship. They are whalers without respect for the whale or proper training in pursuing it. To be blunt, they are sloppy hunters.

The whale they hunt is the bowhead. We know less about this whale than about any of the other great whales. We do know that the total population of the species does not exceed 2,250. Practically exterminated by the New England whalers of a century ago, the bowhead has been slow to recover. Although the Inuit are not responsible for the mass slaughter of the whale, the annual hunt could easily finish the species off. For as the bowhead population has fallen, the Native population has risen. In 1977, 34 Inuit whaling crews joined the spring hunt from Barrow — twice the number that had hunted in the 1960s. The population of Barrow itself has swollen from a few families a century ago to 3,400 today. In 1910, the Inuit slew 13 whales; in 1977, they killed 76.

It is my considered opinion that the bowhead is endangered by this so-called aboriginal whaling. I oppose the Inuit hunt for this reason and also because I have witnessed the United States trade the lives of 6,000 sperm whales to the

Japanese and the Russians in return for a kill of 12 bowhead by the Inuit. That unfair trade had taken place at the 1980 International Whaling Commission meeting in Brighton, England. I had argued with Alaskan whalers there and I would continue to do so here. I would not at this time oppose them. Our mission for the summer was to protect the grey whale. One or two of these whales were killed by the Alaskan Natives every year but the greatest number of killings were the responsibility of the so-called aboriginal hunters of Soviet Siberia.

I returned with Bobby to the bar at the Nome Nugget Hotel, which had no connection with the newspaper of the same name. This place was Nome's answer to New York's Plaza Hotel, though the only true resemblance lay in the prices, which were somewhat higher at the Nugget. We had a talk with Mark from the *Nugget* about sending a reporter from his paper.

"Just think, Mark: the story will be covered from the scene by United Press International, the *Sydney Morning Herald* and the *Nome Nugget*."

But Mark was worried that we might be starting a Third World War, and he wasn't the only one. My crew were getting harassed all over town by people who thought we would be responsible for an outbreak of hostilities between the Soviets and the Americans. One woman had given me hell because she said I would be responsible for getting her son drafted by starting a war.

Where all this was coming from I had no idea until Mark handed me a clipping from the *Anchorage Times*. As he passed it to me, I saw Bobby make haste to leave. After I had read the first few paragraphs I knew why he was making himself scarce. Apparently Bobby had done some interviews in Anchorage on the way to Nome. That was all right, but he had said that we would search out the Soviet whaler and blow its prop off, sink it if need be. He told the newspaper that we had sunk three whalers in the past and this might well be our fourth.

After I had tracked him down, Bobby admitted to having given the interviews but claimed he had been misquoted. He thought that the result was not such a bad thing. He figured the story might stimulate more media interest in the expedition. It sure as hell did that. Both Eric Schwartz and John Chenery were told by their editors to get off the ship. Both refused. They told their editors that they were going on the story and they would take full responsibility for their actions.

"Don't you think the Russians might have some access to this paper or that they might pick it up off the wire?" I asked Bobby.

He didn't see any problem. "It will get them interested without a doubt. I thought you wanted an international incident."

"I do, Bobby. I do. I just hope we haven't pushed them too far. We're talking about the big league here. The Soviet military is not noted for its ability to be understanding."

We would also have less protection than we had previously thought. We were counting on the presence of an NBC news crew to generate the publicity we needed as a shield against possible Soviet heavy-handedness. Word had reached me just hours before our scheduled departure time that NBC had cancelled the deal. We would begin our invasion without network film coverage and without the $6,000 dollars in berth fees that I had counted on to purchase fuel in Dutch Harbour.

Shortly after, we returned to the ship to get ready for departure at 1400 hours. Our stay in Nome was over. We were ready to set out for Siberia. The date was Saturday, August 8, 1981.

It was fortunate that I had returned to the ship early. Quite a few of the crew were still loitering about the town. I put Marc Busch in command of the recall party and he headed in to collect stragglers. It didn't take him long. The only one he left ashore was Stephen Maxwell. Instead of Stephen, I got a note. Maxwell would not return until I gave him a contract stating that any film footage he took was 100 per cent his property and that he would have the say as to what was done with it, and he wanted his $1,000 back. This was his response to the discovery that NBC had cancelled and his was the only film documentation we would have.

He was a poor bargainer, though — he had left his camera on board. I sent Bob Osborn ashore with a message for Mr. Maxwell suggesting that he had better be on board within a half-hour or he would remain in Nome and his equipment stayed with us. I already had a deal with him that he would receive half of the funds from the sale of his film to cover his expenses for film and equipment. Maxwell tried to argue with Bob Osborn but didn't get very far. Bob simply told him to get in the boat and return to the ship or say goodbye to his film equipment.

With the crew on board, we blew the whistles in a farewell blast to the people of Nome and headed west towards Sledge Island and beyond to the Bering Strait.

7

Escape from
the **G**ulag

Only a few hours after leaving Alaska, the *Sea Shepherd II* was anchored two miles (3 km) off the Soviet coast. A few minutes after the anchor hit bottom, I had my hand on the throttle of the Mercury outboard. Our Zodiac inflatable was bound for the Siberian shore.

Eric Schwartz huddled defensively over his cameras. Bob Osborn attempted to brace himself against the pontoons to avoid the impact of the boat when it came down off the swell. Fortunately a strong wind was blowing out to sea, which meant we would not have a heavy surf to contend with. I had selected Bob to accompany Eric and me ashore because I needed an "expendable" engineer in the event that the outboard broke down. Peter Woof was essential if the ship was to return home. I, as her captain — well, I was expendable too. Neil could handle the *Shepherd* without me. This folly was my idea and I would share in the awful consequences, if there were any.

As we approached the shore, I felt as if our little boat was a time machine.

71

The facility on the beach looked like a desolate and remote Basque whaling station from centuries past. There was a timeless quality in the air. I looked back at the *Sea Shepherd II* as she shrank to our stern. That ship! My heart actually seemed to surge when I saw her from the distance. Some say that a man and his ship represent a symbiosis, that they select each other. I know this is romantic hogwash, but . . . there's truth in it. I can honestly say that I loved that ship. I loved the lady that went before her, too, and hated having to scuttle her in Leixoes harbour, but sometimes in a range war, you have to shoot your horse. John Wayne knew of these things. I learned them from him at Saturday afternoon matinees. Call me a cultural apostle of the Duke. His politics were antediluvian. But his style! His style was okay.

Actually, the Duke would have loved this. A landing in Siberia, thumbing your nose at the Commies? Hey!

As the forbidding beach loomed larger, I could make out a few people walking about. And as we drew closer, it became very obvious that two of the figures on the beach were Soviet soldiers with rifles slung over their shoulders. I looked at Eric and Bob — they were both ready and game for anything. Eric was preparing his cameras.

"Well guys, this is it. Just act like we belong here, like we do this sort of thing every day."

We reached the backwash of the gentle surf, white crushed seashells sluicing around us. I opened up the Mercury, hit the stop button and yanked up the prop so it wouldn't smash against the gritty bottom. We rode in on a small wave and skidded smoothly onto the beach.

We had landed about 150 feet (50 m) from the whaling station. Chunks of fresh whale meat were being hacked at by distinctly Caucasian-looking women with blue eyes and blonde hair protected by baboushkas — so much for it's being an aboriginal hunt. Their flensing knives would have made formidable weapons in the hands of the Tatars. There was no whale carcass in sight. Nor were there bones. Just glistening, reddish-black meat chopped into blocks. Astonishingly, the women ignored us completely. I half expected them to run screaming up the beach, yelling something like, "The Americans are coming! The Americans are coming!" But they carried on tossing smaller slabs of whale meat onto a conveyor belt. I could smell the slaughterhouse stench of dead mammals. Gulls hovered everywhere, diving in to grab any scraps they could, and blood stained the concrete deck the women were working on. The blood was so brightly red on that flowerless, rinsed-out beach.

Eric began snapping pictures. He captured the action around the conveyor belt and secured the evidence we needed to prove that Lorino was a major fur-raising community. The conveyor belt was transporting the meat directly to storage sheds alongside the holding pens, which housed either mink, sable or fox. I presumed the pens held sable because that would account for the two soldiers on the beach. The Russians are very protective of their monopoly on sable. I counted more than 50 sheds. Plainly they were shelters for animals: I could see row upon row of cages. The California grey whale being hacked into bits was a cheap source of fodder for this commercial fur farm. I had suspected as much. No wonder the Russians had turned down IWC requests to monitor the happy Asian natives conducting their "subsistence hunt."

Eric's cameras clicked and whirred, pale purple lenses impassively recording the scene. The only thing Russian about the town that I could see was the baroque Russian Orthodox church with its broken cross and onion-shaped steeple. I was beginning to think we could stroll right up the bluff and into town when Bob suddenly spoke up: "I think we're about to have some trouble, Paul. Look over there."

The two soldiers, rifles still slung over their shoulders, were walking along the beach towards us. But these two soldiers didn't seem to be interested in us at all. They were a few hundred yards away, taking their time. Eric continued to take pictures. Bob remained in the boat. I stood and smiled at some of the children who had run down to the beach to see us. Out of the corner of my eye, I watched as the two soldiers approached. When they were about a hundred yards (100 m) away, I quietly said to Eric, "Head back to the Zodiac — slowly."

Eric waded into the water and stepped into the inflatable. I followed. We motored out about 15 feet (5 m), cruised along the shore in the direction of the soldiers, and then passed them. The two soldiers stopped, swiveled around and began plodding after us. They did it with a tired, duty-bound rhythm. Maybe they were hungover or just bored. Certainly they weren't galvanized by our presence. It was easy for us to get several hundred feet ahead of them, take more pictures, then swing around and motor past them one more time, still pretending we didn't see them. And since they hadn't signalled to us in any way, it was possible to maintain the charade that everything was normal for a few minutes more. Once again, methodically, uninspired, the two soldiers turned on their heels and half walked, half wandered after us. It was as if we had picked up two unenthusiastic scavengers trailing in our wake. When we passed them this time, only 60 feet (20 m) separated us. I could make out the red star on their caps. They were both young — mere boys, really — and one of them had been outfitted with a uniform at least two sizes too big. His skinny neck stuck out from the rim of his collar.

Back in front of the whaling station, I aimed for the shore again, landing on the other side of a couple of ancient weather-beaten whaling longboats, beached, with popped planks and a dry brown hide of dead seaweed on their overturned hulls. Without going more than a few feet from the beached Zodiac, Eric snapped more pictures of the whaling station. As before, the women working at the conveyor belt paid no attention to us. The only explanation I could think of, both for the women and for the strangely uninterested soldiers, was that they presumed us to be Soviet scientists or technicians of some kind. Our orange Mustang suits probably gave us the appearance of a survey team. The only real interest we sparked was among a handful of kids, who pointed at us, jabbered among themselves and laughed. They kept their distance. I tossed a couple of chocolate bars in their direction, but they only stared at them with little frowns. I guess there's not much candy going around in Siberia. I opened a bar myself, peeling back the silver foil, and took a bite. They got the idea then, scrambled to pick up the other bars, but remained wary.

Finally, the soldiers arrived, boots crunching, leather squeaking. We couldn't pretend not to notice them any more. They were of Mongolian descent. One, the shorter, wore a peaked policeman's cap, dark green, with a red star badge. The other had a wool Cossack hat, also with a red star. Their uniforms were such a dark green they were almost black.

The taller one asked me something. The semester of Russian I had taken at Simon Fraser University eight years before now paid off finally — sort of.

The soldier called out, "*Shto eta?*"

I turned, smiled and said, "*Da-svidan'ya?*"

The soldier was not smiling. He repeated himself, this time much louder. "*Shto eta?*"

Still smiling, I shrugged my shoulders, noticing that his gaze was falling upon our boat.

I answered, "*Eta* Zodiac."

He was staring at our boat, puzzled, then swung on me. His eyes widened. "*Nyet*," he yelled, "*Eta* Mercury! *Eta Amerikan!*"

I gave him a smile, which caused him to step hurriedly backwards, fumbling for his rifle. The other soldier jerked away at once and unslung his weapon fearfully. It was easy to read their minds. Lights had gone off and bells were ringing inside their heads as they realized that standing before them was . . . the Enemy.

Their boots crunched the finely crushed seashell and gravel beach as the two slack-jawed Russians backed up behind the nearest abandoned longboat. Instinctively they were seeking cover. I guess they expected us to whip out handguns and begin mowing them down, cowboy fashion. A shootout at the Siberian corral, that sort of thing.

One of the soldiers yelled at me. I couldn't understand him. I smiled and pointed to my ship. He yelled again. I was nervous but I fought not to show it. Stepping into the boat, I pulled the engine into activity, the roar drowning out my lack of an answer.

The soldier who had been speaking quickly unslung his rifle and aimed it at my departing back. I felt a cold sweat break out on the back of my neck. Looking ahead, out to sea, I quietly asked Bob to keep me informed and to keep smiling and waving. Eric had wisely decided to quit taking pictures. I was counting on their being confused. That and the fact that these soldiers were young, and most people will hesitate to shoot you from behind, especially if you haven't done anything threatening. I was counting on these two fellows being typical draftees, not yet fully trained killing machines. In the back of my mind, I reassured myself that if these guys were super-efficient soldiers, they would not be doing beach patrol in Siberia.

With the boat moving slowly away from the beach, Bob, who was trying to smile and talk at the same time, said through clenched teeth, "The first soldier has his gun aimed at us and the second soldier is unslinging his . . . Both soldiers have their guns aimed at us but they appear to be puzzled."

"Good," I said, "Keep waving, keep smiling."

Osborn said nervously, "I think we should turn back and let them take us in. Those guys are going to shoot any second."

"No way," I answered. "If we go back, we go to prison. We lose the evidence. Everything'll have been for nothing. If they shoot us, they've got an international incident on their hands."

"Do you think that'll worry the Russians?" Schwartz, the pragmatic journalist, demanded.

"No, but it's a possibility that might worry those two guys with the guns. They don't strike me as the killing type."

"I sure as hell hope not," Osborn managed to say.

I felt strangely confident that the soldiers would not fire, but that small measure of doubt in my own instincts sent a brief shiver up my back. Our Zodiac moved away from the beach. Every yard seemed like a mile, every minute like an hour.

"They've put down their guns," Bob said with obvious relief. "Now they're running up a path to the top of the bluff."

"Probably to report us," said Eric.

We arrived back on board and hoisted the Zodiac up after us through a hole in the barbed wire.

"We got the evidence we came for," I announced to the waiting crew.

Peter Woof was doubtful. "You sure you got proof?"

Eric Schwartz was ecstatic. "I covered that beach like a blanket. Do we have proof? We have proof!" he gloated.

Marly Jones heard that and said, "Thank God. Now we can get out of here."

"Marly," I said, "you seem to have forgotten something."

"What? We got what we came for!"

"Not completely. There's still the *Zevezdny* to find." Ah yes, the *Zevezdny*. Our intelligence reports gave that as the name of the coastal whaler used to conduct this so-called aboriginal whaling. My plan for this expedition was twofold. First, find the evidence. Mission accomplished. Second, locate and disable the *Zevezdny*.

Marly was stunned. "You've got to be kidding! I want a vote taken. You're going to get us all killed!"

"Sorry, Marly," I growled. "When I decide that this ship is gonna be run as a democracy, I promise you, you will be the first to know." I turned to my officers. "Now let's go and look for that whaler."

I left Bob and Eric to describe our adventures on the beach to the crew and headed to the wheelhouse to plot a course with Marc and to brief Neil so that he could contact the ham radio operators in California with the news that we had uncovered illegal Soviet whaling activities.

We headed south along the coast. A Russian freighter was approaching from the south at a distance of five miles (8 km). I asked Marc to keep an eye on it. The two soldiers had not been idle after our departure. Within 15 minutes of our return to the ship, two Soviet helicopter gunships appeared and swiftly overtook us. They flew in low circles above us. The green machines each sported a large red star on their sides and two machine-gunners poised in the doors with their fingers on the triggers of a couple of nasty-looking weapons.

"What do we do now?" asked Marc.

"Ignore them," I said.

A few minutes later, the helicopters began to drop flares on our decks. The crew scrambled to retrieve them and throw them over the side.

"Now what?" asked Marc.

"Ignore them," I repeated.

Eddie Unterman was manning the radar. "Paul, there seems to be a ship moving up on our stern."

I ran out on the bridge wing and peered through the binoculars. It was obviously a military ship and it was moving fast. Stepping back into the wheelhouse I asked Marc to change course back to U.S. waters. It looked like we'd finally stirred up the hornet's nest.

"How far is it to the line, Marc?"

"Just over 20 miles, mate."

One of the choppers banked and headed away towards the oncoming behemoth. Using the radar, I calculated the speed of the pursuing ship at just over 30 knots. She was more than twice as fast as us and it was clear she would be alongside in less than an hour, which would still put us close to 10 miles (16 km) inside Russian waters. I began to prepare a battle plan to buy us time to cover the extra miles.

Marc interrupted me, poking his head into the chart room to let me know that the Soviet freighter had changed course to intercept us.

"What do we do?" he queried.

"Nothing. But ask Neil to relay everything to Los Angeles."

From the radio room, I could hear Roy Harrison's voice. He was a retired Los Angeles police officer living in Van Nuys. As a ham-radio enthusiast, he had taken a personal interest in our welfare and for the last few days we had kept him constantly up to date. It was good to have someone reliable on the other end.

I put the crew to work putting fresh grease on the gunnels, preparing the water hoses, distributing the gas masks and raising the flags. In addition to the red ensign on our stern, we flew the Russian courtesy flag on the starboard side of the aft mast. On the port side, we flew the United Nations flag, under which fluttered flags representing the home countries of the crew: Canada, Australia, West Germany, Scotland, England and the United States.

The freighter was closing in. I took my seat in the captain's chair and took a look at her through the binoculars. Her name was the *Kommunist*.

"An appropriate name, wouldn't you say, Marc."

"How so, mate?"

"We're taking on the entire Soviet system, the Party to be specific. It's us against the Kommunists."

Marc chuckled. "Not to mention the one on our tail."

The *Kommunist* closed in on us and passed behind, then changed course to keep alongside and just slightly back on our port side. Her civilian captain intended to wait for the military ship. Meanwhile the helicopters still darted back and forth overhead while my crew waved and smiled widely at them.

Eric ducked into the wheelhouse, yelling to be heard above the roar of the chopper that still hovered over us like a terrible insect. Closing the wheelhouse door, Schwartz commented, "Those helicopters sure do look nasty."

I looked at him. "Worried?"

"What me worry?" He laughed and ran out the door with his camera.

It did not take long for our pursuer to catch up with us. She was big and she carried a big gun on her bow. Smaller guns stuck out on the sides. Her name was the *Iceberg* and the number 024 was emblazoned in big white letters on her grey hull. A landing platform for helicopters was raised off her stern. She pulled up alongside us, 150 feet (50 m) off our starboard side. My crew could plainly see the Soviet sailors, some of whom were carrying automatic rifles. Her captain looked down on us from his four-storey-high bridge deck. I was beginning to have a few nagging doubts about whether we were going to get out of this. I briefly flashed on the comment by the State Department official that we would find ourselves under an iceberg. Perhaps he was right. We were definitely under the cold stare of a crew from a ship of the same name. Only this iceberg could and might spit fire.

There was something so futuristic about the bristling gunship compared to our old trawler. They were like machines from two vastly different ages meeting in some kind of time warp. Technically, we were aliens. But that pilot and his gunner looked like something out of *Star Wars*.

The Russians raised some signal flags ordering us to stop.

Once again Marc asked, "What do we do now?"

"How far are we from the line?"

"Just over 11 miles."

"Ignore them, keep the present course and speed."

Marc had taken the wheel himself. Except for Neil in the radio room and Eddie standing by the radar, I had placed the bridge off limits to the crew, a few of whom were visibly whimpering. Leslie Fillebrown stamped furiously into the wheelhouse, despite my ban on unauthorized entry. "What do you mean, 'Ignore it'? You have to stop! They'll blow us out of the water! Somebody should stop this ship." In tears, she pointed at me. "He's crazy! He's insane! He's —"

"Would you prefer permanent residency in Siberia, Leslie? Marc, please clear the bridge again. This time lock the door."

"My pleasure, Captain."

As my eyes roved over the deck to keep in touch with how we were doing, they fell upon the witch's broom high up in the mast. I remembered the words of the self-proclaimed warlock who had given the broom to Ben White to place there. "As long as the broom remains on the mast, you won't have any storms. And you will not be boarded by the Russians." So far, the weather had been terrific.

For 10 minutes the three ships moved alongside each other, our crews eyeball to eyeball. The two gunships continued to circle overhead. It was obvious that the Russians did not know quite what to make of us. The warship was ominous with her big grey bow cleaving the water and sending showers of spray onto our deck. It was if a true sea monster had surfaced and was eyeing us hungrily.

The Soviets lowered the flags and ran up a second set. The new message demanded our identification.

"Ignore it," I said again. "They can read."

"He's flashing a signal to us now," Marc reported. "Same message. He wants us to stop the ship." A pause. "Maybe we should?"

"Marc," I said as patiently as I could, "if we stop this ship and let those characters on board, this ship will be theirs and you, me and the rest of the crew will be on pick and shovel detail in the salt mines. Okay."

Suddenly, the VHF radio erupted with a deep voice speaking badly broken English. "*Sea Shepherd, Sea Shepherd*, stopa your engines, immediate!"

I picked up the telephone reluctantly and said, "Stop killing whales."

There was a slight pause on the other end, but then the voice returned.

"*Sea Shepherd*, stop your engines. Prepare to be boarded by the Soviet Union."

I answered with a chuckle, "Sorry, we do not have room for the Soviet Union."

The Soviet captain responded, sounding a little irritated, "Stop your engines now. You are in violation of the laws of the Soviet Union. You are under arrest! This is an order!"

Marc looked at me and said, "Well mate, that's that, isn't it. We have to stop now."

"Marc, the one absolute thing we are not going to do is to stop our engines. I've lost one ship to this kind of bullshit. I'm not about to lose a second."

Marc looked alarmed. "But what if he threatens to fire?"

"Then we call their bluff."

"Then what do we do if they do fire?"

"Then they will have an international incident on their hands and that will surely publicize this illegal whale kill. They won't fire, I'm pretty sure about that."

The Russian's voice interrupted us: "*Sea Shepherd*, you are under arrest."

I answered the Russians, "You are in violation of the regulations of the International Whaling Commission. Your nation is involved in illegal whaling operations. We have already radioed this information to the United States. I do not intend to stop this ship, nor will I allow your men to board us. We do not recognize the authority of a pirate whaling nation."

The Russian did not answer. Instead, he sped up and raced ahead of us and then crossed our bows. Some men on the stern were paying out a thick cable with the intention of fouling our prop. We passed harmlessly over it.

I radioed the Soviet commander. "Captain, we have a protected prop. That tactic will not work."

The Russian did not answer. Instead, he sped ahead once again and then stopped full abeam, directly in front of us.

"Captain," I yelled in to the telephone, "your ship is worth tens of millions of dollars. My ship is worth very little. Please get out of our way or I will run into you. I have no intention of stopping. I repeat, I will not stop."

The distance was closing rapidly. Marc held the wheel steady but he was obviously frightened.

"Jesus, Captain, we can't hit him. There'll be hell to pay if we do and I'll sure as hell never see Melbourne again."

"Marc, don't change course, not even a degree. We cannot be seen to be weakening. I'm not bluffing. He moves or we hit him."

The ball was in the Russian's court now. I spoke into the transmitter for the ship's intercom. "Stand by for a ramming. Hold tight and make sure you have your life jacket."

Things were unfolding quickly. Everything rested with that Russian captain. He had to assume that I was crazy. He had to weigh the cost of explaining a damaged ship to his superiors. He had to be aware of the responsibility he had to his crew and to the property of the State. It was like drag racing when you're a teenager. The guy with the battered old wreck could always take chances that the kid with Daddy's fancy sedan could never risk. If we survived the impact, there was the problem of escape, but in that regard, I had the tactical edge. The *Sea Shepherd* wasn't that much smaller than the *Iceberg*, when you got right down to it. Moving at 15 knots, our absolute top speed, we could deliver a hell of a blow amidships. With a hole punched in their side, the Russians would have a lot harder time staying afloat than we would with a smashed-up bow. As well, our bow was high and sharply angled forward, excellent for can-opener duty. Of course, he had his guns, and there were the armed helicopters overhead, but . . . if I could have tromped on the gas, I would have. As it was, our game of chicken was transpiring at breathtaking speed.

She was looming closer. From the bridge we could see very little water separating the two ships. Finally, to our immense relief, the Russian destroyer lurched forward and out of our way, allowing us to pass behind her stern by less than 50 yards (50 m).

I could sense that her commander was angry now. The warship moved and steamed around us. The *Kommunist* fell back. The *Iceberg* moved back into position on our starboard side. This time just 60 feet (20 m) separated us. Soviet sailors were whipping the tarpaulins off deck guns mounted on her bridge deck.

I yelled down to the crew. "Stand your ground, keep smiling and keep waving."

Turning to Marc and Eddie, I said, "All we can do now is confuse them and pray that we survive this."

I could hear Neil calmly appraising Roy and the other ham operators of the situation. I left my seat in the wheelhouse and stepped outside to look across at the Russians. I could see the sailors loading an ammunition belt and then waiting for orders. This was the moment of reckoning. It looked to me as if the Soviets now intended to rake the deck with 50-calibre machine-gun fire and then board us. Other sailors were now preparing two launches. The silence over the radio was ominous. No more talking.

Then the miracle occurred.

If there hadn't been so many witnesses, I wouldn't dare to report this. I'd be in the position of somebody who had just seen a flying saucer. Who would believe me? But this is what happened. There was a sudden cheer from the deck. It seemed senseless. I thought at first that some of my crew were flipping out. But it wasn't just my crew. The Russians had stopped their attack preparations and they were pointing wildly at the water.

For suddenly, without warning, the space between the two ships erupted in a shower of water. It obscured our view of the Russian ship for a moment and then the mist dispersed in rainbow-tinted droplets. My crew continued to cheer wildly. The Soviets looked surprised.

A large California grey had surfaced between the two ships and spouted. It remained for a few moments then dove beneath the surface. The space between the two boats opened as the Soviets turned to starboard and Marc instinctively turned to port.

A whale! A glorious, beloved, wonderful whale! Like a hand coming up from the sea between us and the Russians. I shuddered. Damn! Nobody who experienced this moment could help but feel that something mystical had taken place, something beyond the pale of anything we had a rational hope of expecting.

Years before, a man who knew more about whales than I ever will told me that if I could ever get my act together enough to get out to sea and go to aid the whales, I could depend on the whales for help. "The whales will come to you when you need them," Paul Spong had promised. "You can trust them to be there." I had put the thought aside, preferring to depend on the realpolitik and real economics of making the sea a no-man's-land for whalers. I would depend on pistons and willpower and ask nothing of Nature that Mother Gaia could easily grant. Oh, but by a miracle, here was a whale, a lone California grey whale, coming up out of the water between the warship and ourselves! Just as I had put my body between harpooners and cetaceans, Leviathan now had placed its body between mine and the naval vessel that would have destroyed us. We could not have been more astonished, more awed, if an angel had intervened.

Eric raced up to the bridge. "Christ, did you see that? It was incredible." I didn't answer.

The Russians were falling behind. One of the helicopters suddenly turned around and a few seconds later it was followed by the second. It was a relief not to have the thudding roar of their jet engines above us.

Eddie was looking into the radar. "We have land up ahead," he shouted. Marc interjected, "It must be St. Lawrence Island."

I ran into the chart room and made a few rapid calculations before returning to the bridge.

"Gentlemen," I said, "we are safely back in American waters."

We who would shepherd the whales had been shepherded by a whale through the valley of the shadow of death.

The Dolphins
of Iki

Would I die for a dolphin?
The answer without hesitation is yes.

Dexter Cate, The Fund for Animals

In late February 1978, fishermen in Nagasaki Prefecture rounded up and cold-bloodedly massacred more than a thousand dolphins, using machine guns borrowed from the Japanese Self-Defence Force.

Wounded dolphins were clubbed and speared on the beaches and in the shallows. The Japanese were careless about where they thrust the spears. The gentle dolphins were wounded repeatedly by spear-thrusts to the tail, the head and the body. This was no display of efficient, "humane" killing. The fishermen appeared to derive sadistic pleasure from the dolphins' dreadful torment. They were in a festive mood and obviously unconcerned about public opinion. The spear-thrusts were accompanied by laughter and smiles directed towards the cameras of Japanese television crews. The killers displayed their barbarity to the world with all the satisfaction of a trench-coated pervert flashing his genitals. The tortured bodies of the dolphins were finally towed out to sea and dumped for the sharks to feed on.

The fishermen boasted before the cameras that they had dealt with these gangsters of the sea, these dolphins. They said that they slaughtered the dolphins to teach them a lesson. The lesson was that the fish of the sea belonged to the fishermen and not to thieving bandits like these finned "demons."

A month later, another 100 dolphins were netted and clubbed to death on Tsushima island. With fish populations drastically reduced owing to overfishing and pollution, the fishermen were doing what fishermen the world over are inclined to do. They chose a scapegoat to vent their anger upon. They ignored the deadly contribution made by man to the impoverishment of the sea, and killed the dolphins as punishment for the excesses and crimes they had committed themselves. The government of Japan condoned and encouraged this butchery, offering a $12 bounty for every dolphin slain. Officially, the bounty was described as "a subsidy for countermeasures against harmful maritime mammals."

By 1980, the bounty had risen to $85 and the dolphin bodies were being disposed of in a giant meat-grinder financed by the government and set up on Iki island. The ground-up meat was being used for pig fodder and fertilizer. In the spring of that year, the civilized world outside of Japan was horrified by film and photographs showing the wholesale slaughter in the Japanese islands.

Blood-red waves lapped along the sandy shore. Dolphins thrashed about in pain, attempting to avoid the slashes inflicted by the spear-wielding fishermen. Hundreds of terrified creatures screamed in a language we do not yet understand as the fishermen continued the killing, relentlessly and without pity. By late afternoon, the bay was boiling with blood and the shore was a hellish canvas splattered with the mutilated corpses of the animals. The next day the killing continued. The lance blades were long and heavy. Nine inches (23 cm) of razor-sharp new steel plunged repeatedly into the smooth unresisting flesh of one dolphin after another. The dolphins screamed out at their tormentors but still the grotesque carnage continued and the dolphins continued to suffer and die.

Outraged North American conservation groups sent representatives to Iki to attempt to reason with the fishermen. They patiently tried to explain that it was pollution and too many fishermen that were responsible for the reduction in fish. The dolphins were being forced to come close to inshore fisheries because the vast Japanese offshore fisheries with their overwhelmingly efficient technology were wiping out the traditional food fish of the dolphins.

To no avail. The fishermen would not listen. The Japanese public and the government paid little attention to the concerns of foreign troublemakers. The killing continued.

But not without challenge or interference. On the last day of February 1980, one man launched a kayak under cover of darkness. He crossed the polluted bay through schools of blood-mad sharks to the shores of Tatsunoshima island. He felt the wind picking up as the evening became cooler, but this was a job that could not wait; it had to be done that night. On shore, he beached his small craft and quickly ran to the holding nets. He sliced the ropes binding the nets. But the dolphins did not move; they did not swim away. The healthy and strong dolphins refused to leave the injured and weak members of their own kind. This man, a member of the species that had been responsible for the netting and the slaughter, jumped without hesitation into the midst of hundreds of dolphins. He pushed and shoved and got them moving, one at a time out of the nets to freedom. The teeth of the dolphins could have caused serious damage to this one frail human among them. Yet on the part of the captured cetaceans there was no hostility. Three hundred of them were saved. Another 500 would be slaughtered later in the day.

Dexter Cate, a field agent for the Fund for Animals, had flown to Japan from his home in Hilo, Hawaii, to help the dolphins. Early the next morning, he was tired, cold and trapped on the island by rough seas and wind, but he was at peace with himself. He had acted and saved lives.

Earlier in the week, the fishermen had caught the 800 dolphins and were keeping them in the nets at Tatsunoshima, an uninhabited islet across Katsumoto Bay from Iki. The day before the release by Dexter, the Japanese had killed and fed 100 dolphin bodies into their meat shredder.

The fishermen arrived early in the morning of the first day of March to begin their grisly work. They found Dexter at the scene of his "crime." He made no attempt to escape. The angry fishermen took him back to Katsumoto and turned him over to the local police, who placed him under arrest.

Dexter's name became legend on Iki. A year later, schoolchildren were acting out a play where Dexter is discovered releasing the dolphins. They dramatically play out the role of indignant and morally correct fishermen beating this criminal senseless as just retribution for his interference in Japanese affairs.

The arrest touched off a storm of international protest. Among those who had taken up the cause was U.S. senator Robert Packwood. He had spoken eloquently on the subject in the spring of 1978. It was a historic address and bears repeating here, as taken from the Congressional Record:

The Iki Dolphin Massacre

Mr. President, I call to the attention of the Senate and the American people an appalling situation in Japan. More than 2,000 dolphins have been systematically rounded up and slaughtered over the past month around the island of Iki. The killing is continuing.

I am raising this issue today because the Foreign Minister of Japan, the Honorable Saburo Okita, is in Washington on an official visit. I call on Mr. Okita to inform his government and the people of Japan upon his return that the American people find abhorrent this official campaign to exterminate the dolphins from the Sea of Japan.

Last week, 48 members of the House of Representatives signed a letter to Prime Minister Ohira of Japan. In it they stated that:

"The savage and cruel slaughter of these highly intelligent and social mammals should not be condoned by any civilized nation. . . . There are certainly more humane means of clearing your fishing areas of dolphins. Such cruel and inhumane treatment must come to an end. Certainly, a nation as dedicated to peace and the value of human life as is Japan will not continue to permit the wholesale killing of highly intelligent mammals."

The sentiment of my colleagues is reflected in the law passed here in 1972, the Marine Mammal Protection Act, which grants protection to the dolphins and whales and other mammals that inhabit the sea. This landmark legislation recognizes that these extraordinary creatures must not be harvested without restriction or until they face extinction.

I strongly urge Japan to adopt dolphin protection laws like those of the United States, Canada, and the Soviet Union. The directed killing of dolphins at Iki and in other coastal areas of Japan, totaling many thousands annually, must be halted. We are only just beginning to understand the significance of the dolphins and their close cousins the whales in the web of life. Dr. Hans Gruenberger of the Brain Anatomy Institute in Switzerland has stated:

"Many toothed whales [including the dolphins] have reached such a degree of central nervous system differentiation that, cerebrally, they are on a par with higher primates and human beings."

These findings are echoed by American neuro-biologist Dr. Peter Morgane and others.

Jacques Cousteau observed with sad eloquence:

"The only creatures on Earth that have bigger — and maybe better — brains than humans are the Cetacea, the whales and dolphins. Perhaps they could one day tell us something important, but it is unlikely that we will hear it. Because we are coldly, efficiently and economically killing them off."

Mr. President, I have received an eyewitness account of the Iki dolphin massacre and other killing from a West Coast filmmaker, Hardy Jones, one of the courageous environmentalists who went to Japan to expose the events taking place there:

"We arrived late Wednesday and went into Katsumoto town, the scene of killing in 1978 and 1979. . . . We called the fishermen's union to ask for a meeting but, much to our surprise, were told to leave Katsumoto town immediately. The fishermen had captured 800 dolphins that very afternoon. They were astonished we had shown up when we did and were paranoid about our camera equipment.

"The following morning I noticed what looked like dolphin bodies on the beach at Tatsunoshima island — the place where the dolphins were confined. . . . We approached the area. . . . Fishermen rushed along the shore waving us away. But instead of leaving we circled around a point of land and went ashore. What we saw was appalling. The beach was littered with dolphins that had been confined in nets in shallow water. The outgoing tide had caused them to beach in the hot sun. Many were dead. Others were still gasping for breath, their skin cracking from dehydration.

"Across the bay, fishermen were massacring dolphins. As we approached the killing area the fishermen warned us away. They did not want cameras to record their deeds.

"We walked in among the fishermen and began filming and photographing the massacre of dolphins. Dozens of bottle-nosed dolphins were lying on the beach, dead or dying. Fishermen were wading into crimson water to throw nooses around the tails of other dolphins and pull them ashore to be killed.

"As we worked, the fishermen, of whom there were about 60, would try to dissuade us from filming. One shoved Howard. Others put their hands over his lens. We both continued our work — recording this terrible tragedy so the world would know what happened at Iki.

"It is still staggering to me to realize that if we had not arrived that morning the world would know nothing of this massacre in the town of Iki. . . . The events at Iki were alarming enough. Even more so is the fact that Japan appears to be preparing for a massive exploitation of the dolphin and pilot whale population for food."

Mr. President, this is an extremely distressing situation. I repeat my request that the government of Japan end this killing. The importance to

Japan of food from the sea is well recognized. However, the American public is outraged by the deliberate killing of dolphins and by installation of a "dolphin processor" costing more than $100,000 which grinds up the dolphins for pig food and fertilizer.

I urge that serious scientific analysis be made of these dolphins' food preferences or of effective methods of warning them away from Iki fishing grounds.

I urge that the Honorable Saburo Okita inform his government upon his return that its current practices are rejected by the American public and members of Congress, and hope Japan will reconsider its policies on dolphins and whales.

Not all the protests came from Americans or Europeans. One of the most unusual demonstrations in recorded history took place outside the harbour at Iki island.

On April 1, 1980, Reuters news service carried the following story:

ANGRY DOLPHINS TAKE REVENGE
ON FISHERMEN

In one of the weirdest cases of animal behaviour ever recorded, 4,000 dolphins have massed around a Japanese coastal village where fishermen had earlier slashed and stabbed 200 dolphins to death.

The dolphins formed a massive floating wall around the harbour on Iki island, stopping fishing boats from leaving.

The day before, Japanese fishermen had rounded up 200 dolphins in their nets and slaughtered them.

American experts were unable to explain the apparent act of revenge. Making eerie squeaking noises the dolphins stayed grouped together around the harbour for almost a full day.

Fishermen said the floating wall was so thick it would have been impossible to sail their fishing vessels through it.

Dolphin expert and film-maker Hardy Jones, who visited the island before the incident, said: "I've never heard of a phenomenon like this. I guess it just shows that the dolphins got as mad as hell and decided not to take the slaughter anymore."

Dexter Cate was held in jail for three months to await trial. He was jailed at Sasebo, awaiting an appearance before the Sasebo branch of the Nagasaki District Court. He was charged with interfering with the legal operation of business in Japan.

Dexter began a 10-day hunger strike to focus Japanese concern on the continued plight of the dolphins. Jail was not going to deter him from continuing his fight. The fasting succeeded in provoking a great deal of public sympathy for him and made millions of Japanese people aware for the first time in their lives that some humans are willing to suffer for the sake of their non-human brethren.

Cleveland Amory and the Fund for Animals retained a Japanese lawyer for Dexter's defence. Manabu Arioka, a native of Kochi City, a lawyer who spoke fluent English and was well versed in American law, took the prosecution completely off guard during the hearings of April 9 and 10. He submitted that the dolphin killing violated the Natural Parks Act and the Fisheries Act. The defence argument contended that the area where the dolphins were caught — Iki Katsumotocho — was part of the Iki-Tsushima National Park, designated a specially protected zone under the Natural Parks Act. In this zone, one is not even allowed to break off a tree branch, much less drive dolphins towards shore and kill them on the beach during ebb tide. The beach is land and therefore falls within the jurisdiction of regulations embodied in the Natural Parks Act.

Arioka further contended for the benefit of the defence that a net was stretched across the inlet at Tatsunoshima to catch the dolphins as they were driven in from the sea. According to the Fisheries Act, this constitutes fixed shore net fishing. Since the fishermen's co-operative had not established fishing rights in this inlet, they were in violation of Article 7 of the Fisheries Act, which stated that fixed point fishing not based on fishing rights is prohibited for unlicensed fishing.

On the stand, Dexter Cate admitted his ignorance of Japanese law. He did not consider the act of cutting the nets a crime but a moral act justified by the need to save the lives of the dolphins. The prosecution responded that Cate was guilty since he had admitted to having cut the nets and freed the dolphins, and that the other matters referred to by the defence contending the dolphin kill was illegal were irrelevant to the case being heard before the court.

The hearings continued with testimony from ecology experts brought in from the United States. It ended with a decision being put off until May 9. Dexter Cate remained in jail without being granted bail.

When the trial began on May 9, Peter Singer, a philosophy professor from Monash University in Australia and author of the book entitled *Animal*

Liberation, took the stand to argue that Dexter had acted on humanitarian grounds. The court became impatient with the defence's using the trial as a forum for what they considered academic philosophical discussions. Again they ignored as irrelevant the defence argument that the killing of the dolphins was illegal. The case was dismissed until the end of May for a decision, with the prosecution demanding an eight-month sentence for forcible obstruction of business. They argued that this was lenient since the charge could bring three years' imprisonment.

On May 25, Dexter was given a six-month suspended sentence, released from prison and immediately deported back to Hawaii. He had spent three months in jail.

But the dolphin wars in Japan were only just beginning. The next year witnessed another arrest, this time of Patrick Wall for cutting the nets and releasing dolphins at Futo on the Izu peninsula. Patrick also received three months in jail. He was then ordered deported. On his return to the United States, Patrick joined the crew of the *Sea Shepherd II* for the voyage to Siberia.

But despite the arrests, the publicity, U.S. governmental pressure and thousands of letters of protest, the killing continued. By 1982, with our mission to the Bering Sea completed, the situation in Japan screamed for our attention. But before we could do battle with the Japanese we would have to defend ourselves from environmentalists who felt we had no right to take our protests to Japan.

Before the ship had left Los Angeles, John Duncanson of Greenpeace told the *L.A. Times* that *Sea Shepherd* would be ineffective because the Japanese are "tired of American environmentalists telling them what to do with their fish" (*Los Angeles Times*, November 2, 1981). I responded to this charge by saying that I was not an American, that dolphins were not fish, and that they did not belong to the Japanese. I added that the only way that the *Sea Shepherd* would be stopped was if the Japanese sank her.

I was annoyed with Greenpeace for this unprovoked attack, but there was more to come. In Hawaii, the local Greenpeace organization decided to picket our ship. I was away when the pickets arrived but returned to the ship in the middle of the protest. Greenpeace had a large inflatable whale on the dock and they had members walking about with picket signs printed in Japanese saying absurd things like "Let them eat tofu."

Greenpeace had their own cameraman filming the scene, who turned out to be Stephen Maxwell from our Siberian campaign.

I yelled over to him, "Hey Maxwell, I see that you found us useful as a stepping-stone for employment with Greenpeace."

Maxwell sheepishly ignored me.

I went up to the clown who had organized this fiasco. His name was Steve Sipman, and he was busily engaged in a shouting match with Peter Woof, who had just ripped up a Greenpeace picket sign because Sipman refused to translate it.

"All right, Sipman," I interrupted. "What's all this nonsense about? Haven't you nerds got anybody else to hassle today? Are we your lucky targets this morning?"

Sipman was convinced we were the enemy. "If you go to Japan, you'll only make things worse. The Japanese don't need to see the sons of the conquerors of Japan coming over to preach morality to them. Change has to originate with the Japanese from within Japan. You're interfering in something you don't understand. We've been working for years on this problem and you're going to ruin everything."

Peter, Lins and Marc looked at each other. Marc said, "Wow, like heavy, man."

Lins added, "Whoop-de-do, an expert on friggin' foreign affairs."

Peter just laughed. I almost gave in to the temptation to laugh along with my disrespectful Aussie crew members. As seriously as I could, I ventured to reply.

"Steve, I've heard it before. Greenpeace accused me of spoiling their protests against the *Sierra* because, like a boor, I sunk the poor boat before you could stage a banner-hanging event. Besides, my father never invaded Japan and I'm not going to preach to them. I'm going to explain ecological facts of life to them and I don't really care if I have your approval or not."

Steve countered, "Your violence is going to kill more dolphins than the Japanese, you egocentric bastard . . ."

"Enough of this. I'll give you two minutes to get off this dock because in two minutes my crew is going to slash that balloon, then we're going to break your signs and then —"

"We'll go to the press. We have the right to oppose you."

"I'm sure you do, Steve, but not here. We pay for this dock. It's private property and I don't want you here, so get lost. Peter, Marc, slash that balloon!"

Peter and Marc pulled out their deck knives. Without further ado, the Greenpeace gang left.

But the opposition continued. We received a telegram from the Greenpeace mission in Japan telling us to stay away. I wired back that I had forwarded their message for consideration by our head office. Not that we had a head office but when talking with bureaucrats, it's wise to speak their language. By now we were attracting quite a lot of attention in Japan and I was doing a number of interviews daily with both local and Japanese media. I was losing patience. We had tried other methods of reaching the Japanese. All had failed.

In October 1981, Marc had completed a three-week protest fast against the hunt. In Los Angeles, Susan Weidman had fasted atop the foremast for two weeks over Christmas. Now, in Honolulu, Frankie Seymour was continuing the fasting protest. These campaigns served to arouse support in the communities where they took place and as a result we were able slowly to build a war chest to fund the upcoming dolphin battles.

We had officially opened our campaign in Los Angeles on December 7, the anniversary of the attack on Pearl Harbor. We wanted to address them when they were most sensitive. Even so, the Japanese consul, Mr. Watanabe, refused to meet with us or to speak with the press. We responded by slicing the Japanese flag in half with a Katana, a Japanese sword. We announced that the two pieces of the flag would be sewn together when the dolphin massacres were ended. This act was shown on Japanese television and described as "gross disrespect."

A few days later, Mr. Watanabe agreed to speak to me on the telephone only to say that the *Sea Shepherd* would never be allowed to enter Japanese waters. I answered that he could try to stop us but that, whatever he attempted to throw at us, we would continue on to our planned destination: Iki island.

Watanabe accused me of being a terrorist, then added, "Have you no respect for the territorial and sovereign waters of Japan? What makes you think you can flaunt the law?"

"Freedom, Mr. Watanabe, freedom. The lands of Japan are not your property because you say so. Man does not own land. This is my earth and yours. It belongs to all people, every damn square inch of it. It belongs to the animals and the plants and if not for mankind's unnatural tendency to impose absurd rules like trespass, there would be no problem. I am a citizen of the Earth, Mr. Watanabe. I am not a Canadian; that is just a label. I have as much right as ordained by the laws of nature to walk on the soil of what you call Japan as any Japanese. And to be more specific, I have as much right to protect dolphins as any Japanese and I have more of a right to protect them than you have to kill them. Please, Mr. Watanabe, spare me your archaic concepts of property and laws of trespass. We are going to Japan."

"Japan will never allow it," blustered Watanabe. "You cannot go."

"Japan cannot stop us by force. Japan can stop us by ending the dolphin kill. Sink us, imprison us, kill us — it makes little difference to us. We are going to Japan."

During a recent book promotion tour I had held a press conference at the

National Press Club in Washington, D.C,. for members of the Japanese press. They all attended, and I was encouraged by the knowledge that we had grabbed their attention. I gave them copies of a letter that I had that day delivered to Ambassador Yoshio Okawara at the embassy on Massachusetts Avenue. The letter read:

Dear Mr. Ambassador,

I respectfully request that you transmit the following proposal to your government in Tokyo:

The Sea Shepherd Conservation Society hereby offers to pay the fishermen of Iki island the sum $100 for the life of each dolphin they spare during the next dolphin hunting season beginning in February 1982.

The fishermen would agree to refrain from killing any dolphins and they would be reimbursed up to a total amount based on the average kill over the last three-year period (1979–81) Should this figure be about 5,000 dolphins, we would pay the fishermen a total of $500,000. Our offer of $100 per dolphin is $15 more than the fishermen are presently being paid for each dolphin they kill.

As part of this agreement, we would expect to have permission to station a representative of our Society as an observer at Iki island for the duration of the hunting season.

We respectfully request an urgent reply since, in the absence of an agreement, our conservation ship, *Sea Shepherd*, is now being prepared to sail with an international crew of volunteers to protect the dolphins at Iki island.

Respectfully submitted,
Captain Paul Watson

Although we ourselves did not have the funds to make good on this offer, we had been assured by the Fund for Animals in New York that the money could be raised if need be. The offer was given a great deal of publicity in Japan, but the embassy did not respond.

By February 15, the ship and crew were ready to depart, but we were delayed because of the need for an additional $5,000 worth of fuel. A departure date was set for February 23.

This was a fortunate delay for on February 21 I received a telephone call from Robert Friend, the Bureau Chief for the British Broadcasting Corporation (BBC) in Tokyo. He had just returned from a visit to Iki island, where he found that the fishermen were becoming sensitive to international public criticism and were not killing dolphins.

In response to this information, I took another stab at diplomacy and delivered by hand the following letter to Consul Naotake Yamashita at the Japanese consulate on Nuuanu Avenue:

Monday, February 22, 1982

Consul Naotake Yamashita
1742 Nuuanu Avenue
Honolulu, Hawaii 96817

Dear Mr. Yamashita,

The British Broadcasting Corporation has informed me that the fishermen of Iki island in Japan have made an effort to avoid the mass killings of dolphins. The reporter, Mr Robert Friend of the Tokyo Bureau, spoke to me by telephone on the evening of February 21. He informed me that he had just returned after a week's visit to Iki island.

Mr. Friend told me that the people of the area are sensitive to world opinion and are taking measures to avoid killing dolphins. He said that the fishermen were not making any attempts to round up and herd dolphins in to shore for slaughter.

As you are probably aware, my ship the *Sea Shepherd* and my crew of 18 people from five different nations are making final preparations to depart from Honolulu for Iki island on Tuesday, February 23.

If the BBC report is true, then the Sea Shepherd Conservation Society would not wish to risk losing any benefits given to the dolphins by the fishermen of Iki island. We would like to encourage this conservation effort on the part of the fishermen. We would not want to interfere with a Japanese domestic situation if a solution can be found in Japan by the Japanese people.

For this reason we are prepared to call off our voyage to the island. Before we do so, I would like to request verification of the BBC report from the Japanese government.

I would respectfully request of the Consul to inquire on our behalf as to the accuracy of the BBC information. Specifically, is it true that the fishermen of Iki island are no longer herding dolphins onto the beach for slaughter? And are the fishermen and the Japanese government searching for a solution to the problem that will not involve the massacre of hundreds of dolphins?

I am sure that the government of Japan would wish to avoid a potentially embarrassing confrontation if a more reasonable solution can be arrived at.

I urgently await your answer.

Sincerely,
Captain Paul Watson

The Japanese consul, the Honourable Mr. Yamashita, wired the contents of my letter to Tokyo and delivered an answer to me on February 24. He had called me on the twenty-third to request that I delay departure for one day to give him time to receive a response. I agreed.

After consultation with the fishermen and representatives of the Nagasaki Prefecture, the local government administering Iki affairs, the Japanese government gave in. I was invited to Japan myself to witness the fact that the fishermen would make an effort not to kill dolphins. I would be welcome to meet with them to discuss their situation and possible alternatives.

My crew were partially disappointed, but only partially. We had achieved a victory without sailing and, although deprived of the adventure of the trip, we were elated by the good news and what it would mean for the dolphins. I left for Japan on March 5. Upon arrival at Osaka airport, I was greeted by more than 40 Japanese journalists. I was taken by surprise at the extent of media interest in this story.

Changing planes at Osaka, I arrived less than an hour later at Fukuoka airport, where I was again swamped by a flood of reporters. One of the journalists, a man from the *Asahi News*, guided me to a hotel, where I met Robert Friend of the BBC.

It was an interesting evening. I was taken to dinner by two reporters from the *Asahi Shimbun*. They treated me to a traditional sushi dinner, complete with copious amounts of saki and the company of some rather beautiful Japanese women. It was a very satisfying evening. Although the language presented some barriers, we had fun communicating. I vaguely remember doing an interview with the reporters, but I remember very little after that.

I awoke the next morning with the worst hangover I had ever experienced. I had an early-morning interview with the BBC, and it was a miracle that I was able to pull it off without giving any indication that rockets were bursting inside my head.

Since I had crossed the dateline, the next day was Sunday, March 7. I picked up the second member of my Japan crew. Peter Brown was a cinematographer from Los Angeles whom I was meeting for the first time. With Peter, I felt a little more secure about the next day's journey into the snake pit, the island of dolphin killers. Peter was participating on assignment for NBC's *Real People*. They were working on a piece about me. He quickly demonstrated a deep personal interest in the welfare of the dolphins. This was the beginning of a long-term association between the two of us.

The next morning heralded a difficult flight to Iki island. Peter and I were almost bumped because the flight was booked solid by journalists. It was only when the reporters realized that they would not have a story unless we were on the plane that two of them picked the short straws to stay behind and allow us to depart. Upon arrival at Iki, the tarmac was crowded with even more reporters. Saving dolphins had definitely become a media event in Japan.

I was met at the airport by Mr. Urase, the representative for the Nagasaki Prefecture government. Peter and I then drove in a convoy of journalists, police and government people to the Katsumoto town hall for a meeting.

Our first problem was to overcome the language barrier. I had arranged for an interpreter, but she would not arrive until the next day. In the meantime, the BBC very kindly allowed their interpreter to translate for the Sea Shepherd Conservation Society. This, of course, was with the approval of the government, the fishermen and the other journalists, and with an understanding that this by no means put the BBC in a position of taking sides on the issue. The BBC, however, realized the advantage of their position since the other journalists would not be allowed to attend the meeting; this ban included Peter Brown. A schedule for discussion was set up for the afternoon and everyone adjourned for lunch.

During the lunch hour, Peter taped a recording microphone to my body to enable him to monitor and tape the conversation from outside the meeting room. I decided to use the rest of the lunch break as an opportunity to visit some of the fishermen at dockside. This proved to be very difficult since we were followed by a herd of reporters and any informal discussion with individual fishermen became impossible.

During this walk, I was approached by a young Japanese man. It turned out that he was not a fisherman but rather an employee of Greenpeace from Tokyo. In broken English, he said to me, "Captain Watson, I am Japanese and I think I understand the Japanese people better than you do. You should go home and let us solve this problem. The Japanese people will stop killing dolphins only through their own efforts. You must understand this and leave this to us. You do not understand the people."

I looked at him and his Greenpeace button and answered, "I agree with you that you most probably understand the Japanese people far better than I do, but then again I don't pretend to understand them. I do, however, believe that I understand the dolphins better than you and that is the reason I am here, to save dolphins. I am not here to argue with any Japanese. I am here to say that killing dolphins is murder and that it will stop. There is no cultural excuse for murder."

At the meeting, the press were allowed in for five minutes to film everybody. Although most of the delegation were fishermen, I was in fact meeting with three officials: Mr. Baba of the fishermen's co-operative; Mr. Matsumoto, the mayor of Katsumoto; and Mr. Urase, the man from the Nagasaki government.

The Japanese began the meeting by lecturing me on the need to kill the dolphins. I listened politely and responded by saying that I disagreed with their reasons justifying slaughter. I pointed out that all over the world, fishermen were blaming marine mammals for falling fish populations instead of facing the reality that overexploitation and pollution were the problems. I told them that even if the dolphins were a threat to their livelihood, the killing could not be justified in the eyes of the world. I pointed out to them that if American fishermen feared that Japanese fishermen were a threat to their livelihood, I would not support the Americans rounding up and murdering Japanese fishermen. The fishermen laughed at that comment, taking it with unexpected humour.

One fisherman stood up and drew me a chart showing the dolphins as a threat. As he spoke, the interpreter translated. Pointing to the blackboard with a yardstick, the fisherman said, "There are over 300,000 of these dolphins here. Our fishing area is the only place where the fish are for hundreds of miles. It is a small area. On some days as many as 500 dolphins are on the fishing grounds, stealing our fish."

I answered, "If there are as many as you say — 300,000 dolphins — and your fishing area is the only area where the fish can be found and if there are 500 dolphins in the area on these days and, as you said before, the dolphins are constantly eating, then where are the other 299,500 dolphins? How come all 300,000 dolphins are not competing on your grounds each day?"

The fisherman smiled and answered, "Who knows what goes on in the mind of a dolphin?"

"Ah," I interrupted, "so you admit that a dolphin has a mind."

Another fishermen stood up and asked, "If you had to choose between saving the life of a dolphin or saving the life of an Iki island fisherman, what choice would you make?"

Without hesitation, I answered, "I would save the dolphin. That is my duty. I did not come to Iki to rescue fishermen."

My answer took them off guard. They had expected an indication of liberal hypocrisy. I was finding that the more firmly I stood on my principles, the more respect they were giving me.

The same fisherman added, "So you think that a dolphin life is more important than a human life?"

"No, I think that both are equal in value."

In a dismissive tone, the same fisherman blurted out, "Then you are a fanatic."

"If you choose to call me a fanatic, be my guest. However, this humble fanatic has no intention of allowing the wholesale massacre of these gentle creatures to continue, so maybe you might humour me and desist."

The meeting proceeded with much difficulty. The fishermen on Iki island are stubborn and proud. In this regard they are no different from fishermen anywhere else. Also like most fishermen, they live in their own isolated communities, ignorant of environmental realities. This was quite evident when I pointed out to them that pollution was an important factor in the local decline of yellowtail tuna. The fishermen claimed there was no pollution in their coastal waters. After all, they argued, this was not Yokohama harbour. I pointed out that from where we were sitting, we could look out and see a sheen of oil covering most of Katsumoto harbour.

"And that's what you can see. I shudder to even speculate what chemicals are out there that we cannot see. I do know that the local dolphins have a dangerously high level of mercury in their tissue."

One fisherman answered, "We are not concerned about the mercury because we do not eat the dolphins directly. We feed the meat to pigs."

"Yes, and then you eat pork, which contains a greater amount of mercury than you would have gotten from the dolphins."

But it was no use preaching the finer principles of ecology. My words were falling on deaf ears. Ignorance of ecological facts and basic chemistry was but one of the problems I would have to deal with. There were four other major obstacles to communication. The first, of course, was the language barrier. The second problem was the many previous false reports and stories spread by journalists about the entire situation, which served to compound the third problem, which was the inherent distrust of Iki islanders for foreigners. On Iki, people from Nagasaki and Tokyo are considered foreigners. This led to the fourth obstacle, which was the apparent lack of trust between the Japanese Foreign Office and the Nagasaki Prefecture government, and in turn between Nagasaki and the mayor and fishermen of Iki island.

But my greatest problem was the initial denial of the promises made to me by Honolulu consul Naotake Yamashita. I told them I had been led to understand that the killing of dolphins would be ended and that the message had come from the fishermen to us through the Japanese Foreign Office. The fishermen claimed that what they had said was that they would make an effort to stop the killing but that they would still kill dolphins if they felt the fishery was threatened. I told them I could see nothing positive in such a position and if such was the case, then I had been deliberately misled by the Foreign Office into cancelling my expedition. Angrily, I told them I would retaliate by calling for an organized boycott of Japanese automobiles in North America and Europe. The fishermen were disturbed by the possibility that they would look bad in the eyes of other Japanese whose jobs could be threatened by such a boycott. They did not wish to attract the ire of the people on the mainland. They were even more disturbed by my threat to bring the *Sea Shepherd II* to Iki in the spring of 1983 to interfere with the fishery. I told them that because of the geography of the fishery, the *Sea Shepherd* could sit on the fishing grounds well beyond the reach of Japanese legal authority, and that if we did so we could make life miserable for any Iki fishermen willing to challenge us. I also told them that I would not hesitate to cut their nets. The fishermen were only too aware that I meant what I said. With that, the first day of our meeting was over and we agreed to continue again the next day.

The reporters were more than eager to attend the press conference that I called in the city hall immediately after the meeting adjourned. I angrily informed the press that I felt we had been deceived by the Japanese government, that we would call for and work to promote a boycott of Japanese cars and that we would continue the fight to stop the killing of dolphins with renewed energy.

The next day, the meeting began after we drove to the airport to pick up our interpreter. We were not allowed to see her until the police and authorities had thoroughly grilled her. I was worried for Mina Fukuda. I had not met her, but I knew that she was not expecting the first degree when she agreed to help us. She was doing so as a favour to Al Johnson, one of my best friends and a very dependable crew member. Al is an airline captain for American Airlines; Mina is a stewardess for Air France. Although born and raised in Nagasaki, she lived in Paris and spoke flawless French and English in addition to her native Japanese. In addition, she was a living doll, which had our police escorts falling about her for attention. Peter and I need not have worried about her. Mina was not in the least flustered by all the attention or the presence of police and politicians.

Our meeting began on the Tatami mats in my hotel room. The tone of the meeting had changed owing to the coverage on all the Japanese networks the night before. The Iki islanders did not like being at the centre of national attention. Unless they could reach a solution with us, they saw the conflict continuing for an indefinite period into the future. I assured them that I had no intention of quitting until the killing was stopped.

I opened the meeting by saying, "I have the responsibility to represent millions of people the world over who are morally opposed to the killing of dolphins, and some sort of positive development must be achieved before I will leave this island."

Mr. Urase went on the offensive. "Iki island has already been the victim of violence as perpetrated by Mr. Dexter Cate and I understand that the Sea Shepherd Conservation Society is even more extreme than Mr. Cate. If we do not agree, will you also commit acts of violence against us?"

"Mr. Urase, we are indeed more extreme than Mr. Cate, very much so. You are aware of our history. We have sunk ships and we have damaged property. You can call that violent if you wish, just as you have called Mr. Cate's act of saving lives violent. I will not nit-pick about what you choose to call us, but yes, we will not hesitate to disrupt the fishery or damage nets if we can save the lives of dolphins."

"Then it is true: you are a pirate?"

"Mr. Urase, if you wish to call me a pirate, then I will be a pirate. All I want is for you to understand our position on this matter."

Mayor Matsumoto asked, "Why do you all pick on the fishermen of Iki island? Why do you plague us? We are not the only people that kill dolphins."

"Mr. Mayor, this is true. Iki is not the only place where dolphins are killed. However if we were to go after Okinawans, they would ask us the same thing. If we were to go to Izu, the fishermen there would ask, Why us? The reason you have been chosen is because the media first came here at your request because you wanted to demonstrate what bandits these dolphins were. Why? So you could get a government subsidy. Is it our fault that your ploy also fed film footage of the killing to the international media and caused an international uproar amongst concerned citizens and humane people everywhere. You called the media here, we did not. You are only reaping what you have sown. The world is saying that the killing of the dolphins is unjustified for whatever reason. World opinion is not going to go away and Iki island will be a dirty word in the mouth of millions of people unless a solution is found."

The mayor agreed. "It is unfortunate that this bad thing, this criminal thing, the blood in the water, the spearing on the beaches, took place and that it was filmed. It did look cruel, it was cruel, and it was a mistake. We did not do this this year and I do not think it will happen again."

Hopefully, I replied, "Mr. Mayor, if you can assure me that it will not happen again, then I will be able to say that yes, we have achieved a positive thing here at Iki and perhaps we can defuse some of the world's anger at Iki."

Mr. Matsumoto ventured, "I think we can say that the deliberate mass killings will not take place again."

Feeling confident now, I added, "Can you also promise me that there will not be any further killing of dolphins this year."

The mayor hesitated, then said, "We cannot promise, but I do not believe that we will kill any more dolphins this year. Yesterday there were over 300 dolphins at the fishing area. We did nothing to harm the dolphins. No, there will not be any further killing of dolphins this year."

Of course, the 300 dolphins were not harmed because it would not have been politically wise to kill dolphins while I was there. However, I felt him to be sincere. But I decided to advance one more question.

"One last request, Mr. Mayor. Can you assure me there will be an effort made by fishermen to stop the killing of dolphins here permanently?"

"I believe an effort has been made. The last dolphin killed here was more than a month ago. We have killed few this year and we have made an effort."

Mr. Baba of the fishermen's co-operative added that there would be no roundup and no more mass slaughtering, but he could not guarantee that there would be an end to individual acts of dolphin killing.

We had accomplished all we could. We would have to trust the Japanese to keep their word. Mina, Peter and I returned to our hotel. For security reasons, the police had requested that we stay in a different location each night. This new place was very traditional and provided a fitting treat for our last night on the island. Mina hosted a dinner in her room for Peter and me and we toasted our achievements of the day with a few jars of locally produced sake.

We were in a jolly mood when we received a visitor in the person of Father

Janusz M. Koza. The Polish priest came to thank us for helping the dolphins. He felt that we had demonstrated great Christian compassion by helping a soulless creature like the dolphin. I did not argue with him. I was disturbed that he would regard this beautiful and intelligent marine mammal as soulless, but I had learned many years ago as a boy that it would achieve very little of positive value to argue with a priest. We tried hard to be polite but it was difficult to keep from laughing. Unbeknown to the priest, he was sitting facing us with his back to a display case in the hotel lobby. Inside the case were dozens of fertility statuettes in the form of male genitalia. We tried hard to avoid glancing at them but we couldn't look at the priest without seeing them appear to sprout from his head like horns. The irony of the situation was hilarious. Even our police bodyguard could not repress a laugh.

The next morning we returned to the mainland. Mina flew to Nagasaki to visit her parents. Peter returned to Tokyo to catch a flight to Los Angeles. I waited at the airport for Al Johnson to arrive. He had planned to come to Iki to help, but now that we would not need to do anything more, he and I took a train to Nagasaki to pay our respects to the victims of the Nagasaki nuclear attack. On our arrival we were met by the Nagasaki police, who demanded to know what my intention was in visiting their city. They found it difficult to understand that I only wished to pay respect to the memory of those who were killed by the Bomb. It was only after we called Mina, and she told the police that she would be responsible for us, that we were allowed to remain. One policeman asked Mina if she would like a bodyguard because both Al and I were known pirates and dangerous men. Mina said she felt she could handle us if we stepped out of line.

It is difficult to be a tourist in Japan once your picture has been a nightly feature on the evening news. But the trip to Nagasaki was worth the stares and police shadowing. To stand at ground zero in Nagasaki was to connect with the reality of the nuclear horror. I could feel the desecration of the soil, the evil of the radioactive pollutants and the pain that was and still is being experienced by the earth and the people alike. A walk through the museum was a series of face-slapping assaults of visual horror: the children with their innocence burned away, the women with their beauty violated forever, the men with their bravado replaced with humiliation. Here were the wages of the original sin born at Alamagordo. This was the fate of my generation and our legacy to the future. This city and Hiroshima were the anvils on which the nuclear hell of today was forged.

Flying back, we passed over Hiroshima. It was an eerie feeling looking down from the position Paul Tibbets occupied that fateful day in the *Enola Gay* when he played God and sent Little Boy plummeting down on its murderous one-way trip into a new age.

But Al and I left Japan with a feeling of accomplishment, with the satisfaction of knowing that once again our actions had saved lives.

The last dolphin officially killed on Iki island was on February 11, 1982. The total number of dolphins killed in 1982 at Iki was 163. Since our agreement, the Japanese have kept their word. The dolphin killing did not take place between 1983 and 1990.

Back in Honolulu, most of the crew had returned home. Some new volunteers were arriving and we began to make preparations to return with the ship to Seattle to begin to prepare for a voyage back to the east coast of Canada to protect harp seals.

A woman from Philadelphia arrived. She was young, naïve, gutsy and foolhardy, and eager for a chance to make a stand in defence of the earth. On her second day on Oahu she nearly sacrificed herself to the sea.

Some of the crew were walking along Sunset Beach on the north shore of the island. The surf was pounding in with walls of water 9 feet (3 m) high. Suddenly, without warning, Barbara dove in. I couldn't believe it. The woman had never seen the Pacific before and on her first encounter she decides to go bodysurfing in the worst possible location. Within a few minutes she was 60 yards (60 m) offshore, caught in an undertow.

I hesitated for a moment, thinking to myself that this would be a futile rescue that would only serve to kill me as well as her. Logic dictated that I stay on shore. But to hell with logic. I dove in to the maelstrom of white water only to be slammed to the bottom, with tons of water holding me down. I rose and gasped for breath just in time to see Barbara rise on the crest of a wave.

It was a miracle that saved her. The wave brought her directly to me. I grasped her wrist as she went by, and both of us were hurled violently onto the beach. Barbara was out cold. The retreating surf sucked the sand from beneath my feet and tried to wrest the woman from my grasp. Randy Henkle and Marc Busch had rushed forward and, between the three of us, we stole her back from the clutches of the sea.

We resuscitated her. She opened her eyes. "I gather," she sputtered, "that was not a very smart thing to do."

"You gathered right," I said seriously, but added, "At least now you've been properly introduced to Father Poseidon. I guess he didn't like your looks because he tossed you back."

Barbara shook her long blonde hair and looked up at me. "That," she said, "is not funny."

"Really." I laughed. "The alternative would have even less humour."

In 1983, Barbara left the *Sea Shepherd II* to join the crew of the *Rainbow Warrior* on its trip north to Siberia. She was arrested along with my old friend Ron Precious when they landed on a Siberian beach near Lorino to film whaling operations. I was a little amused. Greenpeace had called me a fool for going to Siberia in 1981. Now they were duplicating the same campaign and pretending that my voyage had not happened at all. Whereas we obtained documentary evidence of Russian whaling activities without arrest or injury, Greenpeace reaped more publicity for having crew arrested and jailed by the Soviets. They also had two serious injuries. They didn't get any film themselves, but hey, no problem! They simply used our film footage and photographs from 1981 to prove the case that we had already proved concerning Soviet violations of the International Whaling Commission regulations. The incident reminded me of something Patrick Moore had said to me years before when he was vice-president of Greenpeace Canada. "It doesn't matter what is true; it only matters what people believe is true. . . . You are what the media define you to be."

9

Odyssey to the Faeroes

**Give me a fair ship so I might
go into harm's way.**

John Paul Jones

A fter the successful intervention at Iki island, I became embroiled in confrontations protecting harp seal pups on the ice floes of eastern Canada that resulted in the seizure of the *Sea Shepherd II* by Canadian authorities. Although we were acquitted of all charges against us in connection with our interference with sealing operations, it took me more than two years to win my ship back from the Canadian Department of Fisheries and Oceans.

I kept myself busy in the west while battling the government forces in the eastern courts. In 1984, I organized a group called Friends of the Wolf and led a campaign to the Peace River district of northern British Columbia to protect wolves from aerial hunters. It was a successful campaign. We saved many wolves at the acceptable expense of making ourselves very unpopular among the northern Canadian rednecks and various elements of the British Columbian government.

At the same time I was promoting an art education project by working with Robert Wyland, a California muralist who had painted what he called a Whaling

105

Wall in Laguna Beach that featured life-size grey whales. Since then, he had struggled to get support to do a second Whaling Wall in California. I arranged to help him sponsor further Whaling Walls, using our contacts and volunteers. In June 1984, we opened Whaling Wall III at Marine World in Palos Verdes, California. This was followed by Whaling Wall IV in White Rock, British Columbia, and Whaling Wall V in Seattle, Washington. The first three walls featured the California grey whale. The Seattle wall featured a pod of orcas. By December 1984, we were ready to assault the blank white wall of the Illikai Apartments in Waikiki, Hawaii, with a 20-storey humpback mural. It was a herculean task costing us over 6,000 volunteer man-hours. In early April 1985, I dedicated the mural as a gift to the people of Hawaii from Robert Wyland and the Sea Shepherd Conservation Society.

I called the project the art of saving whales. I was hoping that exposing the public to life-size whales would motivate more concern for the whales in the wild.

That month, my ship was finally turned over to me by Jerry Conway of the Halifax office of Fisheries and Oceans. It was a disheartening day. My beloved *Sea Shepherd II* had been left to sit for two years with little maintenance or protection. Her once-glistening black hull was now flaking with rust and scale. The paint on her superstructure had peeled and now fluttered in the cold Atlantic wind. She was filthy outside, but the tragedy was inside. She had been looted and trashed — by whom we knew not. The government disclaimed responsibility. Her electronics were useless, her bell was missing — in fact, anything made of brass was missing, including large sections of brass as well as copper pipes in the engine room.

It quickly became obvious that the government had not laid the ship up properly after it had confiscated her. The dozens of expensive electric motors needed to power the steering gear and the pumping systems for fuel, water, lube oil and sewage were all shot — destroyed by condensation. The freezing temperatures of two Nova Scotia winters had split all the fresh water pipes. One of our three generators was permanently seized. It was a heartbreaking, gut-wrenching, frustrating homecoming on board my flagship. The damage, the looting, the dirt and the amused looks of the Fisheries and naval authorities who contemptuously returned my ship told me the story. The government had done this deliberately, motivated by petty vindictiveness, smug in the security of their arrogance and power.

My appeals to the local government officials were simply laughed at. I tried to contact John Fraser, the Fisheries Minister, in Ottawa to appeal directly to him. He ignored me, as did his lackeys, and to make matters worse, the Port of

Halifax officials ordered me to a dock where I would have to pay an exorbitant daily fee to work on the ship until it was seaworthy. Water would be extra, as would waste disposal and parking.

I had no choice but to accept the situation stoically. Whining would get us absolutely nowhere with those heartless bureaucratic bastards. The best revenge would be to repair the damage, sail the hell out of this piss-ass little port of swivel servants and, with a Trudeau salute to the feds, continue our crusade of making life difficult for the forces of oceanic destruction. In the meantime, I retained my friend Kim Roberts, an attorney in Vancouver, to begin a civil suit against the Department of Fisheries and Oceans to recover damages.

A small crew began to arrive to begin the long task of repairing the *Sea Shepherd II*. An engineering team took shape under Jeremy Coon and included Rod Coronado, who arrived from California, and Nick and Steve Taylor, two brothers from England who had been stranded by a yacht in Halifax and were looking for a ship to take them to sea again.

It would take four months of solid work to repair the damage. During this time, volunteers came and went and we faced constant harassment by petty bureaucrats who lurked like vultures waiting for us to break any one of thousands of port regulations. Backing up the Port Authority officials were waves of attacks by the Coast Guard, the Harbour Police, the Customs and the Labour departments and the Department of Fisheries. We took it all with smiles and appeared willing to satisfy their every demand.

As the weeks progressed, the pipes were replaced, the motors rewound, the wiring repaired, new electronics purchased and installed and the engines rebuilt. Jeremy Coon had seized what seemed to me an all but impossible task and through stubborn determination and elbow grease, he and his crew were becoming more and more optimistic that we would go to sea again. In the meantime, I borrowed money from the bank, organized fund-raisers and hustled donations of tools and equipment. Even so, the repairs were eating away every penny gathered and threatening to put me into debt for years. How would I ever be able to afford the fuel, lube oil, safety equipment and provisions for a transatlantic crossing.

As the days ticked by, the work progressed steadily. The crew put in 16-hour days. Mark Heitchue, a redheaded, freckled tree-climber, came from Virginia, sent by veteran Ben White. Gina Goulding, a tall and attractive blonde who described herself as a witch, arrived from California. A trio of French Canadians looking for adventure joined in mid-May. Two of them, Silvain Angers and Eric Dionne, were navigators. Eric's sister Marie Pierre Dionne joined as a cook. By late June, we had 20 crew, all eager to put to sea. All that remained was to complete the repairs, which Jeremy estimated would take two more weeks, and to locate money for fuel. One additional detail remained: we needed to find a campaign.

In all of the hustle to ready the ship, I had had little time to study plans for our next objective. None of the crew had actually asked me where we were going — they had simply assumed that I would tell them when I was ready. I still hadn't raised the necessary funding, but I reasoned to myself that perhaps if I could plan an appropriate campaign, the funding would become easier. Leaving the crew to complete the work, I flew to London for the July meeting of the International Whaling Commission in Bournemouth.

This year was a turning point for the IWC. The 1982 meeting had ruled that zero quotas on commercial whaling would be established at the 1985 meeting. The IWC in fact proceeded to implement the zero quotas. Unfortunately, the whaling nations threatened mutiny and made no secret of their contempt for the moratorium. Iceland announced that they would continue killing under "scientific" permits. The Japanese delegation stated that they "saw no legal or moral obligation to accept any decision of the commission concerning the moratorium."

I remember at the time that we were not worried. After all, the United States had threatened to implement the Packwood–Magnusson Amendment. This alone would force compliance by all whaling nations under threat of crippling sanctions on their fish exports to the United States. What we didn't know was that the Reagan Administration had cut a secret deal with the Japanese in December 1984 according to which the Japanese were given a green light to proceed with whaling until 1988. This information became public at the Bournemouth meeting, much to the disgust and frustration of most whale conservationists. Of course, Japan was just buying time, using its trade clout to manipulate the United States into a deal. Many of the mainstream U.S. groups were optimistic that they could take the White House to court and force compliance with Packwood–Magnusson. I remained sceptical. What the Japanese wanted, the Japanese would surely get. On April 5, 1985, Japanese Fisheries Minister Moriyoshi Sato, in a press interview from Tokyo, had said, "Japan will do its utmost to find out ways to maintain the nation's whaling in the form of research or other forms."

I left the meeting to the moderates to discuss enthusiastically how they would triumph in court against Reagan and the Japanese. I didn't share their optimism.

I intended to track down our British representative in Bournemouth at the IWC meeting. I knew he would be there. I had not been able to contact him for a few months. He had not answered my letters and I could not reach him on the phone. I needed our U.K. branch for two reasons. First, to provide us with funding. After all, we had 4,000 members in Great Britain and McColl had sent us nothing since 1983. The second reason was to get some information from David about our campaign to protect pilot whales in the Faeroe Islands.

I had set up Sea Shepherd in the U.K. in 1979 as a support group for the ship. Dave McColl had volunteered to administer the Society from Glasgow. Since then, he had initiated some local campaigns, including a successful three-year battle against Scottish sealing. He had even raised the funds to purchase one of the Orkney Islands, Little Green Holm, which was now a Sea Shepherd seal sanctuary. A year before, he had turned his attentions towards the sport hunting of pilot whales in the Faeroe Islands. This was something we would be able to use the ship for.

In Bournemouth, I tracked down Dave McColl at a waterfront pub. He was well into his third pint.

"Good to see you again, Dave," I said. "I need your help. We need money for fuel and we need a campaign. I was thinking we could bring the ship to the Faeroe Islands to help this project you want to do to protect pilot whales."

Dave was unusually reluctant to talk with me about the Faeroes, and he did not seem very enthusiastic about the ship returning to British waters.

"Well, Paul, I've been working with the Environmental Investigation Agency, with Alan Thornton actually, on a project in the Faeroes. I don't think he wants you to be involved."

"Screw him. Sea Shepherd is my organization and if you're working on the Faeroes, then I'm already involved."

"I didn't think you would get the ship back, so I made a deal with Alan. We'll use our inflatables and outboard motors and they will provide crew and transportation on the ferry from Denmark."

"Like hell you will," I responded. "I'll not be having a damn thing to do with that disloyal bastard. I recruited him into Greenpeace and he thanks me by treating me as a leper ever since."

Dave was unrepentant. "I run Sea Shepherd here, not you. We'll do things my way. I don't want your ship or your rules and the ship won't get a penny of Sea Shepherd U.K.'s money."

"Dave, I'm a director of Sea Shepherd U.K. and you've kept me in the dark about this. I'll call a meeting of the board to set this straight."

He laughed. "That won't do you a bit of good. I've placed two of the EIA people on the board and we've voted to change our name to SAVE."

"SAVE," I shouted. "What the hell does that mean?"

"It stands for the Society Against the Violation of the Environment."

"It sounds, like an anti-rape group."

"It is. We're against the rape of the environment and we won't be concentrating just on marine issues. We'll be promoting vegetarianism and animal rights, and exposing laboratory animal abuse."

"You will, will you? Not with my membership, you won't."

Dave stood up, shoved his chair back and pointed a finger in my face. "I'll do what I please."

I cursed him as he staggered out the door.

Later, I had dinner with the poet and author David Day. We were joined by my old friend Ross Thornwood and his fiancée, Sarah Hambley. I had worked with Ross in Greenpeace Hawaii back in 1977. He was a hell of a nice guy, although not the most organized man I've ever met. His girlfriend was very attractive, with a polished educated Devonshire accent and an eagerness to get actively involved.

"Sarah?" I asked, "how involved would you like to become?"

She looked a little puzzled. "What do you mean?"

"Well," said I, "I've just acquired a vacancy for U.K. director. You're educated. You've been around this reprobate [referring to Ross] for some time, so you know the history. It's a volunteer position, long hours, dreary administrative details to contend with and a shitload of bother with the bureaucrats."

"Well," she hesitated, "OK."

The next day, I irritated McColl, the Greenpeace crowd and many of the other delegates by attending the British government's reception for the IWC dressed in a British master mariner's uniform. The black uniform with brass buttons and four gold braids on the sleeve, which I was legally entitled to wear as a master of a British ship, seemed to ruffle a few feathers. The conservationist crowd avoided me, which was a blessing since the official delegates, including the mayor of Bournemouth and his wife, engaged me in conversation.

The mayor introduced me to the Icelandic whaling commissioner, who paled visibly as he shook my hand.

"You're the man who attacked the *Sierra*, are you not?"

"That's correct. I rammed her quite effectively actually. It's the only thing you can do with a pirate whaler."

"I disagree," he answered. "There are proper ways of dealing with these problems."

"Not with pirates," I answered. "The solution is to simply sink them."

"That's absurd," he countered. "Do you intend to sink Icelandic whalers also?"

"That depends," I said.

"Depends on what?"

I looked him in the eye, "It depends on Iceland obeying the rules."

"You're nothing but a pirate," he stammered.

I smiled. "I like to think so."

I flew to Glasgow next, where I discovered that Dave McColl had conned me. He had broken one of my primary rules a year ago. I had set up Sea Shepherd as a volunteer group. Dave had quit his job as a draftsman and began to pay himself a salary. On top of that, he had hired two of Alan Thornton's friends and had set up an office that was primarily occupied with fund-raising activities. I was furious.

I called a press conference in Glasgow to denounce the conduct of the Sea Shepherd Conservation Society in Britain. It was well covered. The media loves scandal. I was forced to attack McColl without mercy. I accused him of misrepresenting himself to the membership. He informed them in the newsletter that Sea Shepherd U.K. was supporting the ship and efforts to restore it and had pleaded specifically for funds for this purpose, but no money had come to me for more than a year.

At the same time, I obtained the membership list from one of the remaining loyal directors and arranged a mailing to inform them that the Sea Shepherd Society in the U.K. would now be headquartered in Plymouth under the direction of Sarah Hambley. The membership were told that if they wished to remain loyal to the Sea Shepherd Conservation Society and to the operation of the ship, then they should notify Sarah in Devon.

Having received the support of nearly 90 percent of the membership, Sarah contacted the police in Glasgow to serve a notice on Dave McColl to cease and desist from activities using the Sea Shepherd name and to return Sea Shepherd property to the membership now represented in Plymouth.

I had acted swiftly and without giving McColl any chance to prepare for the onslaught. Within three months, the Society in the U.K. would be safely back in my control and administered by Sarah. I returned to Halifax.

Back on the ship, which was now days away from being ready for a sea trial, I had an objective but I still had not raised enough funding for fuel, oil or provisions. McColl's behaviour was a severe blow and it would be months before we could count on funding from the U.K. Contributions from new crew members had raised only 20 per cent of what we needed to cross the Atlantic and reach the Faeroes.

I kept to myself for days, brooding in my cabin, exploring every possibility of raising funds. My requests from other organizations were turned down or ignored. It was as if they deliberately did not wish to know anything about the Faeroe Islands and the pilot whale slaughter.

Just as it looked like all hope was gone, I was rescued from defeat by a possibility presented by the harbourmaster. Apparently there was a derelict Colombian freighter called the *Dania* rusting away and taking up dock space. The Harbour department gave me the telephone number of the owner and said he was looking for someone to tow his vessel to Haiti. Thinking that a voyage to the Faeroes via Haiti was preferable to no voyage at all, I jumped at the possibility and called the number in Colombia. I reached a maid who spoke only Spanish and after a few minutes convinced her that I needed to speak to Carlos. The harbourmaster had not given me his last name. After a few minutes on hold, a voice came on the line.

"Hello. This is Carlos."

"Carlos, this is Paul Watson. I own and operate a large vessel here in Halifax. The harbourmaster said that you were looking for a tow to Haiti."

"Yes, that is right." Carlos got straight to the point. "How much will it cost me?"

I started at $75,000 but we settled on $25,000, and I insisted on a contract that absolved me in the event that the ship was damaged or lost at sea. He agreed. I also insisted on using his lifeboats and some electronics on his vessel to enable us to meet the safety requirements to leave Halifax. He agreed to this also and said that he would send up a cheque right away along with a contract.

Things were looking up. At least we could get out of this port, and with luck, we could cross the Atlantic by way of the Azores from Haiti to Falmouth. I whistled to myself as I left the phone booth and returned to the ship.

It was only after I had agreed to tow the ship that I discovered why it was in Halifax in the first place. Apparently, a year before, the ship had been caught lurking off the coast of Maine. The U.S. Coast Guard pursued it into Canadian waters, where the pursuit was picked up by the Royal Canadian Mounted Police. The Mounties were able to board, arrest and tow the ship to Halifax, where it was given a very meticulous search. Nothing was found and although an empty Colombia freighter, with a crew dressed in tropical clothing, lurking in the waters off Maine was viewed as suspicious, there was no case without the contraband. The ship was released but not permitted to sail because of lack of safety equipment. The crew quit and were deported back to Colombia. Now this mysterious Carlos with no last name wanted the ship brought to Haiti.

The ship was not worth $25,000, so I had a sneaking suspicion that something was still stashed on board somewhere. The last thing we needed was to be apprehended on the high seas towing a Colombian ship carrying drugs. Perhaps it was a setup by the government. I wouldn't put it past the bastards.

I called the Drug Enforcement Administration in Washington and told them the deal. They said that they saw no problem with it and I requested that they place my call on the record to prove that I was concerned in the event the ship was later found to be carrying narcotics.

The deal seemed even more suspicious a few days later, when I received a certified cheque from a bank in Aruba. It was a company cheque from Joe's Garage in Aruba. It was, however, a good cheque and I quickly cashed it and bought diesel fuel and lube oil before Carlos had a change of mind. I called him back and verified that the money had been received. I told him, however, that I still needed a contract.

I waited 10 days for the contract. Carlos did not send it. I was unable to reach him by phone. Finally, my patience exhausted, I told the crew to prepare for departure.

Jeremy Coon was worried. "I don't know, mate. I wouldn't double-cross a Colombian drug lord, if I were you."

"I'm not going to double-cross him. I told him what the deal was. I needed a contract. He has not sent it. We have to get going if we're going to make it to the Faeroe Islands this summer. When we do reach Carlos, we'll tell him that the deal was cancelled because we didn't receive his contract. We'll pay his money back to him and that'll be the end of it."

Jeremy was not convinced. "Have you ever heard of a Colombian necktie, mate? These drug lords teach lessons by slitting your throat and tugging your tongue through the gash. It ain't a pretty sight."

"Jeremy, I'm sure Carlos is first and foremost a businessman. Hell, we don't have any real evidence that he is involved with drugs at all, but I'm sure he would rather we pay back the money than kill me before asking."

"It's your funeral, mate. How do you intend to pay Carlos back his money if you don't have the money?"

He did have a point. "Well," I answered, "we'll deal with that problem when we get to it." I laughed. "Besides, the Faeroese will probably kill us first."

Finally, on Sunday, July 28, the *Sea Shepherd II* was ready to depart. I called a pilot and we let go the lines at 0715. The engines appeared to be running smoothly. We were away and it was with great satisfaction that I watched the dark grey, gloomy coastline of Nova Scotia slip away behind us.

My contentment was premature. At 1530 Jeremy stopped the engines suddenly. Shouts from the engine room heralded Mark as a messenger.

"Paul, Jeremy says we have a major emergency. The main lube oil pipeline to the engine has just split down the middle. We've lost a few barrels of oil and the pipe cannot be repaired. We'll have to get towed back."

"Goddamn it, we are not calling for help. We can't afford to be towed back. Tell Jeremy that we'll drift out here until he does get it fixed."

This resulted in some heated arguments with the chief, but I insisted that we not turn back. Finally, after 15 hours of intense labour by the engine crew with help from the deck crew, Jeremy managed to patch up the lube oil pipe with liquid steel, wire and rubber. By 0800 on Monday, we were under way again. I decided to stop at the French islands of St. Pierre and Miguelon to ensure proper repairs. We berthed at the French fishing port on Wednesday evening. Jeremy discovered that we could not proceed without rewinding our steering gear motors. The electrical shop in Halifax had taken our money but apparently had not done the work.

The voyage from Halifax to St. Pierre was too much for a few of the crew. Isabel Bliss left and unfortunately took Steve Taylor with her, which was the only real loss. He was a good engineer. The four others who left were all expendable. I felt that if they were going to be spooked by an engine breakdown, they would be of little use to us in a confrontation. Their loss was more than made up for by the return of Peter Woof, who managed to make his way from Australia to meet up with us on these lonely islands off the southern coast of Newfoundland. I appointed Peter electrician to minimize professional jealousies with Jeremy. It quickly became evident to me, however, that the only thing worse than not having a chief engineer on board was having two.

The French were very helpful with the electrical repairs and we were able to leave the dock on August 5. We were rapidly running out of summer. The voyage to the Faeroes was becoming an odyssey. I set course for Iceland. We needed to pick up a couple of crew and take on some water, and I wanted to get a look at the layout of the harbour and the whaling ships there.

Six stormy, wave-tossed days later the *Sea Shepherd II* docked behind the Greenpeace ship *Sirius* in Reykjavik. Ben White was there to greet us. The Greenpeace crew looked downright hostile. Across the harbour I could see the evil-looking bows of four Icelandic whalers, their harpoons wrapped in brown canvas tarpaulins.

I yelled down from the bridge. "Hey Ben, great to see you. What's with the surly crowd up forward?"

Ben laughed. "Just your typical milquetoast Greenpissers. I think we're raining on their parade here."

I walked down the gangplank after we'd cleared Icelandic Customs. Shaking Ben's hand, I asked him what the Greenpeacers were doing.

Ben smiled. "That's a good question. Last night they invited some of the whalers to dinner, which ended with them all singing songs and hugging. I think the whalers were interested in doing more than hugging with some of the girls. Anyhow, both the whalers and the wimps seem to have agreed on a pact to discourage us here. They wouldn't even allow me to give you a call on their VHF before you arrived. Apparently they're under orders not to allow any *Sea Shepherd* crew on board."

I laughed. "Not that we're interested."

"Something else," Ben interjected.

"What?"

"The fuel companies have said that you won't be able to buy fuel here in Iceland. They refuse to sell it to us."

"Oh, they do, do they. The funny thing is that we don't need any, but it's got the makings of a confrontation. Tomorrow morning, go down to the fuel dock and tell them we want to order 20 tons of diesel. In the meantime, do they have any good restaurants in this burg."

"That they do," said Ben, "and the girls here are incredible."

"Lead on then, Ben. Lead on."

The next morning, Ben went to harass the oil companies. I sent Rod Coronado to map the location of the whalers and to investigate the whale processing plant some 25 miles (40 km) north. Meanwhile, the Icelandic media were gathering like flies on shit at the foot of our gangplank. A police van had shown up and two armed guards were deployed beside the ship.

Ben returned to say that Greenpeace had issued a release to the media that the *Sea Shepherd II* was a terrorist ship and that we were here to sink Icelandic whalers. In addition to the guards watching us, the whaling ships were being closely guarded and the police had deployed divers in the water.

With the media scrambling for a response, I walked down the gangway and confronted them.

"Captain Watson. Are you here to sink our whalers?"

"Is it true that you are a terrorist?"

I waved to them to quiet down. "Look," I said. "The Sea Shepherd Conservation Society is not a terrorist organization —"

A reporter interrupted, "But Greenpeace says you are."

Irritated, I snapped back, "I couldn't give a damn what Greenpeace thinks. We don't protest whaling like they do. We enforce violations against International Whaling Commission agreements. As I understand it, Iceland is not yet in violation of any of the regulations. The ban on commercial whaling will not become law until the end of this year. We are on our way to interfere with the unregulated whaling of pilot whales by the Faeroese."

One woman reporter looked up and shouted, "What will you do if Iceland does kill whales next year?"

Smiling, I said, "The young lady has asked what we will do if Iceland kills whales next year. Ladies and gentlemen, the killing of whales next year will be a violation of the commercial moratorium imposed by the International Whaling Commission, which is the only international whaling regulatory organization in existence. If Iceland decides to violate this moratorium, the Sea Shepherd Conservation Society will take action against Iceland."

"What kind of action?" asked another reporter.

Very seriously, I answered, "We will sink your ships."

The ploy by Greenpeace to cause us problems now backfired on them. The media, Greenpeace's *raison d'être*, now ignored them. Why report on a group that babbles when some real-life pirates are in port.

The fuel companies turned us down, but Ben notified the police and we charged them with discrimination. It was a showdown that lasted for the remainder of the afternoon. The police wanted us out of their jurisdiction. The cost of guarding the whaling ships was a factor, and they were also worried that we might be attacked by some Icelandic whalers. We argued that we could not leave without fuel and if we could not carry on with our campaign to interfere with the whaling in the Faeroe Islands, then we would just have to stay and harass Icelandic whalers.

The police convinced the Icelanders to sell us fuel. Their argument must have been very convincing, because when the fuel trucks arrived and found that I had no cash, they pumped on the 20 tons anyway and said they would send a bill.

On the afternoon of August 14, we left Reykjavik, the whalers, the media and the Greenpeace crowd on the dock and headed seaward for the three-day run to the Faeroes.

10

The Ferocious Isles

The dark green peaks of the Faeroese islands of Vaagö and Steymoy rose from the early-morning shroud of fog like bearded wraith warriors. My first impression was one of enchantment. All the old Nordic sagas that my Danish maternal grandfather had read to me as a child had painted a picture in my mind of the realm of the Vikings. These rugged fairytale islands brought those childhood images back to me in Odinesque landscapes of winged Valkyries, two-handed swords and dragon ships.

The Faeroe Islands, the lair of ancient Norsemen, the first stepping-stone to Iceland and then on to Vinland, were breathtakingly, savagely beautiful. These remote islands, from whose rocky beaches, a thousand longboats had been launched to rape and plunder the known Norse world and beyond, the unknown lands of the ochre-painted Beothuks of Vinland — these emerald promontories were now before our bow. We had made the crossing, despite continued breakdowns, exploding fuse boxes and the routine bursting of pipes. We had made it to the Faeroes.

I dropped the hook off Tórshavn, or Thor's House, and waited for a wary party of Faeroese Customs officers to board us. They came, escorted by the police.

The first officer came straight to the point. "What are your intentions in the Faeroe Islands?"

With a straight face, I said, "Tourism."

His jaw dropped. "Tourism?"

"Yes, tourism. We heard you have a regular bloody tourist attraction here and we're here to see it."

He was puzzled by my approach. "What do you want to see?"

"Why," I answered, "the *Grind* of course — your tradition of butchering innocent whales for sport."

"Do you intend to cause trouble?"

"No, not at all. We're just here to make sure no whales show up for your spears and knives. You could say that we're here to prevent trouble."

Because the Faeroese had no history with us and could not really understand what we were about, they gave us clearance to land.

Family units of pilot whales migrate north each year in search of squid, their principal food. As they enter Faeroese waters, scores of small whaling boats intercept them. With a spear called a *vakn*, a knife known as a *grindaknivur*, stones with attached lines called *fastakast* and a vicious hook named a *soknarongul*, the Faeroese whalers wound and herd the whales, or *grindaval*, onto nearby beaches where they are cruelly slaughtered. The pilot whales are actually dispatched by hacking through the back to sever the spinal cord. According to the Faeroese government, this is both a humane and necessary hunt.

The whales are not killed for commercial purposes. The slaughter is more like a ritual. When the whales are sighted, children leave their classrooms, adults leave their place of work and they all run down to the beach to participate in the *Grind*. The whales are killed for sport and because it is a tradition. The Faeroese call the *Grind* a gift from God, and although as a nation they enjoy one of the highest per-capita incomes on earth, they insist that they need to kill the whales to supply meat for the table. However, the Faeroese Ministry of Health has ruled since the late 1970s that it is illegal to eat whale meat more than once a week because of the high concentration of mercury in the bodies of pilot whales. Every year more than twice as many whales are killed as are eaten. The surplus bodies are hauled out to sea as carrion for sharks and sea birds.

But for any who have witnessed it, the *Grind* is a primitive orgy of blood and violence, the ultimate expression of human contempt for nature. It is human cruelty pathetically justified by weak appeals to tradition and blasphemous pronouncements of rights and actions condoned by God. Only a people completely insulated from present ecological reality could wade into that blood and gore with lust and laughter. Here was proof indeed of the reality behind the legends of the berserkers and red Vikings. It is easy to recognize these people as the children of the rapers of Ireland and executioners of the Celts. Substitute bleeding children, violated, screaming women and decapitated men and this could be a beach from the last millennium running red with Irish blood. Same people, different times, and now that the slaying of people for sport is no longer acceptable, the intelligent creatures of the sea serve to feed the bloodlust of these Viking offspring. Having witnessed this slaughter made me ashamed of my half-Danish ancestry.

We were in for a fight. It became clear to us, when we talked to some of the people on shore, that they would not easily give up their *Grind*. The Faeroese are fiercely proud of their bloodlust. They had slain whales for a thousand years, they said, and vowed to continue for a thousand years more.

We returned to the ship and began to patrol Faeroese waters. I set the crew to stand watch for whales. Over the next week we were able to locate three pods of migrating whales and by running the ship in front of them, at the same time making noise with trumpets and drums, we were able to deflect the pods away from shore and death at the hands of their killers waiting there.

It wasn't long before the Faeroese heard what we were up to. A number of small fishing boats filled with angry, cursing citizens came out to berate us for our interference.

One woman screamed at us to go home. Because of our red ensign, she assumed we were British.

"Go back to England and hunt foxes. We don't want you here telling us what to do."

I shouted down from the bridge wing, "You have no right to slaughter the pilot whales."

Furious, she stood up in the boat and threw a rotten egg, missing Rod Coronado on the lower deck by inches. Shaking her fist, her face reddened with rage, she screamed, "Who the hell are you to tell us we have no right to kill whales, you bastard?"

I replied to her and her companions with calculated calm. "I am a friend of the whales," I said. "That gives me the right to tell you not to kill them."

"Ah, go home. We don't want you here." A flurry of rotten eggs followed, splattering the deck.

"Madam," I answered, "I am home. The ocean is my home and if you throw any more eggs at us, I'll turn my water cannons on you all."

My challenge was answered with an immediate volley of eggs. Nick and Rod accordingly unleashed a torrent of accurately directed water into the boats, soaking the occupants and sending them shoreward in full retreat.

When they returned to shore, the Islanders told the police that I had fired rifles at them and attempted to kill them. Over the VHF radio I attempted patiently to explain to the police what really had happened, but they advised me to leave Faeroese waters. I refused.

The next day, Ben and I requested and received permission to meet with Faeroese prime minister Atli P. Dam, a fat, cigar-chewing bureaucrat who ignored our arguments and babbled on about the whales being a gift from God and how it was the divine right of the Faeroese to kill them. We left the Althing, known to be the oldest democratic Parliament House in the world, shaking our heads, frustrated at our inability to communicate the need for whale conservation. The prime minister had admitted that they did not know how many whales there were. He was satisfied, however, that God would send an endless supply.

"Well, Ben," I said, "we tried talking to the bastards and they won't listen as usual, which means that we'll just have to continue blocking the whales, and if they get into a hunt, then we will have no choice but to get into the thick of it."

No whales were killed as the *Sea Shepherd II* stood guard in the waters around the Faeroe Islands. It was an uneventful vigil. Some successful campaigns are just that — routine and boring. It was a simple matter to intercept the migrating whales and turn them away from the islands. We knew that the Faeroese were not very happy with our continued lurking in their waters but they appeared to be at a loss over how to deal with us. Finally, at the end of August, with the whale migrations close to an end, I set a course for Scotland, only a day's journey to the southeast.

We dropped anchor off the shore of a barren, grassed island, one of the many rocky dots in the Orkney group. This island, however, named Little Green Holm, was special to us: it was our very own.

Back in 1979, Scottish Sea Shepherd commandos in inflatable Zodiacs had first challenged the killing of grey seals in the Orkney Islands. My crew of men and women had physically pulled the rifles out of the hands of the sealers and defended the grey seal pups with their own bodies. It was the beginning of a five-year battle to save Scottish seals, and that first year saw the costs of policing our activities exceed the profits of the sealers.

My crew returned to the Orkneys in 1980, and again in 1982, 1983 and 1984, until it became quite obvious that our interference of the sealers would be an annual activity. Each year, dozens of our people were arrested, and each year they were acquitted at great expense to the state. At the same time, the confrontations and the arrests were publicizing the seal hunt and helping us enlist a lot of supporters — so many, in fact, that we were able to raise enough money to purchase one of the Orkney Islands and declare it a Sea Shepherd Seal Sanctuary. We then announced our intention to raise money each year to buy the islands one at a time and turn them all into sanctuaries. Perhaps because we were now officially landed gentry, the government began to take us more seriously. Finally, in 1985, the fifth confrontation with the sealers was avoided when the Scottish Office announced that the hunting of seals was henceforth banned.

Our efforts in Ireland had also been successful. After our Irish crew camped on the seal rookeries in the Irish Sea in 1982 and physically challenged the sealers, the Irish government responded by shutting the hunt down. In 1984, the Scottish crew had also successfully interfered with the English seal hunt in the Farne Islands. Thus, in five years the Sea Shepherd Conservation Society had been instrumental in banning all sealing activities in the British Isles.

It was with a great deal of satisfaction that I set foot on the pebbly beach of Little Green Holm. All around were young seals and nesting gulls. When I turned to look back at the *Sea Shepherd II* riding at anchor, I saw the distance between the shore and the ship filled with the curious bobbing heads of hundreds of grey seals.

Gina Goulding had come ashore with me. "Why are they all looking at us?"

"I don't know," I answered, "perhaps they're checking out the landlord."

We left the island to the seals and gulls and headed to nearby Kirkwall, the largest harbour in the Orkneys. It was nearly midnight when we approached the harbour entrance. I called in to the harbourmaster and he told me to proceed, which I did, lining up on the harbour light.

It was a very dark night. I stationed Ben and Marie Pierre on the bow. The radar was clear, the lights were clear ahead. Suddenly Ben and Marie Pierre began to wave frantically, gesturing me to reverse engines. I ran for the telegraph and pulled the handle back to full reverse, startling the engine-room crew into action, prepared for a collision.

I could see nothing ahead, just the reflected shore light on the water between us and the guiding range light, when a shudder shook the ship as her engines revved into full reverse and then, with a slight jar, the ship came to a stop. We had hit something.

Running out to the starboard bridge wing, I looked over the side expecting to see, well, expecting to see almost anything, except a cow.

"Moo-oooo!"

"What the hell is that cow doing down there?" I bellowed. The cow stood in a few inches of water, its big brown eyes looking every bit as surprised as we were ourselves.

Ben raced up the outside stairwell. Panting, he explained, "We saw tufts of grass sticking out of the water in front of us. It looks as if we've plowed into a mud bank."

Returning to the wheelhouse, I radioed the harbourmaster's office.

"Kirkwall, Kirkwall, this is the *Sea Shepherd II*. I don't know how to put this but we've just missed colliding with a cow and we seem to be stuck on a mud bar."

The official didn't reply for a full 30 seconds and then observed somewhat apologetically, "*Sea Shepherd II*, och aye, ye musta hit the crow's foot. I shoulda told ye about that. Well, not much use whining about it. The tide should lift ye off in a few hours."

By four and the early-morning dawn, the ship pulled free, we bid adieu to the cow, leaving her munching off the beam, and headed towards the dock.

Jeremy had warned me that the engine gear-shifting controls were leaking air; in fact, he told me that I couldn't rely on them. Keeping this in mind, I stopped the engine a full 200 yards (200 m) from the dock to give plenty of time to switch to reverse. I sent a runner down to tell Jeremy that the next engine movement would be reverse.

A small group of fishermen had gathered to watch us dock. The ship moved gracefully forward and I turned to bring her alongside and gave the order to reverse. Nothing. After 30 seconds, nothing. The dock was edging closer and the fishermen were beginning to look worried. A few had even stepped back a bit. A full minute passed.

"Goddamn it, Jeremy, give me that reverse — now damn it, now."

It never came. With a sickening crunch, the *Sea Shepherd II* collided with the pier and snapped two piles like toothpicks before grinding to a halt. I ordered the crew to secure the lines, tried to ignore the smirking fishermen and waited patiently for an answer from down below.

Jeremy came on the bridge deck, covered in grease and sweat. "I tried, Mate; I tried, but the damn thing froze. I couldn't budge her."

The rest of the day saw our ship become the single biggest current attraction in Kirkwall. I think every man, woman, child and dog on the island came down to see the ship that had rammed the dock.

The next morning, with the reverse still frozen, Marie Pierre and Gina talked a fishing boat into towing us around so that our bow faced seaward. The mayor of Kirkwall saw us off with a bill for the damages, which he estimated at £5,000.

"Five thousand pounds!" I had yelled. "For God's sake, man, we just broke a couple of piles."

The mayor was businesslike and polite. "They not be any piles. These piles are of Japanese green wood, we hav'ta get 'em fra' Japan, ye know."

"Why? You don't have any trees in Scotland?"

"No," he answered, "not like these."

"Well," I answered, "a couple of logs from Japan shouldn't cost over $10,000."

Unperturbed he added, "Aye, but then there's labour."

Shaking my head, I took his bill, amazed that a small port in Scotland had to order timber for its pier from Japan.

We carried on down the coast Channel to the mouth of the Thames, where we picked up a river pilot. Sarah Hambley had secured a dock for us at Tilbury, just down the river from London.

We entered the Tilbury lock and headed down a cul-de-sac to a berth at the end. The pilot was taking us in at a fairly good speed.

"Captain?" I asked. "I'm not sure if we have our reverse gear working. It's been giving us trouble. Perhaps we should slow down."

"You don't say. Okay, stop engines."

Relieved, I telegraphed stop. I heard the engines quiet and stop but in the calm water, we were still moving towards the end of the cul-de-sac at a brisk speed and the end was solid concrete.

The pilot looked a trifle panicked. "I'm not used to bringing in a ship with just a forward gear. This doesn't look good."

The solid dead end was looming larger, and this time it was more serious than Kirkwall. I rushed to the bridge wing and screamed at Ben on the bow.

"Ben, drop the anchor, drop it now!"

Ben rushed over, flipped the bar and released the brake. The five-ton anchor hit the water and plummeted to the bottom as the chain tore out of the hosepipe.

"Brake her, Ben. Secure the chain."

Amidst a cloud of rust flakes, Ben managed to secure the brake, but we continued to plunge forward unfettered by the five-ton hook dragging across the filthy bottom. And then slowly, very slowly, we began to slow down. I swung the wheel hard to starboard and back hard to port, and she came alongside the berth, stopping only inches from the wall.

The pilot smiled. "Jolly good. Welcome to London."

11

Black **H**arvest

It is not enough to understand the natural world:
the point is to defend and preserve it.

Edward Abbey

Our first campaign to the Faeroe Islands was successful despite being organized and launched at the last minute. Returning to England would give us the time to prepare properly for a return to the Ferocious Isles in 1986. We had plenty of work to do, a new crew to recruit and media to line up. And, of course, funds to raise.

Tilbury is without a doubt the armpit of Great Britain. Located an hour by train downriver from London, it is a dock town sunk into a desperate economic sinkhole. Its outstanding features are derelict port facilities, boarded-up buildings in which many of the windows have been replaced with sooty cardboard, the whole mess mired in grime, industrial slime and a suffocating air of hopelessness. The Customs official warned us that it was a high crime area and to watch our backs at night. I had to accept the fact, however, that the primary reason we were here was because we could afford nothing better. The Sea Shepherd Conservation Society had run out of money. This was not unusual, but this grubby dead dock town so reeked of decay and filth that it was a struggle to contemplate recovery.

As usual, most of the volunteers jumped ship. I didn't blame them. I didn't relish the prospect of spending months in this Thames River backwater either, but there was no alternative. Jeremy immediately began a complete overhaul of the ship's mechanical, electrical and plumbing systems. I told him to send in the motors for repairs and we would get them back as we raised the funds to pay for the work.

A few weeks later, I was confronted with a mutiny. It started when one of our new British volunteers dyed his hair pink and purple and took to wearing a large penis earring dangling from his left ear. Each and every time a journalist appeared to interview us, this guy Jason Pettigrew would make sure that he was front and centre, and since the media loves to capture an opportunity to discredit any movement, I was concerned that Jason and his dangling willy would soon grace the local newspaper.

I approached him early one morning where he was washing up in the galley. "Jason."

"Yeah."

"Would you please refrain from wearing that earring on board the ship. I can live with the hair colour if you keep your head covered with a hat when reporters are near, but the earring has got to go."

"I have a right ta wear what I wish," he said defensively.

"Not on my ship, you don't. I want you to take it off."

When I returned to the mess for lunch I noticed that Jason continued to wear the earring. I didn't bother to talk to him again. I told the cook, Steve Hutson, that I wanted to see him in my cabin in 10 minutes' time.

Steve arrived and took a seat. "What's the problem?" he asked.

"The problem is that I gave Jason a direct order to remove that earring of his. I won't tell him again. You tell him, and if he continues to wear it when I get back, he's off the ship. I'll be in London until five."

When I returned I saw Jason on the deck. He was still wearing the earring. Patiently controlling my anger, I demanded, "What are you going to do about that earring?"

He smiled slyly and said confidently, "It stays, man."

"Fine. Here's your passport. You go. I want you off this ship immediately."

He smiled again. "I don't think so."

"Come again?" I asked.

"The crew agrees with me right to wear what I wish and if I go then they will all go," he said smugly.

I looked around. A dozen or so people were looking at me defiantly. I turned back to Jason. "Jason, get your things and get the hell off this ship within the next 10 minutes or I'll call the constables to come and remove you." Turning to the crew looking on, I calmly said, "You are all welcome to go with him. The crew does not run this ship. It is my ship and I run it. If you cannot accept that, then bugger off."

None of them left, but I quickly determined who was in on the "earring conspiracy." A few days later, I called the crew to the mess room and instructed all those who had agreed to back Jason's blackmail attempt to leave the ship immediately. This included three-quarters of the crew, leaving me with Rod Coronado, Jeremy Coon, Nick Taylor and Steve Hutson.

Meanwhile, Sarah was able to recruit some British shore volunteers to fill the gap. She was also able to organize a few fund-raisers throughout Britain. One of Sarah's volunteers, Alex Dandridge, was a comic juggler who gave a daily performance at Covent Garden. He and a visiting American street musician named Artiste organized a street musicians' fund-raiser at Covent Garden. Artiste is the world's foremost virtuoso with spoons and he, Alex and an assortment of clowns, jugglers, acrobats, magicians and musicians managed to fill four large buckets passed about by my crew with heavy British change. The event was so successful that it was a bit of a problem hauling the loot back to the boat. The buckets were too heavy to be carried. The crew frantically made the rounds of pubs, stores and shops exchanging coin for paper until the remaining cash was light enough to be manhandled off the streets, onto the Underground, transferred to the train and hauled bodily back through the crime-ridden streets of Tilbury to the ship. At the end of the day, we found that we had increased the ship's bank balance by over £2,500, mostly in one-pound coins.

Needless to say, we encouraged the artists to make the Sea Shepherd charity performance a regular Saturday event, and it was this activity that raised the bulk of the funds we needed to complete repairs on the ship.

Over the next few months we recruited zoologist Veronica Behn from Mexico; a retired travel agent, Al McKay, from Canada; and a schoolteacher, Gabriella Rennie, from the United States. A crew was slowly beginning to take shape.

David Howitt, a bicycle mechanic from Cornwall, came by and joined the engine-room crew. Rod Coronado quickly became friends with the Cornishman.

They were both young and eager to become ecological gunslingers and I kept a close eye on the two of them. They had too much energy to keep themselves from getting into trouble. That kind of energy and potential trouble can be a positive force if directed properly.

Another local to join the engine crew was Peter Winch, from Plymouth. Jennifer Riley, who lived in the Devon countryside, also joined. Another Devonshire man, Jeff Goodman, working for the BBC out of Plymouth, met with us and requested our permission to produce a BBC documentary when we returned to the Faeroe Islands in the summer of 1986.

By the end of 1985, we had repaired the ship, recruited half the crew needed and had a documentary film crew ready to join us on our second campaign to the Faeroes. We still needed to raise funding for fuel, equipment and other operating expenses. We were also able to secure a new berth in Mill Bay, Plymouth, closer to Sarah's office and surrounded by a more supportive population. This move enabled us to raise the rest of the funds. In the early spring, schoolchildren from Plymouth and Exeter organized a walk for the whales in Edgecumbe Park in nearby Cornwall. By June 1, because of Sarah Hambley's diligent efforts, we had secured all the necessary funding and recruited all the needed crew. We were ready to return to the Faeroes. But first we would sail to Malmö, Sweden, to attend the meeting of the International Whaling Commission.

I rented two inflatables and the BBC hoisted their own boat from shore. I was rather proud of the hand winch on our boat deck. We had salvaged it from a wreck on the mud flats at the mouth of the River Plym. With the mud and rust removed, the bearings greased and the unit painted, it looked as good as new.

I had few opportunities to return home to Vancouver during this period, but I took advantage of what time I could get to do so. My daughter Lilliolani was five years old and I missed her terribly, being away most of the time. I was separated from her mother. I had never felt that a person's vision should be forsaken because of parenthood. In fact, to follow one's bliss is in my opinion the single most important example a father or a mother can set for their child. I would never abandon my dreams for domestic enslavement. I would not abandon my responsibility for the consequences of fatherhood either. I knew that I could have both, but Starlet insisted that I could not. She insisted that I abandon Sea Shepherd and get what she referred to as a "real job." Since it was her way or the highway, I took the highway. I also assumed the responsibility of coming up with $1,000 a month in child support in return for unrestricted visitation rights with my daughter until she was 18.

This financial obligation meant that I had to find more lectures, which had been my only source of income. I absolutely refused to be paid by the Sea Shepherd Conservation Society. I set it up as a volunteer organization and that was the way it had to be. I would not see the primary purpose of the organization being to provide a livelihood for me or anyone else. We were in business to put ourselves out of business. In April, I received a request by the Swedish Green Party to undertake a two-week lecture tour of Sweden. This would provide me with six months' worth of child-support payments and would guarantee me the rest of the year to dedicate to the whales.

I returned to Vancouver in early May in time for Lani's sixth birthday. Unfortunately, I had little time to spend with her. There were so many final preparations back in England. I returned to the ship in mid-May.

We left Plymouth in mid-June and headed up the channel towards the North Sea. Bad weather and a generator breakdown forced us into Dover for a few days. After repairs, we headed towards the mouth of the Rhine and entered the Kiel Canal for the 50-mile (80-km) crossing to Kiel on the Baltic. From there it was a short haul to Malmö.

We were not a welcome sight to the whalers as our grey ship with a pilot whale painted on the side entered Malmö harbour. Our crew threw the lines to Ben White, who was waiting for us on the dock. Ben had arrived as Sea Shepherd's official observer at the International Whaling Commission. I secured the ship directly in front of the hotel where the IWC was meeting.

After Customs clearance, a posse of reporters crowded on board to ask about our intentions.

"We are here," said I, "to receive instructions for actions against the whalers."

"Do you take instructions from the IWC, Captain Watson?" asked one reporter.

"No," I answered. "We observe the decisions of the IWC and act accordingly in response to those decisions."

"What does that mean?"

"It means that once the IWC has outlawed an activity by ruling against it, then we recognize that ruling as our mandate to intervene, interfere, shut down and destroy the illicit activity."

I continued, "A moratorium on commercial whaling has been ruled. We intend to see what measures the IWC will take to enforce this ruling. If they do nothing to uphold their own rulings, then we will take it upon ourselves to uphold their rulings for them, whether they [the IWC] like it or not."

"So," said a woman from the Icelandic newspaper *Dagblad*, "what will you do if Iceland goes whaling against the wishes of the IWC?"

I smiled. "That's simple, if the IWC does not stop Iceland and if the United States does not sanction Iceland, then we will sink your whaling ships."

Another reporter asked, "What gives you the right to take the law into your hands?"

Patiently I looked at the reporter, "You know," I said calmly, "I have never understood why those who wish to champion peace, life, liberty and environmental sanity are always asked this question. Why do you never ask this of the whalers, of those who wage war or those who ravage the Earth? However," and I raised my voice, "I attended the 1972 U.N. Conference on the Environment in this country. That conference condemned whaling, and since 1972, *every* international organization and treaty that has dealt with the issue of whaling has ruled that whaling must stop. Yet all of the warnings, all of the rulings, all of the studies have been ignored with contempt because the voices of the international community are stifled by the political muscle purchased by that most notorious whaling nation — the barbarous whale-killing state of Japan."

A Japanese journalist interrupted me. "That is a racist statement. Admit it, you are opposed to whaling for the same reason that most of the anti-whaling nations are opposed to whaling —because it is a way to punish Japan. It is a plot against Asians. You are a racist. You are —"

I interrupted him in turn. "The Japanese have earned no right to whine about racism. In Japan, if you are not Japanese, you are second class. I will not accept a charge of racism against me from a representative of the media of the most racist nation on earth. There is no plot against Asians. We do, however, plot against Japan, and Norway, and Iceland, and Russia and any other nation that flagrantly violates international conservation law and then has the audacity to hide behind the skirts of racism. Personally, I find it extremely offensive that an issue as important as racism should be used as a tool to justify illegal whaling."

The Japanese reporter wasn't about to retreat. "You are just manipulating the facts. There are plenty of whales. You have your own agenda."

"That's correct. I do have my own agenda. It's the agenda of saving lives, saving whales, and I admit it differs radically from your agenda of profits at the expense of life and beauty, your agenda of slaughter. But, if you want to talk about manipulation, perhaps we should ask why the whaling commissioners of St. Lucia, St. Vincent and Trinidad were replaced by their governments last week in favour of commissioners more sympathetic to Japan. Perhaps you can enlighten the other media here as to what deals were made, promises made and palms greased, to buy the votes of three nations."

"I know nothing about this," he answered.

I responded, "That's the problem. You know nothing about this issue. Perhaps you should investigate the real issue here — greed."

Meanwhile Iceland was attempting to prostitute science by requesting an IWC permit to kill over 200 fin whales for scientific research studies. The reason given was that it would benefit the whales to kill them because it would be the only way to conduct the research necessary to determine what was causing fin whale populations to decline in the North Atlantic.

By the end of the meeting, it became quite obvious that the United States had joined the Caribbean sell-out nations and the Reaganites were all smiles as they licked Japanese boots. It was evident that the U.S. would not impose sanctions. The Reagan Administration had decided to discriminate on the application of U.S. law. Conservation organizations including Sea Shepherd filed a legal protest. Both the lower courts ruled that the president was obliged to apply the law without prejudice. The Reagan Administration retaliated by appealing to the highest court in the nation. The U.S. Supreme Court voted 5–4 to reverse the two earlier court rulings that had sided with our demands that the U.S. government exercise sanctions under Packwood Magnusson. This ruling gave the Reagan gang and the Japanese their victory and guaranteed continued illegal whaling. The Supreme Court had in effect knocked the teeth out of any IWC rulings. The moratorium was doomed to failure and the United States had engineered its defeat. Author David Day wrote after this decision in his book, *Whale War*: "If the administration had sanctioned Japan — as the American people wished it to do and American legislation had required it to do — Japan's and all other whaling operations would have ceased, and the Whale War would have ended."

As usual I was not very popular among most of the delegates at the IWC meeting. The Greenpeace crowd were irritated that our ship was in the harbour and overshadowing them. David McTaggart was his usual arrogant self and his regular troupe of ass-kissers followed him around begging for scraps of importance. The whalers were absolutely furious with us — the Faeroese delegation especially, since we were highlighting their annual whale massacres by flying anti–Faeroese whaling banners from our ship in constant view of all the delegates.

Ben White introduced me to a couple of the Russian delegates. I told them that we once had the pleasure of visiting Siberia when we intervened over their illegal killing of grey whales.

One Russian who spoke good English frowned. "I remember that affair. It was a very low affair, very low. You had no right to enter our country without permission."

"Yeah, well, you had no right to kill those whales, so stick your moralizing where the sun don't shine, Ivan."

I had had enough of these petty primate squabbles by a bunch of hominid demi-gods who presumed to decide the fate of creatures vastly superior to them. At last, the meetings with all the boring rounds of rhetoric and pathetic posturing were over. I prepared the ship for sea. While in Malmö, I lost a couple of crew who decided that the venture was too risky. All three of my navigating officers were concerned that they would have their licences lifted if the Faeroese protested our actions to their government. The trip sounded good when they were in Plymouth and eager for some sea time. Now that we were about to commence on the final leg of the journey, however, they all got cold feet and left. I found only one replacement, a young Swede named Magnus Alpadi.

At the request of the local chapter of the Swedish Green Party, we headed up along the coast to sit offshore of a nuclear power plant while Green Party demonstrators assailed the fences. The Green Party had asked us to be around to annoy the government, grab the attention of the media and worry the authorities. We did our part and then resumed our course, headed out of the Skagerrak and set a course for the Faeroe Islands.

On June 18, 1986, I dropped the hook off of Tórshavn and watched as a launch ferried Customs officers and police to us. Customs saw us first and gave us official clearance. They were very businesslike and calm, but told us that the police wished to speak with me after they were through.

In contrast to the Custom officials, the police were immediately hostile. Three uniformed officers entered my cabin and requested at once that I leave Faeroese waters. They did not identify themselves but got down to business straight away.

"Well, Captain Watson, I have been told to inform you legally to leave Faeroese waters — that is to say, Faeroese territorial waters must be left immediately by you and your ship and your crew. You are not allowed, you or your crew, to enter any harbour in the Faeroes."

I was a little confused. After all, we had just received Customs clearance and had been legally and officially admitted into the country, and now a few minutes later the police were officially requesting that we leave.

"Sir," I ventured, "you have not given me any reasons why we cannot enter Faeroese waters. In fact, we have already legally entered."

"Well, ah, the — what do you call it — the Parliament in the Faeroes simply don't want you in Faeroese waters."

"So you are telling me that we are expelled without having done anything then?"

"You are requested. I am requesting you to leave Faeroese waters."

"Oh," said I, "then this is not an order but a request."

"If you don't, you will get a proper sentence."

Surprised, I asked, "How do we get a sentence without getting charged?"

"Well," he answered, pulling some papers out of his briefcase, "you will get it from the government, and the government says here that there will be no negotiations at all."

It was obvious that the police officer was embarrassed. His argument was political and not legal and my attempts to point out the facts of our defence were flustering him.

"You have your warning," he said as he stood up, closed his briefcase and left my cabin.

Jeff Goodman, who had been filming the encounter, turned his camera on me and asked, "So, Paul, what do we do now?"

"We did get official Customs clearance," I answered. "So legally we can go ashore. However, the police have advised that we shouldn't go ashore. But I don't believe that there is much validity in that advice."

In Tórshavn, the BBC had a second film crew operating independently of their three-man crew on my ship. Producer David Spires met the police officers as they returned to their station. The officer who had spoken to me was confronted with a camera as he stepped from the police van.

"What do you intend to do if the *Sea Shepherd* crew do not leave?"

The officer hesitated, then responded nervously, "Well, the consequences of refusing to leave would probably be something like an arrest, and the ship would be boarded. That's my point of view, but —"

Spires interrupted, "And what will happen to the crew if you board the *Sea Shepherd II*."

"I don't know, haven't a clue."

Back on board the ship I was eager to test the resolve of the Faeroese. There was no purpose in waiting. I decided to send a party ashore in the morning.

I selected an unintimidating group for the first landing. Clean-cut Magnus Alpadi would pilot the inflatable in. Veronica Behn, looking sweet and innocent, and white-haired, white-bearded Al McKay, looking like a kind elderly gentleman, would be the point squad. I selected them, keeping in mind that the three of them represented four nationalities. Veronica had dual Mexican and Swiss citizenship. Magnus was a Swede and Al was a Canadian. This would allow us to contact four embassies to intercede if need be, and it would also provoke interest in the media of these nations.

As they left, I told them that there was a significant possibility that they would be arrested. However, not to worry. It wouldn't be for anything serious, and the publicity would be a good thing.

Three hours later they still had not returned and we had heard nothing from shore.

Rod Coronado and Nick Taylor took the second inflatable. Their mission would be to recover the first inflatable. They raced shoreward accompanied by the BBC crew in their own motor launch. Rod was American and Nick was British, thus increasing our diplomatic card by two extra countries.

As the two boats entered the harbour, they immediately spotted the lost inflatable. Our crew could not be seen but a small crowd had gathered and there were a few police vehicles and officers watching our boys approach. They did not look very friendly.

Nick roared up alongside our captured boat as Rod leaned forward to cut it loose with a knife. The police, loudly encouraged by the citizenry, jumped into the inflatable and wrestled with both men. Rod tossed the knife into the water to prevent an accidental wounding. Rod and Nick were subdued by force of numbers and dragged bodily from the inflatable to the low stone quay. One officer shoved Rod hard against the police van as Rod yelled, "You're making a big mistake. What am I being charged with? I am an American citizen and I demand to know what I am being charged with."

The police did not answer. The men were tossed roughly into the police van and driven to the jail, where they found, not surprisingly, our three missing crew.

Two independent reporters taking photographs of the arrest, Gary Chambers, a freelancer from Britain, and Jerry Free of the Australian Broadcasting Corporation, were also arrested. They did not touch the BBC crew, so they must have assumed the two reporters were with *Sea Shepherd*.

A half-hour later, members of the Faeroese media asked permission to come on board the *Sea Shepherd II* to obtain my response to the arrests. I made a pretense of surprise and anger that my crew had been arrested. The reporters informed me that none of them had been charged with any offence. This was my opportunity to address the Faeroese. I turned towards the TV camera.

"The fact is that your police state here has just taken people into custody without charges, without having committed a crime. We cleared Customs in the proper manner. We have the proper papers. We were invited here by Julianna Klett, the Faeroese delegate to the IWC, who said that all people are invited to come to the Faeroes and view this whale hunt. Well, we happen to be human beings and therefore we qualify in the category of 'all people.' So what kind of double-dealing methods are this government utilizing? They are hypocrites."

The Faeroese must have believed that holding my crew would persuade me to leave their waters. Instead, it gave me the opportunity to call the different embassies in Copenhagen. At the Canadian embassy, we found Randy Stanfield on the other end of the line, the same Mr. Stanfield whom I had encountered on the telephone a few years before, when he called me in Percé, Quebec, concerning the sinking of the *Sierra*.

I explained the problem to Mr. Stanfield and to the other consular representatives and then spent another two days doing ship-to-shore interviews with world media contacts. Within a few days, the relatively unknown islands of the Faeroes were being introduced to the world media as a barbarous little enclave of islands where the residents torture and slaughter pilot whales and subject whale-savers to arrest and detainment without charge.

In an attempt to intimidate us, the Faeroese sent out their only gunboat, a grey trawler almost identical to our own ship but with a mounted deck-gun set forward on the bow. The *Olivur Haglur* approached, came close alongside and radioed for us to give ourselves up.

I answered, "Give ourselves up for what? What charges do you have against us?"

The captain of the gunboat did not seem to understand my question. He responded by asking, "So you do not intend to give up?"

Bri Rennie at the wheel said, "Hell no!"

I laughed, picked up the mike and said, "We have just begun to fight."

The gunboat chased us around off and on for the next five days. It soon became tiresome. One morning I decided to turn the tables on them. I ordered Bri, who was at the wheel, to bring the ship hard over to port. This caught the

Olivur Haglur completely by surprise. They turned to their starboard as we completed a circle and came bearing down on their stern.

The radio crackled and a panicked voice intruded, "*Sea Shepherd, Sea Shepherd,* do you intend to ram us. Do you intend to hurt us?"

"No," I said, "we have no intention of ramming or hurting you. We just wanted to illustrate how annoying it is to be chased around all the time. Besides, why should you have all the fun. It's our turn to chase you for a change."

After their terrified reaction, it was a little hard to maintain any respect for the crew on the gunboat, so most of the time we ignored them. After a week of playing tag and other fun games, the police finally contacted me and said they would like to make a deal. They would return my crew if I agreed to voluntarily sign an expulsion order barring me from any Scandinavian country for three years. This was extortion without precedent. They would return crew members that they had not charged if I agreed to bar myself from Scandinavia, although I had not committed a crime.

I agreed. An expulsion order signed under duress would not be morally binding as far as I was concerned.

So the police boarded once again and I gave them a signature in return for Rod Coronado, Nick Taylor and our two inflatables. The other three were flown off the island to Copenhagen and expelled from the Faeroes. Magnus returned to Sweden, Al to Canada and Veronica travelled to Scotland to rejoin the crew.

I took the *Sea Shepherd II* back to Scotland — to the Shetland Islands to refuel, take on provisions and to purchase barbed wire. Veronica rejoined us in the Shetland port of Lerwick.

We returned to the Faeroes immediately. En route, the deck crew barricaded the ship behind barbed wire. We knew we would be deliberately violating the expulsion order and I had no intention of making it easy for them to board, if they decided to try.

"Rod," I yelled down to the deck. "Prepare the water cannon and haul the pie filling from the fishhold."

If they intended to board, I intended to meet them with our secret weapon, the pie cannon. Years before, I had loaded into the fishhold seven 45-gallon drums of pie filling, which had been donated to us by the U.S. Department of Agriculture. We never attempted to eat any of it. The different flavours — lemon, chocolate, Boston creme, vanilla and cherry — looked as fresh as they did when I brought the cargo on board in 1982. I've always had a policy that we don't eat what bacteria, mold and insects won't touch. I left a barrel of the cherry open once for a few days. It didn't attract flies. It was, however, sticky, messy, sweet smelling, colourful and ideal for throwing or blasting from a water cannon.

The *Sea Shepherd II* re-entered the three-mile (5 km) exclusion zone. We had picked up evidence of a hunt near Gotwick Bay. We were too late — 19 whales lay butchered on the dock and beaches. I felt terribly frustrated and angry.

"Goddamn these bastards. Goddamn them to hell."

We patrolled close to the beaches and sat defiantly outside the harbour at Tórshavn, challenging the authorities to expel us. The barbed-wire barricades made our ship look both sinister and intimidating. The Faeroese were uncertain of what course of action they should take. A visiting Danish frigate ignored us. The last thing Denmark needed was an international incident over the whaling issue. Denmark also had a problem with helping the Faeroese because the pilot whale hunt is a violation of the Berne Convention of the European Community (EC). Denmark is an EC member and the Faeroes, under Home Rule, are not members. Because of this, Danish hands were tied. The frigate returned to Denmark without communicating with us.

Danish reluctance to interfere, however, did not keep Greenpeace Denmark from jumping into the fray, shooting off press releases from the lip and stirring emotions in an attempt to whip up both hysteria and violence against us. One of the five Faeroese weekly papers (one each day representing different political points of view) carried a headline interview with Michael Nielsen, the titular head of Greenpeace Denmark. Nielsen openly called me a "terrorist" and was quoted as saying, "Paul Watson will have no moral hesitation about killing a Faeroese fisherman if he gets in his way."

Although Greenpeace USA was sending out millions of mail-outs collecting funds from Americans to oppose the killing of pilot whales in the Faeroe Islands, Nielsen defended the hunt as "aboriginal" and "traditional." I told Jeff Goodman I couldn't understand how the organization that raises the most in contributions to protect whales can publicly denounce the organization that raises the least. The irony of it is that the organization with the money, Greenpeace, takes the money to end the hunt, does not even send a ship or crew to interfere with it, then publicly endorses the hunt as traditional.

Jeff was philosophical about it. "Business is business. Is Greenpeace in the business of raising money or is Greenpeace in the business of saving whales? They make a contribution in educating the public, I suppose."

Angered, I snapped back, "A contribution! It's fraud. The whole damn animal-welfare and environmental movement is a fraud, filled with greedy, disloyal individuals who will say anything, compromise with anybody and do anything to protect their ass. What really makes me mad is that this so-called peace organization has just endangered our lives by telling the Faeroese that we are terrorists. They'll probably come out shooting after that story."

"Surely," said Jeff, "they're not that foolish. Why should they listen to Greenpeace?"

"They wouldn't listen to them if they condemned whaling but by condemning us they are simply telling the Faeroese what they want to hear." I said. "And to make matters worse, Ian MacPhail of the International Fund for Animal Welfare is on shore giving comfort to the enemy."

Another story had appeared about MacPhail's meetings with Kai Hoydal, a Faeroese Fisheries scientist, and Birgir Danielsen, the managing director of Faroese Fisheries. He had taken great pains to distance himself, the Environmental Investigation Agency and IFAW from any association with Sea Shepherd. He was quoted in the newspaper as saying that Danielsen laughed when MacPhail said it was a pity that the French Secret Service had not sunk the *Sea Shepherd II* instead of the *Rainbow Warrior*. And to demonstrate what a sensitive man he was compared to me, MacPhail spent most of the time discussing Faeroese art, and received an invitation to return to the Faeroes at any time. MacPhail said that the two were welcome to visit his home in London.

"God, I could puke. The bastard would probably serve them whale meat if he could. And listen here, there's more. He accused me of attending the IWC meeting in 1985 as a Walter Mitty character in the guise of a British commodore with gold braid from my sleeves to my elbow. It's obvious that he can't tell the difference between a British Merchant master's uniform, which I am entitled to wear, and a British commodore's uniform. Then he goes on to say that I am 'a dangerous psychopath who should be avoided at all times.'"

"Tough talk," said Jeff. "These guys seem to hate you more than the Faeroese do."

"They probably do. However, the important thing here is that both IFAW and Greenpeace have placed us in extreme danger. Damn them for their selfish, irresponsible jealousy."

Jeff asked, "What are you going to do about it?"

"I think we should move down to Sudaroy Island, 30 miles [50 km] to the south, and patrol that coastline for a few days. That will give the police here in Tórshavn a chance to cool off."

I set the course south to pass Sandoy and Skuvoy to starboard. We watched as the lights of Tórshavn faded to our stern. At this latitude in the summer, the nights are very short and the seas usually very calm. Visibility was very good when I woke at 0300 hours for my watch. The dawn had passed and the sun was up although muted behind an overcast sky. The southern end of Sudaroy was five miles (8 km) away.

I was told a boat was approaching from the north. It didn't take long before we could identify her as the *Olivur Haglur*.

"*Sea Shepherd*, this is the Coast Guard vessel *Olivur Haglur*. You are under arrest. Please stop your engines."

I ignored them. We could see them lowering inflatable boats into the water. A few minutes later, four large inflatables each carrying five uniformed officers came racing towards us. I stepped out onto the starboard bridge wing as one of the vessels came alongside. I yelled down to them.

"Do you wish to arrest us?"

For an answer, one of the policemen stood up and aimed a shotgun at me. I could see that the other officers were heavily armed and two of them carried what looked like automatic weapons.

I laughed. "What are you going to do — shoot me?"

I saw his response. His trigger finger moved and I saw a spurt of flame, heard a whining buzz and felt an explosion to my right. Something struck me in the side of the neck and then I couldn't see. I was blinded, my eyes stinging painfully.

The bastard shot at me. I heard a second shot and the green running light above my head exploded in a shower of glass. I dove through the wheelhouse door.

"Everybody put on your gas masks," I yelled as I reached for mine. I realized that the stinging in my eyes was tear gas. My student demonstration days in the 1960s had taught me to recognize the stuff, if nothing else. I found out later that the officer had fired a tear-gas grenade at me. It had shattered against the bulkhead only three inches (8 cm) from my head, a piece of the fibreglass striking me in the neck.

Gabriella came running to me with a wet towel and pressed it against my face.

"Thanks, Bri. Put on your mask and take the wheel."

I grabbed a parachute flare and stepped back on the bridge wing with my gas mask on. The officer stood up to fire again. I aimed the flare, pulled the cord and sent a rocket flying into the side of their inflatable. The officer dropped his rifle overboard and dove for the deck on top of the other officers. The officer at the controls quickly fell back.

On the main deck, Rod Coronado waited until an inflatable came up along-side on the port. He crouched on the deck and watched as an officer tried to position himself to jump on board. Suddenly Rod stood up with a firehose in his hands as Peter Winch opened the fire-pump controls. A jet of water caught the officer in the chest and hurtled him back into the arms of his soaked comrades.

On the stern, Nick Taylor and Veronica Behn saw two tear-gas canisters land on the deck. Nothing came out of them. They ran and grabbed them. The officers had forgotten to pull the pins. They hid behind the gunnel and waited for the inflatable to come alongside. When it did, they pulled the pins and tossed the canisters into the inflatable. Unlike us, the police did not have any gas masks and that boat, too, fell behind as they struggled to throw the canisters over the side.

Back on the bridge, I deployed the line rockets. These are devices for firing lines to other ships or to shore, usually in emergency situations in heavy weather. Deploying the units both from starboard and port, I was able to attach the lines to fixed points and then fire the rockets. This laid down 200 yards (200 m) of line on each side of the ship and as the line drifted quickly backwards, we were able to snag the propellers of the two outboards on one of the inflatables. The boat was brought to a quick halt as the line wrapped itself around the propeller blades, whipping the small vessel around before fouling the props. It was quickly obvious that at least this inflatable was down for the count.

Behind us, the Faeroese gunboat was slowly slipping back. We knew that we had an extra half-knot on her. Down below, David Howitt, oblivious to the battle on deck, was tending the main engine, nursing every possible extra revolution out of her.

On deck, we had a brief respite. It actually looked as if we had won and the police had had enough. All the pursuing inflatables fell back. One was out with snagged props, a second crew were nursing stinging eyes and a third crew were soaking wet. The fourth boat was untouched.

It was this fourth boat that led the other two for a second assault. The tear-gas grenades and shotguns were met once again by our flares and water cannons. One officer shot a volley of machine-gun fire across our bow, peppering the water with dozens of little eruptions.

With amusement, we watched as an inflatable sped in front of us, the officers jeering and smiling as they released a large net in front of our bow. They were actually attempting to foul our prop. I laughed. Our prop would spit that net out in little pieces, and the smiles of the officers turned to surprise as little pieces of their secret weapon rose up in our wake.

It was time to unleash our secret weapon. We waited as two of the inflatables roared up alongside and three officers unslung their automatic rifles. Before they could pull the triggers, Rod unleashed a torrent of banana creme onto the crew of the closest boat, drenching them with sticky yellow liquid. They looked as embarrassed as a tomcat dropped into a bubble bath. The second inflatable retreated before the onslaught of 45 gallons (200 l) of cherry-pie filling.

With a cheer from my crew, we watched as they returned in defeat to their mother ship, now three miles (5 km) to our stern.

I set course for the Hebrides, where the BBC got off with their film for the next broadcast. We then stopped at the Isle of Skye before proceeding through the Irish Sea to the port of Bristol.

It had been a successful voyage. The bullet-scarred ship gave us a news story that along with the BBC film was very dramatic and thus we were able to inform the world of Faeroese atrocities against whales in the North Atlantic. A year later, the BBC documentary film *Black Harvest* aired in Britain, Denmark and North America, increasing awareness of the killing. Our drama had provided the action foundation that enabled Jeff Goodman and his crew to tell the world of the real tragedy in the Faeroes — the continued senseless slaughter of thousands of defenceless, intelligent and harmless beings.

The IFAW, EIA and Greenpeace could and did rave on about how we accomplished nothing. However, during the three-week period in June that we lay in Faeroese waters, not a single whale was killed. This was the first June in Faeroese records that recorded no kills. Perhaps it was a coincidence. Perhaps our critics were right, but it is a fact and one that supports our belief that direct action speaks louder than words and confrontation achieves more than rhetoric. My crew had fought for the whales while the others talked. I was content to let them keep talking.

Nineteen whales had died in July before we could return from Scotland. However, the kill figures for July were lower than previous kill statistics on Faeroese record for the same time period. If our critics had chosen to support our efforts and had directed funding towards direct action instead of direct mail, we would have been able to paralyse Faeroese whaling for the entire summer.

During 1986, 1,677 pilot whales died — again, the lowest kill figures since the Faeroese increased their kills in the late 1970s. This may be compared with the following figures officially recorded by the Faeroes government:

1985: 2,500 kills
1984: 1,921
1983: 1,689
1982: 2,652
1981: 2,973
1980: 2,773
1979: 1,672
1978: 1,183
1977: 898
1976: 531

Despite this, I decided that we would not be able to return to the Faeroes in 1987. Two years of campaigning there had exhausted our funding, and the publicity we had attracted had served to advertise a lucrative cause for other animal-welfare and conservation groups to exploit. Now it seemed that every group was jumping on the Faeroese pilot whale hunt bandwagon. At least, I thought to myself, we had elevated it to recognition and perhaps it would now be best to leave the campaigns to the other groups. Perhaps with their big budgets, big memberships and big mouths, they could finish what we had begun.

Because we were unable to afford maintenance on the *Sea Shepherd II*, I tied her up in Sharpness in Gloucestershire in September 1986. I left her in the charge of Sarah Hambley along with her capable new husband, Sten Borg. I needed to return to North America to raise funds, and I needed a rest.

It was becoming too much. I had responsibility for operating the ship, for organizing the campaigns and the media, for raising funding and writing the newsletter. Our membership remained small, as few people had heard of us. This was my fault. I refused absolutely to turn over the reins of my organization to fund-raisers and administrators. Direct mail, adopt-a-whale programs and whale merchandising were not the course I wanted to take. I would rather be poor and committed than rich and idle.

Before leaving, I met with Rod Coronado and David Howitt over some beers. I told them they had shown great courage under fire in the Faeroes.

"David, you kept those engines going. Here's to the unsung hero of the Faeroes and the skirmish off Sudaroy."

Rod and David had come forward with a plan to attack the Icelandic whaling fleet. It was a good, solid, workable plan, and even if we did not have adequate resources, they were convinced they could do the job. They said they could leave for Iceland at the end of September.

"Cheers," said David raising his glass of Guinness.

"Cheers," answered Rod.

I raised my glass. "Go for it," I said. "Send the bastards to the bottom."

12
Raid on
Reykjavik

We had given our first warning to the Icelanders on the docks of Reykjavik in 1985. The message was clear: Obey the moratorium or Sea Shepherd will sink your whaling ships. We had given a second warning at the International Whaling Commission meeting in Malmö in 1986. We had waited for the United States to uphold sanctions as stipulated by U.S. law. By September 1986, we had exhausted all conventional means of forcing Iceland into compliance with the whale conservation regulations. The moratorium had failed, betrayed by the Reagan Administration. The floodgates were opening and other nations were watching Iceland. Japan announced it would send a "scientific research fleet" to Antarctica. Norway and Korea picked up the loophole of "research" whaling. The Philippines announced its intention to resume whaling.

In fact, the only thing that the moratorium had achieved was to relieve public pressure against whaling. The public now believed that a moratorium was in effect and that therefore there was no further need for concern or action. It looked as if the whalers had won the whale wars. It was absolutely imperative that we strike a blow against whaling and that we do it soon. We needed to dramatize the fact of continued whaling to keep the public aware of its existence. We needed to send a lesson to all of the whaling nations that their flouting of the law would not go unchallenged.

Rod Coronado was a small boy of 12 when he first heard of the Sea Shepherd Conservation Society. That was the year we rammed the *Sierra*. He had written me a letter, which I answered. In 1983, he sent us $200 to buy fuel for a campaign. In 1984, a month after graduating from high school, Rod travelled north from his home in California and searched me out in Vancouver. He wanted to get involved. I sent him to Hawaii to work with Wyland on the Whaling Wall. He worked every day for five months, preparing the wall, hanging scaffolding, painting the background and being treated like a servant boy by Robert Wyland.

When I saw him a month later in Waikiki, I asked him how he was doing.

"Wyland's a self-centred, conceited jerk," he said. "But I'll put up with his crap for the whales."

And he did, until the Whaling Wall was completed in April 1985. I understood how he felt when I listened to Wyland at the wall's dedication ceremony. Dozens of volunteers in addition to Rod had put in over 6,000 hours on the project, but Wyland never said a word about the contribution they had made. Adding insult to injury, he told the media that, "I did it all by myself, from scratch to finish."

I apologized to Rod and the others for the slight. What most impressed me about Rod is that he just shrugged and said, "Well, it is a hell of an educational project. It's an impressive promotion for the whales, but what I would really like to do is to fight for them."

I sent him immediately to Halifax to help prepare the *Sea Shepherd II* for the 1985 campaign to Iceland and the Faeroe Islands. In the year since he had proven to be the most loyal, dedicated and hardworking of my crew. Now he was ready and eager to lead his first field campaign.

When the *Sea Shepherd II* was in Reykjavik in the summer of 1985, Rod was assigned the task of reconnoitering the whaling ships. He had made things very clear to me. He wanted to lead a field campaign and both he and I decided that Iceland would be his first field command. He wanted only one other crew member.

David Howitt had joined us in March 1986 in Plymouth. He was very quiet, at first glance more an observer than an activist. This suited his training as a natural history photographer. His other skill was as a bicycle mechanic, which landed him in our engine room. Advancement is quick in Neptune's Navy, and two months after he joined, David was serving as second engineer under Jeremy Coon.

More research into the location and security of the Icelandic whaling fleet was needed. Accordingly, on October 15, 1986, Rod and David landed at Keflavik airport in Iceland, taking the bus into town, where they registered at the Salvation Army Hostel. They spent hours drinking coffee at small cafés across from the dock, watching, keeping an eye on the four whaling ships and taking notes on the movements of the crew and security guards. Bit by bit they picked up tools from different hardware stores: a bolt-cutter, a large crescent wrench, a heavy monkey wrench. They hitchhiked 30 miles (50 km) up the coast to the whaling station at Hvalfjördhur that the ships used during the summer. They had heard that the factory station gave tours, so they played tourist. Howitt brought his camera. When they arrived, the place was deserted. The plant had been closed for the season. They took pictures, made maps and planned to return to the plant.

In an effort to locate where the summer's take of whale meat was stored, Rod applied for a job at the Reykjavik meat-processing plant. He reasoned that a meat plant was the best place to look for a meat stash and he was able to earn money to cover the high cost of staying in Iceland. It was amazing that he was not viewed with suspicion. Rod is from an old Spanish California family; in fact, his roots go back centuries to an ancestor he is not very proud of — Francisco Coronado, the conquistador "discoverer" of the Grand Canyon. Over the centuries, the Coronado family had picked up some Native blood, which explained Rod's dark-complexioned good looks. They were the kind of looks that did not exactly blend in among the fair-haired, fair-skinned blue-eyed Icelanders.

Rod recalled later with a grin, "There I was, the only dark-skinned, non–Icelandic-speaking vegetarian working at this meat-packing plant. And they didn't get suspicious."

On November 1, Rod narrowly avoided deportation when Icelandic officials discovered that he was working illegally. Because of his arrest only months before on the Faeroe Islands, despite the fact that he was not charged or convicted of a crime, he had been banned from entry into all Scandinavian nations for three years. The immigration authorities ran a background check on him but failed to discover the expulsion order. He was told that he could not work in Iceland, but he was not expelled.

On November 6, David and Rod mailed their photos, drawings and notes to Sarah Hambley in Plymouth. Aside from myself, she was the only person who was aware that the two were involved in a Sea Shepherd mission in Iceland.

On Saturday, November 8, the planned attack on Icelandic whaling operations was set in motion. Their agenda was to rent a car, eat dinner at Reykjavik's only vegetarian restaurant, drive to the whaling station and sabotage it, return to the docks, sink the whaling ships and then drive to the airport and catch a plane to Luxembourg.

Back in Vancouver, I was keeping tabs on the two field agents by phone although I was deep into a political campaign, running on the Green Party ticket for Vancouver Parks Board commissioner. I had no illusions about my chances of winning, but it was an effective forum for addressing environmental concerns. On Saturday morning, I had talked on the phone with Sarah in Plymouth. She gave me a coded message to be prepared for developments within the next 48 hours.

On Monday, Sarah rang again. Very calmly she said, "We've got two on the bottom and the boys are home."

That was all I needed. I had the media releases ready to go. The Icelanders were furious. Greenpeace predictably went public within the hour with releases of their own condemning the action.

The operation had been a complete success.

Rod and David drove their rental car to Hvalfjördhur and arrived at 2000 hours just as a snowstorm began. They parked the car in a quarry, changed their clothing, slipped on day packs containing tools and flashlights and walked towards the whaling station. As they approached, they were almost spotted by a man operating an excavator.

"We immediately dropped to the ground and lay motionless for close to an hour, waiting for the man to finish his work," Rod said later.

It was a cold, wet and miserable wait, but the man finally shut down his machine and left for home. The snow was falling heavily now and it gave them excellent cover. They circled the compound under the glare of the mercury vapour lights that illuminated the entire facility. After confirming that there were no people about, they entered through an unlocked door, located the main circuit box and flipped the switch, killing the power.

They began to systematically attack the machinery of the facilities in a controlled assault. The objective was to inflict as much damage as possible. The first target was the computer room. The video monitors exploded under their heavy crescent wrenches. They smashed the terminals, the printers and everything that looked expensive. They worked over the six huge Caterpillar diesel generators that powered the refrigeration units, severing lines, breaking and dismantling expensive parts. They carried many of the smaller bits of machinery, along with flensing tools, to the pier on the fjord and dumped them into the deep water. The refrigeration units then came under the blows of the wrenches. Then on to the whale-oil centrifuges and hydraulic-driven machinery, methodically dissecting the robotic apparatus the Icelanders had recently used to cut up the whales.

The storm outside kept people off the road, and would have explained the blackout at the facility to anyone who was in the vicinity. The storm also muffled the racket of destruction: the broken glass, shattered equipment and dismantled engine parts that fell to the concrete floor. Not satisfied with shutting down the power plant for the freezers, Rod and Dave broke open the freezer doors and discovered tons of whale meat inside. They jammed the doors open to expose the meat to the warmer air of the plant.

Outside they found a small trailer containing a couple of desks and microscopes and a few containers of whale tissue samples.

"It wasn't a laboratory," said Rod. "It was a pathetic excuse for a lab. They had a couple of microscopes and a few test tubes to justify what was obviously a very large commercial operation."

The saboteurs appropriated the "scientific notes" and other records after breaking into the foreman's office and smashing the radios used to communicate with the whaling ships. "They had this stereo unit, which they used to play classical music to the workers as they cut up the whales," said David. "We toyed with the idea of leaving a whale song tape for them to discover and then thought, what's the point."

Dave swung his wrench like a Viking warrior and wasted the stereo on the spot, its smashed components scattered across the room when he left the office. Rod had found a stockpile of whaling ship engine parts, which both men lifted and lugged to the dock. These, too, were tossed into the deep inky-black waters.

They felt good, damn good, and later when they told me how liberating it felt, I understood what they meant. Years of frustration at watching whales die had finally found an outlet. The sense of helplessness vanished bit by bit with every swing of the monkey wrench. They understood, as I had discovered when I rammed into the side of the *Sierra*, that it was possible to strike back for the whales.

The rampage went on for more than four hours. Finally, they felt that they had worked over the whaling station really thoroughly. Just as they were about to leave, they discovered gallons of a liquid chemical in a storehouse. A brief investigation showed that it smoked, fumed and foamed when it came into contact with metal, so they poured it liberally over the plant. It was cyanic acid.

And then they left, closing the door carefully behind them, and walked calmly back up the road. They recovered their car from its hiding-place in the quarry and proceeded to drive through the pelting snow back to the harbour, where they parked in the harbour parking lot.

They knew from their earlier observation that only one watchman was around. They verified that his car was parked where it should be. Three whaling ships, rafted together, were moored at the pier. The fourth whaler was in drydock. The watchman would be on the outermost ship. They made a quick dash across the home pier towards the whalers. The wind was howling and the harbour water was choppy.

Rod felt good about the weather. "The storm was a blessing. It kept people inside and the wind masked any sounds."

The two target ships were the *Hvalur 6* and the *Hvalur 7*. I had instructed them not to take any risks with any person's life.

All the lights were on in all three ships. The doors were unlocked. David made a quick run through the first ship, Rod took the second. Every bunk was checked. There was no one on board. Rod cautiously stepped on board the third ship and peered through the galley window. The watchman was lying back on a bench snoring.

With the check for personnel completed, both men entered the open door of the engine room on *Hvalur 6*. Their experience in the engine room of the *Sea Shepherd II* paid off. They lifted the heavy deck plates and quickly located the sea valve. This is the large seawater intake valve that allows the cold ocean water into the cooling system for the engines and provides water for the fire-fighting systems and the toilets. David closed the sea valve and then both men went to work removing the heavy bolts to dismantle the main seawater pipe from the valve.

With the first ship primed and ready to blow, they boarded the *Hvalur 7* and went to work on the second valve. When the bolts and the pipe were removed, Rod opened the sea valve. As the wheel turned, seawater began to piss through the crack. It became a high-pressure stream as the valve widened. Rod worked the wheel fully open until a torrent of water blasted from the bottom of the ship, a geyser that hit the overhead bulkhead and rained down on them. Both men were soaked. The roar of the water was unnerving but they were undeterred. Jumping onto the first ship, they ran down to the bottom of the engine room and opened the second sea-cock. Both ships were sinking and sinking fast.

Running up to the deck, they vaulted the rails back onto the second ship and severed the mooring lines of the third ship with knives that they carried for that purpose. The hapless guard was sent drifting into the harbour like an oblivious baby Moses.

Rod quickly dumped the tools into the harbour, then they both ran across the lighted pier and jumped into their car. It was 0540 hours when they drove away. They looked back towards the harbour and saw that the ships were listing noticeably. There was no time to enjoy watching the results of their labour, however: they still had to escape from Reykjavik.

A minute out of the harbour, a police cruiser flashed its lights behind them.

Rod muttered, "They can't be that quick. They can't be that good." They pulled over to the side of the road.

Two officers stepped out of their car. One cop stayed with the police car and the other walked up to Rod and asked him to step out, too. It was then that Rod became acutely aware of his wet, grease-stained clothing. He smiled and got out of the car. The officer requested that he take a seat in the back of the police cruiser, leaving David sitting by himself in the passenger seat of the rental car. Rod handed them his California driver's licence and smiled.

The two police officers spoke to each other in Icelandic for a few minutes and then one of them asked, "Have you been drinking any alcohol?"

"Of course not. I don't drink." He responded.

"Okay. Have a nice trip."

"Thanks, officers."

Rod got back into his car and they drove off. David had sat nervously waiting, debating if he should make a dash from the car, but then where could he have gone if he did? Iceland is an island.

Unknown to both men, the police had discovered the scuttling of the two ships just about the time Rod was sitting in the back seat of the police car. The ships had hit the bottom in just half an hour.

Their flight was at 0730 hours. They waited anxiously for the plane's crew to announce that it was open for boarding and then their hearts began to pound when it was announced that there would be a half-hour delay due to the weather conditions.

Meanwhile, back at the harbour, police cars were gathering and word was quickly spread throughout the town that two of Jon Loftson's ships had sunk. Loftson was the sole owner of Whales Limited, Iceland's only whaling company. This night was very costly for him.

The police did not suspect sabotage at first, and this was the reason they did not announce an all-points bulletin for suspected saboteurs. By the time they did finally realize what had happened, Rod and David were in the air and bound for Luxembourg. From there they took a bus to Belgium, boarded the ferry to Dover and caught a train to London.

They had called Sarah from Luxembourg. She called me and I issued the press releases. I claimed responsibility on behalf of the Sea Shepherd Conservation Society and stated that it was our objective to cripple illegal Icelandic whaling operations.

The attack was expensive. Icelandic officials conservatively estimated the cost of damage to the ships at more than US$2 million; the damage to the whaling station was set at more than US$2 million; and the loss of whale meat due to spoilage at over US$4 million. My men had delivered an $8-million punch to the Icelandic pirates and they were reeling.

If nothing else, we had got their attention.

Prime Minister Steingrimur Hermannsson called an emergency cabinet meeting and a debate in the Althing, the Icelandic Parliament. Afterwards, Hermannsson delivered an angry speech on Icelandic radio and television.

"The saboteurs are regarded by the Icelandic government as terrorists," said the prime minister. "All efforts will be made to get the people who are responsible prosecuted for this inhuman act."

Attorney General Hallvardur Einarsson said that he would use all possible channels to have the saboteurs extradited and then prosecuted in Iceland. I immediately contacted the Icelandic police and the international media to inform them that I would welcome extradition proceedings and the opportunity to defend our actions in an Icelandic court.

Back home in British Columbia, the provincial attorney general, Brian Smith, forgetting his place as a provincial rather than a federal power, announced that he would have me investigated for conspiracy, terrorism and anything else he could get on me, and then he would send me to Iceland himself. He was not too pleased when I responded by telling him to investigate his own powers first. This was not a matter of any concern to the provincial government of British Columbia.

A day later I was a guest on a former British Columbian premier's talk show on CJOR radio. David Barrett was questioning me when the manager announced that the building would have to be evacuated. A caller had said that a bomb had been planted in the radio station to protest our violence in sinking the whaling ships.

On the sidewalk below, reporters from all over the city descended for an impromptu press conference with me and former premier Dave Barrett. I told them I thought it was a little puzzling that someone would threaten to kill innocent people to protest our violence against illegal whaling equipment.

Just then a reporter thrust a microphone into my face and asked, "What's your response? Greenpeace Canada has just issued a release condemning your actions as terrorism."

I defended myself with a quick sound bite. "Well," I said, "what do you expect from the Avon Ladies of the environmental movement?" I was referring to the army of door-to-door salespeople who beg for money for the Greenpeace coffers. Greenpeace has never forgiven me for that remark. I guess I came too close to the truth.

Charges of terrorism, from whatever source, have never bothered me much. Terrorists do not take precautions to protect people from death or injury. Terrorists attack innocent people, and we had attacked an illegal operation as defined by international wildlife conservation regulations. Terrorists do not hold news conferences to announce what they have done, and, finally, terrorists do not offer to turn themselves in to address the legal and moral consequences of their actions.

My offer to surrender to the Icelandic authorities went unanswered.

Rod called me when he was safely back in Plymouth. I asked him to catch a flight to New York City, where Cleveland Amory would host a press conference at the offices of the Fund for Animals at which he would introduce Rod to the public. David had decided to take a vacation in Greece.

In New York, I met Rod at the airport.

"You did good, Rod. You did damn good. We're proud of you."

Rod handled himself brilliantly before the press. He never wavered from the position that Iceland was a "hooligan whaling nation in violation of international law." The American media were, as usual, more receptive than the Canadian media. For the most part, we were warmly received, getting positive write-ups in *Time*, *Newsweek* and a bevy of national publications.

I sent Rod on a talk-show trip and then he returned to California for a rest. I felt wonderful. Half the Icelandic fleet down, a whale-processing plant destroyed, no injuries, no arrests, extensive media coverage and, most important, a financial blow to the profits of Icelandic whalers.

Following up our victory, I sat down and typed up a letter to the President of Iceland to address any possible charges that the government of Iceland might wish to pursue against the Sea Shepherd Conservation Society or any of its members. I sent a copy by mail to the prime minister of Iceland and faxed copies to the Icelandic police and the Icelandic media. In doing so, I took the moral high ground away from the Icelanders. They had talked tough about their intention to prosecute. I was ready to call their bluff. We *wanted* our day in court.

13

Return to
Reykjavik

My first letter to Iceland went unanswered. I wrote a second and a third. A reporter for the Icelandic newspaper *Dagblad* called me and said that the authorities in Iceland were determined to have us extradited. I told them that there was no need to do that. They simply had to invite us and we would come, the date and the place to be of their own choosing.

Nothing. I heard nothing from them at all.

In the meantime, we had work to do in the North Pacific. It was time for somebody to do something about the expanding Asian drift-net fleets. Nobody else was doing anything except talking. If no one else would act, then we would.

It was a daunting task. Conservative estimates by the United States National Marine Fisheries Service indicated in excess of 1,700 Japanese, Taiwanese and Korean drift-netters. Each one of the large 150-foot (45-m) to 220-foot (67-m) vessels carried a net that averaged some (64 km) 40 miles in length. Each and every day, more than 60,000 miles (96,000 km) of monofilament nets were set

across the North Pacific. Each year, according to estimates by the U.S. Department of Commerce committee on drift-net fishing, these curtains of death caused
more than a million incidental bird kills and a quarter-million incidental marine
mammal kills. It was wanton pillage on an almost inconceivable scale. These
organized gangs were strip-mining the oceans.

With the *Sea Shepherd II* broken down in England, I searched for and located
a repossessed American tuna seiner, the *Bold Venture*, in Seattle. A wealthy donor
from Virginia gave us $100,000 and we bought it for $60,000. Unfortunately,
although it was an ideal vessel, it became painfully obvious that we would not
be able to repair and prepare the ship in time to reach the summer drift-netting
operations.

The donation that made possible the purchase of the *Bold Venture* had been
arranged by Ben White, one of the directors of the Sea Shepherd Conservation
Society. Ben had been with me since 1981, when he served as bosun on the Siberian campaign. After that, he had returned for the seal campaign in 1983 and the
Faeroes campaign of 1985. He had a tree care business near Fairfax, Virginia,
and the donation had come from one of his genteel customers. We were all grateful that the donation had secured a new ship for us, but Ben insisted that he be
rewarded with the position of expedition leader for the first drift-net campaign.

Scott Trimingham, another board member, supported Ben's position. They
argued that Sea Shepherd had become a one-man operation and insisted that I
delegate both responsibility and some control to them. At first, I thought it would
be a good idea; if nothing else, it would broaden involvement in the organization. I did not, however, think much of their disdain for a military organizational
structure: both Ben and Scott wanted to democratize Sea Shepherd. I remembered too vividly the perils of democracy from my days in Greenpeace.

I agreed to their demands reluctantly. Ben would lead the expedition and I
would skipper the ship. My position as captain was politically subservient to the
board of directors. But then I found myself on my own in Seattle having to recruit
a crew, prepare the ship and make all the logistical arrangements, which I had
always assumed were the responsibility of the expedition leader. Ben stayed in
Virginia to attend to his business. He apparently felt that the donation he had
brokered was enough of a contribution to justify his leadership.

My first problem in Seattle was the ship itself. We had spent the money only
to discover that it was useless to us for a summer campaign. The ideal vessel for
us was berthed at Pier 75. It was called the *Gratitude* and had recently been
donated to Don Tipton of the Park West Children's Fund. Don was a Christian

missionary and his wife, Sondra, was a former Sea Shepherd volunteer. Their dream was to build a fleet of relief ships to transport food to Third World nations.

The *Gratitude* was a sleek former Japanese skipjack tuna vessel built in 1972 and ideal for our purposes. The *Bold Venture*, with her larger cargo capacity, was a better vessel for Don's group. He agreed and we officially traded ships.

The month of June 1987 was a hectic scramble to ready the new ship for a voyage to the North Pacific. I had painted on her bow the new name *Divine Wind* and underneath we added the Japanese characters signifying *Kamikaze*. The Japanese term originated with the typhoon that destroyed the armies of Kublai Khan when the Mongol ruler attempted to invade Japan. It was the wind, the *kaze*, sent by the gods, the *kami*, that protected the Japanese from the Mongol hordes. I wanted the name to reflect divine intervention protecting the whales from the drift-net hordes. By doing so, I hoped to get an edge on the opposition — most uneducated sailors and fishermen are superstitious.

Don's people, as part of the deal, worked on the ship with my crew from sunrise to midnight. It was remarkable how well our two crews worked together. Tipton's volunteers were all devout, proper, chaste and fervent in their Christian beliefs. They prayed constantly, talked in tongues and preached to us incessantly. They were, besides, heavy meat-and-potatoes people. My crew were biocentric, deep ecologist, primarily vegetarian and had nothing but contempt for the idea of Jesus Christ as saviour of anything. One group worked to save souls and the other to save whales. Despite the philosophical chasm that divided us, there was a great deal of mutual respect based on sharing hard, dirty and unpaid labour in an effort to bring life to a steel hull driven by a Japanese Yanmar power plant. Our welder might believe in Darwin and their welder certainly was passionate about Christ but they could talk welding. Nonetheless, it was amusing to see 700 Club and Jesus Saves bumper stickers on cars parked alongside other cars bearing such slogans as Love Your Mother, Don't Rape Her and Bring Back the Pleistocene.

Our crew included veterans David Howitt and Rod Coronado, and Alex "The Juggler" Dandridge. New crew members included my girlfriend, Joanna Forwell, and three women biology majors from the University of California at Davis, Sue Rodriguez Pastor, Myra Finkelstein and René Grandi. Bob Hunter's daughter Justine joined us as a reporter for the *Vancouver Province*. Returning also was Jeff Goodman and his crew from the BBC, including soundman Adrian Allery and veteran Peter Brown, who would be shooting film for us.

When everything was set to go, Ben White arrived and took over. His idea was to head north to the Aleutian Islands and then follow the chain westward to look for drift nets. He was relying heavily on information he had obtained in Washington, D.C., information that I did not trust. Our first disagreement began after a day at sea. I questioned the validity of his information.

"I don't know, Ben," I asked. "This info on possible drift-net locations is coming from the beltway bureaucrats. I have a feeling that we would be better off to head due west and intercept them some 800 miles [1,280 km] south of the Aleutians."

Ben looked at me patronizingly. "What evidence do you have that they are there?"

"I have a feeling that that's the place to look."

He smiled and remarked, "A feeling ain't much to go on."

"It's always worked for me," said I.

"I don't think so this time," answered Ben. "I think the co-ordinates I have will be sufficient."

"Ben," I said, "it doesn't make any sense for the Japanese to be using drift nets so close to U.S. territory."

"It may not," he snapped, "but the beaches are polluted with drift nets, and that's where the guys in the know in Washington say they will be."

"Well," I argued, "I'm for heading straight out."

Ben became angry. "You agreed that I would lead this campaign, or maybe our critics are right, maybe this isn't anything other than a one-man operation."

Resigned, I muttered, "OK, I'll take it where you want me to go."

I began to feel the frustrations I had felt many years before with Greenpeace. It was difficult to surrender my intuition and allow myself to be led where I had no wish to go. But I felt that perhaps Ben was right and I should share the control.

What followed was a three-week voyage without a target or a confrontation. Ben insisted on hugging the coastline of the Aleutians, putting in to different islands to search out a telephone to call his contacts in D.C. He didn't want to use the radios for fear of giving away our position to the Japanese.

It was nice, however, to see the lush green islands of the Aleutian chain again, to see sea otters, Steller's sea lions, northern fur seals and the thousands of puffins. At least up here, things still lived.

The day we pulled in to Amchitka Island was a landmark for Justine Hunter.

"Hey, Justine," I shouted across the deck. "You've made it to the place your father didn't."

She laughed. "I know and it's great. I can't wait to ride him on it."

Seventeen years before, her father and I had tried to reach this island in time to stop a five-megaton underground nuclear test. We failed, but not without attracting international media attention to the needless destruction the Atomic Energy Commission was causing to the surrounding marine environment.

That voyage was the genesis of a group called the Don't Make a Wave Committee, which in 1972 became the Greenpeace Foundation. Justine Hunter was a little girl at the time. Now she was a tall, slim, very attractive woman not much younger than my girlfriend Joanna. But I couldn't help but see her as that little girl.

We cruised out past Agattu and Attu, where Ben went ashore to use the telephone at the Coast Guard station. This precipitated my second argument with Ben. Because of a severe williwaw, which is a sudden Aleutian windstorm, I anchored the ship on the north, lee side of the island. I then gave permission for the crew to go ashore. As the storm worsened, most of the crew returned to the ship, but I hiked inland and climbed the rugged hills of the island to watch the North Pacific rage on the south shore. I got back a few hours later and picked up the remainder of the shore party who were awaiting my arrival before returning with the inflatable to the ship.

It was a harrowing return as the rising winds howled over the steep hills and funneled down over the ocean. The swells rose dramatically between the shoreline and the ship, which was anchored only a half a mile out. The thick kelp beds made it a tricky passage. Peter Brown, Peter Wallerstein, Ben White, Pearl Shore and I were tossed about and nearly thrown overboard. There's no doubt that some dangerous manoeuvring was required to haul the boat onto the deck of the *Divine Wind* amid the heaving swells and fierce wind, but it was an exhilarating ride just the same. All but one of us enjoyed it.

Once the inflatable was safely stowed, Ben laid into me. Red-faced, he blew up, "Just what the hell did you think you were doing? You could have killed or injured one of us. Of all the foolhardy, imbecilic stunts."

"Ben, for God's sake, don't blow a piston. Nothing happened to anybody. This is what we do. Hell, it's not that dangerous."

"Oh yeah," he countered. "You wouldn't be talking so smart if you had lost somebody, would you?"

"Hell, they would have fallen out and I would have retrieved them. What's your problem?"

"My problem, mister, is you. You may feel that you're immortal, but you just can't go around risking people's lives. Who the hell do you think you are?"

"I'm the captain, Ben, and risking our lives is what we do — not that there was much risk in that little jaunt."

"I can see risking our lives for the cause but not for a joy ride."

"Ben, look on it as training. You should stick to your trees and keep your criticisms to yourself concerning me and my ship and crew."

"Your crew." He looked pissed. "Your ship. I raised the money for this ship. So it's just as I thought. It's a one-man organization after all, isn't it?"

"I don't know about that. I founded the group by myself. I raised the initial funding and worked my ass off for years to win credibility for this organization without much help from anyone else, but I am willing to share in building it. Ben, I'll follow your directions — I agreed to do that — but I will not captain a ship unless I *am* the captain, and I will not be dressed down in front of my crew by you or anyone else."

The next day, when I tried to talk Ben into heading south, he ignored me and decided to retrace our steps north of the Aleutians to the Pribilof Islands, which we reached a week later without finding anything. If nothing else, the Aleuts will remember our visit for the show Alex Dandridge staged when he juggled six cod heads while dressed in black tails and top hat.

It was the first expedition I had ever taken out that had failed to find the opposition. Ben left the ship in the Pribilofs and returned to Virginia. I took the ship back to Vancouver to begin the task of reorganizing for the next campaign. So much for democracy — it didn't do a damn thing to improve our effectiveness. All we had to show for our efforts was some washed-up remnants of drift nets on the beaches of a few of the Aleutian Islands. The BBC crew packed up and returned disappointed. Adrian Allery elected to remain as mate until we reached Los Angeles. He was looking for some sea time to sit for his yacht master's ticket in England.

I took the ship farther south and anchored off Santa Cruz to raise funds. We carried on down to Los Angeles and, because of the prohibitive and costly berthage fees, I anchored the ship in San Pedro harbour. By now, as usual, most of the crew had departed, leaving David Howitt, Adrian Allery and Linda May on their own. I left Adrian as first mate in charge of the ship and David as chief in charge of the engine. I warned them that the ship could not be left unattended. I had to go on a speaking tour to raise additional funding and some new volunteers for the crew.

While I was away, all three decided to go see a movie, leaving the ship unattended. A sudden squall came in and drove the ship, dragging her anchor, against the breakwater, causing some structural damage below the waterline. It was not overly serious but I was angry enough to want to sell the ship then and there. I felt that the three of them had betrayed my trust, but then I discovered that director Scott Trimingham, who was now the president of the Sea Shepherd Conservation Society, had told them it would be all right to see a movie and not to worry.

I was being undermined by directors who knew nothing about ships, who countered my orders to prove that they were in charge. My position was being threatened by people who knew little about what we actually did. Scott was an administrator and Ben was an arborist. Of the other directors, Peter Brown was firmly on my side and Peter Wallerstein seemed loyal, and with their continued support I could still outvote the other two. But if either of the Peters switched sides, I could be turfed out of the organization I had established and dedicated the last 10 years of my life to building.

To ensure the security of the ship, I decided to move her back to Washington State and berth her in Poulsbo. I did not have the time to move the ship myself so for the first time I entrusted the vessel to a volunteer who had excellent papers qualifying him as a ship's master. Walt Simpson would deliver the *Divine Wind*. Joining him on the voyage was another new volunteer, a diesel mechanic from Arizona by the name of Ron Frazier. They both seemed to be capable crew members and David Howitt, serving as chief engineer, thought highly of them.

I had met both Simpson and Frazier at the Earthfirst! rendezvous in Okanagan, Washington, during the summer of 1988. Frazier had been giving lessons in monkey-wrenching heavy machinery. Simpson was hanging around with another Earthfirst! activist from Arizona named Mike Fain. I remember reading Walt's crew application. In response to our question asking why he wanted to join the *Sea Shepherd* crew, he had written, "to kick ass."

They delivered the ship without incident and fortunately we were able to sell the *Divine Wind* for a profit. I used the money to repair and refit the *Sea Shepherd II*, which was still sitting forlorn and virtually abandoned in Sharpness in England.

Jeremy Coon offered to help. I sent him over to England to begin work on the ship. We had it towed to Dartmouth and anchored it in the River Dart, and Jeremy began what he did best: he started at the bottom and worked his way to the top, addressing each problem a step at a time. He next had the ship towed to a berth in Torquay to complete the work. It would take just over a year to make her seaworthy again. But with patience and frugality, the *Sea Shepherd II* would point her sturdy bow seaward once more.

Meanwhile I had become impatient with waiting for an answer to my queries from Iceland. I fired off a press release and informed the Icelandic media that I would be arriving in Reykjavik on January 18, 1988. Joanna would go with me and we would be joined in London by Sten Borg, who spoke his native Swedish.

It was a gamble. I knew it was important that we carry through and occupy the moral high ground. I would not have us perceived as outlaws when the real outlaws continued their illegal killings. It was obvious to me that the Icelanders did not really want to apprehend us. If they had, they would have answered my correspondence. Putting myself deliberately in their hands could force them to take action just to save face. Then again, a trial would help to publicize the issue of illegal whaling and embarrass Iceland further. The danger in which I was putting myself was that I could be convicted and imprisoned under their laws, which would deny me further opportunities to carry on the fight against whaling.

It was a situation ripe for the classic Br'er Rabbit ploy. I would tell the Icelanders that I wanted them to arrest me. They would then believe that, since it was what I wanted, there must be some advantage to me in getting it. If there was an advantage to me, then there must be a disadvantage for Iceland. I set out eagerly and enthusiastically to seek an arrest in order to provoke an essentially contrary reaction. That was my plan in theory. Now to put it into practice. I reinforced the Br'er Rabbit ploy by utilizing what I called the Oliver North gambit: I made sure to wear my gold-braided merchant marine master's uniform.

So it was that in mid-January 1988, Joanna, Sten and I boarded an Icelandic airline flight from Luxembourg bound for Iceland. We arrived at Kleflavik airfield in the early evening. When we stepped off the plane dozens of uniformed police officers gathered on the tarmac to greet us. They were a little taken aback by my uniform. Not one of them touched me.

A man in a grey suit approached us.

"Captain Watson, I am the Chief Immigration Officer. How long do you intend to stay in Iceland?"

I laughed. "Well, I don't really know. Five minutes, five days, five months or five years. I'm afraid that only Iceland can answer that question."

"I see." He seemed confused but added, "Will you come with us to the police station for questioning?"

Smiling, I answered, "That's what I'm here for."

I kissed Joanna goodbye and she and Sten were free to enter Iceland.

The police hustled me out a side door into a waiting car and drove towards town. Meanwhile, back at the airport, the Icelandic media descended on Joanna and Sten. They found out that four Icelandic journalists had been arrested for attempting to get by police lines to intercept me.

Sten and Joanna were met by one of our supporters, Magnus Skarpedinsson, who had formed the Whale Friends Society (Hvalvinurfelag) shortly after the Icelandic whalers had been sunk. Magnus had recruited some 200 members to his organization and, in the summer of 1987, organized the first-ever protest against Icelandic whaling by Icelanders in Iceland. A few members of Hvalvin-urfelag had chained themselves to the masts of the two undamaged whaling ships to prevent them from leaving port. Magnus invited Joanna and Sten to stay as his guests in his home.

The drive to the police station was pleasant. The officers were friendly and pointed out the sights. They were especially proud of a geothermal green-house that produced Icelandic-grown bananas. At the station, I took a seat, they brought me coffee and I waited for two prosecutors, the Canadian consul, a state-appointed lawyer and some additional officers to arrive.

At last, one of the prosecutors addressed me. He got straight to the point. "Is the Sea Shepherd Conservation Society responsible for sinking the two ships and for damaging the whale meat–processing plant?"

"Of course," I said, adding, "and we intend to sink the other two ships at the first opportunity."

"What was your role in this action?"

"I am responsible for all activities undertaken in the name of the Sea Shep-herd Conservation Society. I give the orders."

"Did you give the orders to sink the ships?"

"I did."

"But," and the prosecutor paused before continuing, "you yourself did not actually sink the ships."

"No, of course not. I'm too well known in Iceland, and at the time I was under an expulsion order, since expired, from the Faeroes, that would have prevented me from getting into the country, or it would most certainly have red-flagged me. Therefore it was not possible for me to have participated."

Appearing clever now, the prosecutor said, "Hah! So the people who actu-ally did this thing, the people that we want to arrest, will not come to Iceland?"

"They'll both come if you ask them to. You have not officially requested any arrests or charges. I have repeatedly requested charges and my requests have been ignored. Give me a phone and I'll ask them to come here on a plane tomorrow, although I'm afraid you will have to buy the tickets, since they can't afford it themselves at the moment."

The other prosecutor turned red. "It is not your place to decide who and when to bring charges. That is our prerogative. We don't have to respond to your requests simply because you make a request. Our investigations dictate our actions."

I chuckled. "What investigations and what actions? The situation is simple. Iceland kills whales illegally. My crew retaliated by sinking two of your ships. We did it although we will plead not guilty for the benefit of a show trial — it's quite straightforward. What do you need to investigate? A deed was done, the perpetrators admit doing it and we throw ourselves before you to do with as you will, and you respond by doing — nothing. Frankly, gentlemen, I'm a trifle confused."

One of the officers interrupted. "Captain Watson, are you hungry?"

"No, I'm not." He looked a little hurt, so I added, "Unless of course you're all hungry."

"We are," he answered.

"Well then, let's eat," I said.

All in all it was great fun, this questioning. We chatted through dinner and then continued with further questioning.

"So," said the first prosecutor, "you admit, then, that you did not yourself participate in the sinking of the ships."

"That's correct. I did not do it myself. However, I did conspire to do so, I did support the actions and I will continue to do so."

"But" — he smiled — "you did not yourself actually go on board the ships and help to sink them."

"No, I did not."

"Thank you, Captain Watson. That will be all. We'll talk to you in the morning."

I was then taken to a cell and escorted by a gorgeous blonde female prison guard to one of the most comfortable jail cells I had ever seen. If this is prison, I thought to myself, it isn't half bad. I could catch up on my reading here, learn a little Icelandic and do some writing.

After a restful sleep, I woke up and had breakfast. I ignored some chunks of suspicious-looking meat on my plate, which I later found out was whale meat. Very funny. I asked for a pen and some paper.

The Chief Immigration Officer came to my cell around ten o'clock.

"Captain Watson, please get ready. We will be taking you to the airport."

"To the airport? You can't do that," I protested.

"You are being deported," he answered matter-of-factly.

"Deported?" I asked. "How can you deport me without first convicting me or even charging me with a crime?"

The officer looked at me and smiled. "You will understand when I say, I am just a deck hand. This makes no sense to me. I'm just following orders."

I was escorted by four officers to a waiting car. Some Icelandic reporters were being kept some distance away by police. One of them yelled across the parking lot.

"The police say that you deny any involvement with the sinking of the whaling ships. Is this true?"

I shouted back, "No, it is not true. I told the police that Sea Shepherd is responsible for sinking the ships and I am responsible for the actions by Sea Shepherd."

Before another question could be asked, I was pushed into the back of the police car and driven to the police station at the airport. It was a cushy place, more like a country club than a cop shop. It had television, a pool table, dart board and shuffleboard. Joanna, too, was escorted to the station. She arrived with a bottle of champagne. We drank the champagne and I showed the officers some pool tricks, winning a couple of Icelandic kroner from them on the side.

Joanna would talk with the media after I left to tell them what had happened. Originally, Magnus had invited me to give a public talk in Reykjavik. This would not be possible but I had written out what I would have said if given the oppotunity. I gave a copy to Joanna to give to the newspapers to run as an opinion piece.

At seven, I was taken to the plane and escorted all the way to New York City by two very friendly police officers. They seemed pleased at the opportunity to visit New York. One of them openly expressed his admiration for our efforts.

"You know," he said, "we have not had this kind of thing in Iceland since the days of the Vikings. I do disagree with you sinking the ships, but it is a good spirit, a spirit that we once had and have long since lost."

In New York, I shook hands with them. "I'll probably see you again, I hope soon, when we return to get your other two ships."

They laughed and waved goodbye.

Two days later, Joanna arrived in New York and handed me a newspaper. My speech to the Icelandic people had been translated and printed uncensored in *Dagblad*, the largest Icelandic daily.

So the Icelandic people would be given the opportunity to understand why we acted as we did. I wrote, in part, as follows:

An Open Letter to the People of Iceland

I would like to address the people of Iceland as an ambassador. I do not represent any form of human government. I am speaking to you on behalf of the Cetacean nation.

I am representing whalekind in an effort to reach a state of co-existence with humankind.

My credentials in this regard are simple. I am a human who has swum with, communicated with, studied and respected the great whales all of my life. I have repeatedly risked my life and freedom to protect and conserve the whales. My love for the whales is such that I would not choose to live upon this planet without them.

I have touched and I have been touched by the whales. I have been with them when they frolicked freely in the seas, knowing that their mighty hearts were filled with the joy of life.

I have been with them at the moment of their birth when they have taken their first breath. I have been with them in death. I have felt their hot blood on their skin as the life ebbed slowly away after the horrendous, shattering impact of the grenade harpoon. Once on the rolling Pacific swells I comforted a dying child whale, a young sperm killed illegally by a Soviet whaler. I felt its last breath against my face and closed one of its large eyes, but not before seeing my own reflection in that eye and the despair reflected back from my own eyes. I knew then, as I know now, that the survival of the whales is the most important objective for my life.

In 1975 Robert Hunter and I were the first people to physically block a harpooner's line of fire when we intercepted a Soviet whaling fleet and placed our bodies between the killers and eight fleeing, frightened sperm whales. We were in a small inflatable boat, speeding before the plunging steel prow of a Russian kill boat. As the whales fled for their lives before us, we could smell the fear in their misty exhalations. We thought we could make a difference with our Gandhi-inspired seagoing stand. Surely these men behind the harpoons would not risk killing a human being to satisfy their lust for whale oil and meat. We were wrong!

The whalers demonstrated their contempt for our non-violent protest by firing an explosive harpoon over our heads. The harpoon line slashed into the water and we narrowly escaped death. One of the whales was not so lucky. With a dull thud followed by a muffled explosion, the entrails of a female whale were torn and ripped apart by hot steel shrapnel.

The large bull sperm in the midst of the pod abruptly rose and dove. We had been told by whale experts that a bull whale in this situation would attack us. We were a smaller target than the whaling ship. Anxiously, we held our breath in anticipation of 60 tons of irate muscle and blood torpedoing from the depths below our frail craft.

The ocean erupted behind us. We turned towards the Soviet ship to see a living juggernaut hurl itself at the Russian bow. The harpooner was ready. He pulled the trigger and sent a second explosive missile into the massive head of the whale.

A pitiful scream rang in my ears, a fountain of blood geysered into the air, and the deep blue of the ocean was rapidly befouled with dark red blood. The whale thrashed and convulsed violently.

Mortally wounded and crazed with pain, the whale rolled and one great eye made contact with mine. The whale dove and a trail of bloody bubbles moved laboriously towards us. Slowly, very slowly, a gargantuan head emerged from the water and the whale rose at an angle over and above our tiny craft. Blood and brine cascaded from the gaping head wound and fell upon us in torrents.

We were helpless, we knew that we would be crushed within seconds as the whale fell upon us. There was little time for fear, only awe. We could not move.

The whale did not fall upon us. He wavered and towered motionless above us. I looked up past the daggered six-inch teeth and into an eye the size of my fist, an eye that reflected back intelligence and spoke wordlessly of compassion and communicated to me the understanding that this was a being that could discriminate and understood what we had tried to do. The mammoth body slowly slid back into the sea.

The massive head of this majestic sperm whale slowly fell back into the sea. He rolled and the water parted, revealing a single solitary eye. The gaze of the whale seized control of my soul and I saw my own image reflected back at me. I was overcome with pity, not for the whale but for ourselves. Waves of shame crashed down upon me and I wept. Overwhelmed with horror at this revelation of the cruel blasphemy of my species, I realized then and there that my allegiance lay with this dying child of the sea and his kind. On that day, I left the comfortable realm of human self-importance to forever embrace the soulful satisfaction of lifelong service to the citizens of the sea.

The gentle giant died with my face seared upon his retina. I will never forget that. It is a memory that haunts and torments me, and leaves me with only one course to chart towards redemption for the collective sins of humanity. It is both my burden and my joy to pledge my allegiance to the most intelligent and profoundly sensitive species of beings to have ever inhabited the Earth — the great whales.

I found out later that the Icelandic attorney general, Hallvardur Einarsson, had given a speech before Parliament that made a mockery of his earlier position that all efforts would be undertaken to make sure we "terrorists" would be brought to justice for our "inhuman act."

Einarsson said, "Who does this man Watson think he is? He comes to our country and demands to be arrested. Well, we are not going to play his game by his rules. We're not going to do it. I move that he be deported and banned from entering any Scandinavian country for five years."

It was so moved and I was so deported.

Back in Vancouver, I called a lawyer in Iceland to investigate the possibility of suing Iceland for illegal deportation. He said that he would look into it but suggested that I not hold my breath.

A few days later, as I was walking through Stanley Park, a middle-aged man approached me. He pointed his finger at me and scolded me for the Icelandic action.

"I just want you to know," he said, "that your actions in Iceland were criminal, reprehensible, irresponsible, despicable and totally unforgivable."

"So?" said I.

He had not expected that. "So, I just wanted you to know that that's what I think of you."

"So?" I said softly.

Perplexed, he asked, "What do you mean, 'So'? You're a terrorist, nothing but a common criminal."

"What's your name?" I asked.

"My name? What do you want my name for?"

"What's your name?"

"John."

"John," I said, "what makes you think that your opinion means anything to me. Do you think that I should have asked, Gee, I wonder what John will think if we sink some illegal whaling ships? John, let me tell you something, we sank those ships for the whales. Not for you and not for any other goddamn human being on the surface of the Earth." I raised my voice steadily as I continued. "John, I don't care what you think. I don't give a damn what any human being thinks about what we did. We did it for the whales, John, for the whales. As for your opinion about what we did, well, quite frankly, I couldn't give a good goddamn. Just who the hell do you think you are, John? I'll tell you what you are. You're anthropocentric slime, John, nothing but a self-centred, overly glorified, conceited ape, a divine legend in your own mind and your opinion don't mean shit to a tree, John, and less to the whales."

He actually ran away while I was berating him. But what John represents is the problem itself and explains why we must do what we do. It's because people like John can't see through the petty little concerns of our own species. John was concerned that we saved animal lives at the expense of profits because in John's reality, profits are first, people are second and other life forms are irrelevant. In my reality, interspecies diversity and the laws of ecology are all-important and human greed at the expense of diversity is an evil that is best eradicated.

John the anthropocentric had just crossed swords with me, a biocentric, and the encounter dramatized the struggle that's been going on since Cain the farmer slew Abel, the nomad, symbolizing the dominance of agricultural and later industrial man over the people of the Earth, the hunter-gatherers and the Goddess-worshipping pagans of the Early and Middle Pleistocene.

Only now things were beginning to change. Biocentrics were fed up with the trashing, the killing, the poisons and the waste. We were beginning to fight back, for the Earth, for our fellow species and for our children and descendants.

14

The Last Days
of the Dolphins

Any further controversy over our actions in Iceland was now irrelevant. We had taken the appropriate actions. I had made myself available for charges. Iceland refused to bring charges and thus refused to resolve the issue in a court of law. Because of this I had no patience with those who accused us of terrorism or criminal behaviour. The action had been successful. We prevented Iceland from continuing the killing in 1987, and every subsequent year until 1994. We had helped to buy time for the whales and we could only reflect on this achievement with pride.

By the end of 1988, the whalers were in retreat. So-called scientific whaling by Japan and Norway continued, but it was illegal. I decided to withdraw from the whale wars for a few years in order to allow the moderate forces and the IWC to work on the moratorium and its loopholes. It was time for us to address the devastation caused by drift nets and by the dolphin-targeting purse seine nets of the U.S. and Central American tuna fleets.

Although the tuna fleets were not exploiting dolphins directly, they were hunting them in order to locate yellowfin tuna. There is a relationship between three different species of dolphin and the tuna. It is a relationship we do not understand, but it is known that the tuna swim under the dolphins. Once the tuna boats spot spinner, spotted or Pacific white-sided dolphins, they know they will find the tuna underneath. Because of this they have devised a method of fishing called "fishing on porpoise."

The large tuna seiners hunt the waters of the Eastern Tropical Pacific, that vast area of the Pacific between Central America and Tahiti. Each ship carries a helicopter to spot dolphins. Once they are spotted, the chopper directs the ship to the dolphins. The ship then drops a half-dozen high-speed boats to chase and herd the dolphins into a tight circle, terrorizing them with the roar of their outboards and by tossing "seal bombs" — small sticks of dynamite — into the water. As the dolphins are herded tightly together, the tuna beneath them are also corralled. The tuna boat then deploys a mile-long purse seine net around both dolphins and tuna. The net is closed on the bottom and both tuna and dolphins are entrapped. In terror, many dolphins panic and become entangled in the nets and drown. Some are crushed in the power block when the net is winched on board. The incidental kill is devastating. Since 1970, according to United States Department of Commerce estimates, more than 17 million dolphins have been killed in these nets.

After a year of frustrations, meagre funds and unreliable volunteers, the *Sea Shepherd II* was finally repaired and ready to return to sea. Volunteers joined from Great Britain, Australia, Canada and the United States. We took the ship to the Netherlands to complete repairs. I had more faith in Dutch workers than British workers to complete the machinery overhaul. This included a comprehensive overhaul of our water pumps. My 14-year-old nephew, Trevor Van Der Gulick, arrived for his first voyage. His Dutch relatives delivered him to us when we arrived in the Dutch port of IJmuiden. Other crew members would meet us in Key West, Florida, where we would continue on through the Panama Canal to the Eastern Tropical Pacific (ETP).

Scott Trimingham told me to look up Walt Simpson in The Netherlands. He said he was skippering the MV *Greenpeace*. I called the ship in Rotterdam and located Walt. He was unusually nervous when he realized it was me. Instead of asking how I'd been, he immediately snapped, "How did you get this number?"

"The Greenpeace office in Amsterdam gave it to me, Walt. Hey, since we're in the same neck of the woods, why don't you drop in and visit us? I'll show you around the *Sea Shepherd II*."

He hesitated. "I don't think I'll have the time. We're pretty busy here."

"I'm surprised you're working with Greenpeace, Walt," I said. "The last time I spoke with you on the *Divine Wind* you said they were wimps. How would you like to join us for a trip to kick ass among the tuna seiners in the ETP."

"I don't think I can, man. I made a commitment to take this ship down to Australia. They may be wimps but they pay better than you do. I need the money."

"Okay, just thought that I would ask," I countered.

"Thanks, man, but I can't. Wish I could. Good luck, hey," he said.

"Walt, how about dropping by for a beer."

"Sorry, man, but I can't get away. Can't afford the bus fare actually. Have a good trip, hey." He hung up, leaving me with a feeling that something wasn't right. He seemed really uncomfortable to be speaking with me. Perhaps he was just nervous that Greenpeace would discover his previous association with us.

In June 1989, we left Holland and I plotted a course to Key West, Florida. A day later, as we were moving along the southern coast of Great Britain, disaster struck. Our recently repaired primary saltwater pump was now acting so efficiently that the saltwater cooling pipes split under pressure. We limped into Falmouth for emergency repairs and tied up at the Falmouth Shipyards directly behind a gleaming white, multimillion-dollar, 200-foot (70 m) yacht named the *Land's End*. The shipyard said we could have the statutory 48 hours for emergency repairs. We would be charged if we intended to stay longer. Worse, the cost of replacing the entire saltwater cooling system would be thousands of pounds in parts and labour — much more than we could afford.

After all the hard work, and now with our cash reserves practically exhausted, I was finding myself wearied with the effort of keeping it all going. The endless strain of raising funds, organizing campaigns, repairing and maintaining the ship, besides supporting myself independently of the Sea Shepherd Conservation Society, was becoming far too stressful.

That night I had a dream that I was invited on board the yacht the *Land's End*, where her owner presented me with an expensive dinner and asked me if there was anything he could do to help. I woke up feeling curiously elated. I called Rod Coronado up to my office.

"Rod, I want you to visit the yacht in front of us and see if you can find out who owns her."

Rod returned a half-hour later. "The first mate is on board," he said. "He told me that the ship is owned by Alex De Savary, the same man who owns the shipyard."

"I know who that is. He's an entry for the America's Cup race. He's an extremely wealthy individual."

Sitting down at my desk, I wrote a letter and handed it to Rod.

"Take this and give it to the mate on the *Land's End.*"

In the letter, I made a formal request to Mr. De Savary for help in repairing our ship. A few hours later, Rod delivered a fax given to him by the mate on the yacht. It was from Alex De Savary from his office in London. He gave us a free berth, use of the facilities at the shipyard and labour costs. We need only pay for the parts. Thanks to his generosity, it took only a few days to complete the repairs. In the meantime, we had lost a couple of crew and recruited a couple more. Joanna flew in from Seattle to be our medical officer. A local master mariner, looking a bit like the ancient mariner himself, came on board and requested permission to join the crew. He was a big man with white hair and a full white beard. His name was William Towel.

I felt a little awkward interviewing Bill. He was one of the most qualified skippers I had ever met, with experience on ships going back to the late 1920s. Two vessels under his command had been torpedoed beneath him by German U-boats, and since the war he had commanded everything from fishing boats to super-tankers.

"I don't know, Bill," I ventured. "It's a little intimidating to give you the position of first officer, what with your experience and all. You should be captain."

He chuckled. "I'm 68 years old and I just want to go to sea again before I die. I retired three years ago and it's been hell here on shore. I'm becoming a crotchety burden to my wife and I'm bored. I'm not interested in command — just want to shoot the stars and tend to the navigation."

"Well," I answered, "I'm proud to have you on this crew."

The next morning, Bill Towel arrived at 0500 hours, jolly and ready to head to sea. Stepping on board he spoke to a few of the crew.

"It's a beautiful morning," he said. "You know, I kissed my wife this morning and she said, 'Bill, you've never kissed me goodbye before.' I answered her by saying that I had never felt so good about going to sea, and this the first time ever that I've shipped out without pay."

I greeted Bill as he entered the bridge. "Bill, this is your home port. Would you like to take her out."

He smiled. "I would be honoured."

We threw off the mooring lines. Rod Coronado took the wheel. I left the wheelhouse to Bill's command and stood outside on the port bridge deck to enjoy the departure. It was a warm sunny morning. The *Sea Shepherd II* pulled away from the dock and then Bill suddenly telegraphed full speed ahead. The ship surged forward towards a protruding jetty, much to the surprise of some local yard workers, who stood slack-jawed at our approach.

Bill knew what he was doing. He had gauged the clearance brilliantly and the ship turned slowly, in time to avoid striking the dock. It was impressive. This man knew his stuff.

The ship's bow pointed towards the mouth of the harbour and we were on our way. Suddenly, I heard Rod cry out my name. I ran into the wheelhouse to see Bill lying on his back, his face turning blue.

"Keep her on course, Rod," I yelled as I called down to the deck. "Joanna! Adrian! Get up here."

It was evident that Bill was suffering a massive heart attack. Adrian and Joanna ran into the wheelhouse and began treating him. Joanna immediately began mouth-to-mouth resuscitation while Adrian checked vital signs. I had grabbed the radio and help was on the way. Amidst the chaos, rain began to pelt down and visibility became extremely reduced. I notified Harbour Traffic and they directed me through the shipping channel to the closest anchorage. On route, a Royal Life Boat pulled up alongside, followed, seconds later, by a Royal Navy helicopter. Within eight minutes of Bill's collapse, two doctors and four medics were at his side.

Regrettably, it was too late. Bill died and the doctors escorted his body off the ship to the shore. The police requested that we anchor overnight to await an autopsy.

The next morning, I had Joanna return Bill's effects to his wife. She asked us to keep his binoculars so that a part of him would complete the trip. The police gave us permission to proceed.

The local newspaper called and asked me about Bill's death.

"I think it was poetic," said I.

"What do you mean?"

"It was obvious that Bill was dying on shore. His life was the sea and it was to the sea he wanted to return. He took the helm and under his command, the ship headed towards the ocean. I believe that his spirit just continued out to sea. If I was him, I couldn't imagine a more fitting way to die — doing something he loved within the element that he loved. I'm happy that we were able to serve him in this manner. I feel that he died happy and I'm happy for him because of it. It was a good way, a good day to die."

We hauled anchor and headed south towards the Azores, then cut across westward towards Bermuda. I anticipated a 16-day crossing. Instead, it became a three-week ordeal. Most of the crossing was windless with a merciless sun beating down upon us. The seas were flat as glass and this only helped to raise the water temperature. Our ship, a North Sea trawler built to run with a sea-cooled system that worked most efficiently in a northern climate, was severely taxed. In spite of our reduced speed we had numerous breakdowns due to overheating.

During one of the breakdowns in the mid-Atlantic, to escape the oppressive heat, we jumped over the side to spend an hour swimming. I love to give the crew as many opportunities as possible to swim in the deep ocean. It's an exhilarating feeling to swim through the water hundreds of miles — sometimes more than a thousand miles — from land. The sun beams down through the layered, darkening blues until it's swallowed, hundreds of feet below, in inky darkness. Swimming in miles-deep water gives you a thrill and stimulates the imagination, especially when something as wonderful as a large shark swims casually by.

A friend of mine, Doug Peacock, once gave a lecture entitled "The Importance of Big Fierce Animals that Can Eat You." Although I have little fear of sharks, I respect them, and understand that you have to know how to behave in their territory. It is a valuable lesson in humility to be within the killing range of a more powerful animal.

Joanna and I followed one shark for a distance and then doubled back when we spied a sea turtle going in the opposite direction. We had so much fun trying to race the sea turtle that we began to race each other. I caught her and we coupled in the ocean. The thrust from a pair of flippers allows humans to mate almost as easily as dolphins in the ocean. We came together three-dimensionally, falling through the depths along shafts of light, and then kicking to the surface and rolling on the gentle swells. When we surfaced and looked around, the ship was at least a mile away, practically invisible from our limited horizon. We struck out towards it, swimming strongly against an easterly current until we reached her. The crew had lost sight of us. No one was too worried. I had often swum out of sight before. I liked to do so at night sometimes, for the peace of being alone, cradled in the bosom of the sea. At such times, I have felt a delightful sense of bliss in being a conscious mote of sentience balanced between the planet below and the stars above, surrounded by the living sea.

By late July, we reached Key West and berthed at the Truman Annex pier, which had been generously offered by a dedicated ecological developer by the name of Pridim Singh. The word's "ecology" and "development" usually clash, but Pridim had demonstrated that he could make money by development of lands that had been formally considered toxic. The former Naval Annex and site of the Truman White House was an ecological disaster before Pridim got his hands on it. It cost him big bucks to remove the toxic soil and contaminated buildings and equipment but when finished he had prime Key West waterfront property.

For years, I have said in lectures that a person did not have to be a radical activist to make a difference. I did not expect every person to ram a whaling ship or sabotage a bulldozer to be effective. The difference between those who help make a positive contribution and those who do not is motivation. If all people enlisted their talents, skills, imagination and energy in the service of the Earth, that would be sufficient. Pridim had demonstrated that he could be both developer and ecologist. He had restored ugly toxic land to a condition of usefulness and beauty. From a place of danger, he had created a safe haven for homes.

At his docks, we were able to replace some crew, bringing on Rosemary Waldron as our nurse, and ecology folksinger Dana Lyons and his guitar. We also refueled, reprovisioned and raised some funding with an open house on the dock to recruit members. The *Sea Shepherd II* officially became a part of the Navy of the Conch Republic of Key West and I was given an honorary citizenship as a Conch.

Cartoonist Berkley Breathed, the creator of Bloom County, came by to visit with his wife, Jody Boyman. We were able to talk Berke into painting a mural of Opus the penguin on the starboard side of the superstructure. Opus stood with clenched fist and sporting the words "Environmental extremists" on his feathered chest. He looked like a logo mascot on a Second World War bomber, and this gave us the idea to paint "kill" flags on the side to symbolize our past victories. The crew painted on three pirate flags to represent the *Sierra*, the *Susan* and the *Theresa*. Two Spanish flags to represent the *Ibsa I* and *Ibsa II* and two Icelandic flags to represent the *Hvalur 6* and *Hvalur 7*.

Adrian Allery remained as first mate. Ben White had sent down his selection for second mate, a tall, gangly Norwegian Floridian named Gary Neilsen. Our vegan crew, always ready to jump on every recruit, seized upon Gary.

"Are you a vegan? Are you a vegan?" they demanded.

Puzzled, Gary replied, "Ya, I guess I am a Nordvegan."

About a third of our crew were vegans, people who used absolutely no animal products. I had always tried to promote vegetarianism on the ship. The vegans, however, despite their admirable choice of dietary lifestyle, were unbearably irritating with their holier-than-thou preaching. They dismissed meat-eaters as absolute barbarians and directed their ire at vegetarians because they should know better. I called them the veggie Jesuits. However, some of my best crew, including Susana Rodriguez Pastor, David Howitt, Rod Coronado and Myra Finkelstein, were part of the vegan brigade.

One potential crew member became something of a Sea Shepherd legend. With bushy black hair and Rasputin-like cold blue eyes and all energy, he didn't so much apply to volunteer as demand to be on the crew. He hung around the entire time we were on the dock at Key West. He ran errands and begged and pleaded to go with us. We called him Dolphin Dave. The problem was that he believed that he was a dolphin from a planet of dolphins and that he had been stranded on Earth with the other dolphins until he, who was their spy among humans, could decode the Bible, which was actually an elaborate cryptic set of instructions that would allow the dolphins to return to their home planet and, of course, take Dolphin Dave with them. Finally I had to break the news to him that he would not be able to go.

"Give me just one good reason why I can't go," he pleaded.

"Okay, I'll be honest with you. You're crazy."

Non-plussed, he responded, "Can you prove that?"

"Well," I ventured, "first of all, you are not a dolphin."

He looked at me seriously and asked, "Can you prove that?"

I laughed. "I rest my case. Dave, you can't go because I said you can't go."

He was devastated but I couldn't risk having him on board. He was already criticizing us for being too aggressive. In addition, he was standing around with a Bible in his hand denouncing one of my crew as a witch and another as a vampire.

Ben White flew down to meet us and to organize some of my crew to interfere with the capture of dolphins on the northwestern coast of Florida. I tried to unload Dolphin Dave on him but Ben was not appreciative. He said he would fly down to Puntarenas, Costa Rica, to join the expedition.

The *Sea Shepherd II* left Key West and voyaged south through the Panama Canal and on up the coast to Costa Rica. As we entered Costa Rican waters, a small plane flew overhead and made radio contact with us.

"*Sea Shepherd II*, this is Walt Simpson. Do you copy?"

I was dumbfounded. I picked up the transmitter. "Walt, what the hell are you doing here?"

I heard his voice as he circled above us. "Hi, Paul. I thought you could use my help. Ben's in San José and wants you to head for Puntarenas. There are a couple of tuna boats anchored in the harbour there, hey."

"Thanks, Walt. We'll head that way. Tell Ben we'll see him there."

Watching the Cessna fly off to the north left me puzzled. Here was a guy who couldn't afford the bus fare to visit us when we were in Holland and he was only a few miles away. Now, a month later, he had flown himself to Costa Rica and had chartered a plane to locate us just to deliver a message for me to proceed to a place that I was already heading for, and where Ben White had already agreed to meet us.

The next morning we pulled into Puntarenas. There was a single Venezuelan tuna boat complete with helicopter and speedboats, fully equipped to kill dolphins in their quest for of tuna. Her name was the *Pan Pacific*. We passed close by her, dropped our anchor and took care of the paperwork with Costa Rican Customs.

Ben White was not on shore. Walt Simpson was there, however, along with Marc Gaede, a photographer and a well-known eco-warrior from the days of the Black Mesa Defense Fund in Arizona. I took an instant liking to this former U.S. Marine who had stood with the Hopi and the Navaho to defend land besieged by mining companies in Arizona in the 1960s. He was dressed in khaki, armed with his cameras and ready for action.

The first thing he said to me was, "Who is this Walt Simpson?"

"He's a volunteer," I answered. "Sometimes he works for Greenpeace and sometimes for us."

Marc grunted. "Well, I don't trust him. He got the smell of infiltrator all over him."

I didn't comment and asked instead, "Do you know where Ben White and Peter Brown are?"

"No, I haven't seen them."

I called Scott Trimingham at our headquarters in Redondo Beach.

"Scott, do you know where Ben and Peter are?"

"Yeah, Peter is flying in this afternoon and Ben's at his hotel in San José. He's been meeting with Costa Rican officials about doing something about the tuna boats."

"What!" I was taken aback. "Scott, he knows that Sea Shepherd doesn't do meetings. Other groups participate in that crap. This is a shock troop group, for Christ sakes."

"Well, I don't know, Paul. We should try and talk with these people. Ben feels confident that he can convince them to ban tuna boats in Costa Rican waters."

I was getting a little angry now. "Scott, our role is to provoke an incident to

While sailing off the coast of Siberia, I spend a quiet moment on the bridge of
the *Sea Shepherd*.

The *Sea Shepherd,* docked in Bermuda in the spring of 1979, is seaworthy and ready for action.

July 18, 1979. Chief Engineer Peter Woof (left), 3rd Engineer Jerry Doran (right) and I on the *Sea Shepherd* in the Portuguese harbour of Leixões after ramming the *Sierra*.

After the ramming the pirate whaler was badly damaged but awaiting repairs.

On February 6, 1980, sabateurs were successful in sinking the *Sierra*, finally ending the ship's illegal whaling career.

Moments after this photo was taken in August 1981, these two Soviet soldiers had their rifles aimed at our backs. We hastily returned to our ship with filmed evidence of illegal whaling operations off the Siberian coast.

Sea Shepherd/Eric Schwartz

As we sailed in Siberian waters, the deck crew rigged barbed wire barricades on the *Sea Shepherd II* to protect against hostile boarding.

The slaughter of pilot whales like these for sport by the Faeroese fishermen was prevented during the month of June 1986 while the *Sea Shepherd II* stood guard.

Sea Shepherd/Gerry Free

On November 9, 1986, Sea Shepherd commandos Rod Coronado and David Howitt scuttled these two ships in Reykjavik harbour thereby destroying half of the Icelandic whaling fleet.

The *Sea Shepherd II* prepares to ram a Japanese drift-net ship in the North Pacific.

August 1990. The *Sea Shepherd II* rams the Japanese drift-net vessel *Shunyo Maru #8* in the North Pacific.

Lisa Distefano and I off the west coast of Vancouver Island in August 1992.

create a climate for publicizing this issue. If you talk to him before I do, I want you to tell him to get down here as soon as possible. I intend to ram this bastard and sink her here in Puntarenas harbour. I need Peter Brown to record it."

"I don't think that's a good idea," Scott responded. "We could get into trouble doing that and all of Ben's work in San José would have been for nothing. I would advise you not to get rash, Paul."

"Scott, I couldn't give a damn about what Ben is doing in San José. We don't talk, we act. We've been working for months to get this ship here for one reason and that is to provoke an international incident over the issue of dolphins being slaughtered by the tuna industry, and now I'm supposed to be worried about upsetting a couple of days of meetings that Ben took it upon himself to set up with some low-life politicians. No way. Scott, we are ready to take action now and I need Peter Brown."

Scott was quiet and then he said, "If you ram that ship and if anybody is hurt, I will be the first to denounce this action. I hope you understand that?"

"I understand that it's easy to moralize from your desk. It's all academic to you. It's our asses on the line, not yours."

Defensively Scott said, "I have a reputation to —"

I interrupted him, "A reputation? Scott, listen to yourself. You're the president of a radical, controversial, in-your-face, kick-ass conservation organization and you're worried about your reputation."

"I can't be responsible for any violence," he protested.

"You won't be. I'll be responsible." Fuming, I slammed the phone down and walked back to the beach.

I called Adrian Allery and Gary Neilsen ashore and had a meeting in a local sidewalk café. I told them that I had to make a decision about taking action against the tuna seiner. Sue Rodriguez Pastor had been listening to the scuttlebutt on the beach and found out that the *Pan Pacific* was preparing to leave in the evening. Both officers agreed with me that we should ram and disable her if she attempted to leave. It was decided that we would make our stand for the dolphins today in this harbour.

I needed Peter Brown. I called Ben's hotel in San José and left a message. For the rest of the day I called or had a crew member call the hotel every half-hour in an attempt to reach him.

Returning to the ship, I saw Marc Gaede waiting on the deck.

"Marc," I said, "we're going to ram that boat. How do you feel about that?"

"That's what I'm here for," he said with a wide smile.

The crew received the news with mixed reactions. Walt Simpson immediately grabbed his bags and headed shoreward in the inflatable. I yelled after him. "Hey Walt, where ya going?"

"This kind of action is a little heavy for me, man," he replied.

"Walt," I answered, "it's what we do."

Joanna disappointed me by leaving the ship. She also criticized the tactic. Both she and Walt got hotel rooms on the beach. Apart from Marc Gaede, only Rod Coronado and Sue Rodriguez Pastor seemed to be enthusiastic about my plan.

As the day turned to dusk, I put the crew on action alert and we watched the *Pan Pacific* for any sign of pulling up their anchor. I sent Rod ashore every hour to call Ben's hotel room. It was a tense situation. Although the Venezuelan crew were unaware of the potential threat, my crew were very much aware and the more time spent waiting, the more time they spent weighing the consequences, and fretting and worrying. I was fretting only because I had committed myself to act when the tuna seiner made the move and I was reluctant to go into action without film backup.

Finally, at 2300 hours, Rod returned. He had at last reached Ben.

"He's pissed," he reported.

"Drunk?" I asked.

"No, he's mad. He was calling you a lunatic and told me to tell you to do nothing until he gets here. He should be here in two hours. I told him that we would ram that bastard if he moves and we would not wait for him. He said I was as crazy as you, for which I thanked him for the compliment."

I shook my head. "Why is it that these guys are going wimp on me? This is what we do. What's the surprise?"

Two hours later, Rod reported that Ben and Peter were on the beach. He and I took the inflatable to greet them. It looked as if the *Pan Pacific* wasn't going anywhere, at least until morning.

I beached the boat in the slight surf and Rod and I walked up the beach to the sidewalk where Ben was waiting with Peter. It was a calculated move on his part. He could have met us on the shore but he wanted us to come to him.

As we approached, I could see a deep frown and a look of scolding disapproval. He spoke first. "Are we having fun yet, boys? Getting our rocks off, are we?"

"What the hell are you talking about, Ben?" I answered. "You directed us here. You reported to Walt to tell us that a dolphin killer was here in the harbour. You were not here to meet us when we arrived and now you want me to let the bastard just sail away. What did you think I would do — take pictures?"

"I've been meeting with Costa Rican officials and talking to them about banning tuna seiners in their waters. This effort will be in vain if you do something stupid like ram or sink a ship in Costa Rican waters. Don't you ever think about consequences?"

"Yes, I do, Ben. When did we ever start to meet with politicians or bureaucrats? Who authorized that? We are shock troops, Ben, not negotiators. We act; others talk. As a matter of fact, I have thought long and hard about the consequences and here is what the result will be. Step one: we ram and disable that ship. Step two: we force the crew to abandon. Step three: we ram her until she sinks. Step four: we head out to sea. We can prevent boarding by the Costa Rican Coast Guard. If they board anyway, then the consequence of arrest is acceptable. Because the objective is to blow this issue sky high in the media, to bring awareness to people around the world that these bastards are killing hundreds of thousands of dolphins each year. People will support us when they understand what we are fighting for. Unfortunately, the only thing that will focus media attention on the plight of the dolphins is drama. Our footage of dolphin slaughter on the deck of a U.S. tuna boat was ignored. They media will not ignore this and our footage of dolphin atrocities will be guaranteed the coverage it deserves."

Ben ignored me. "You have 20 crew whose lives you're playing with. You are screwing up my negotiations and I think it's all because you're upset that Joanna left you. You're letting your emotions control your actions. Because you're feeling suicidal over some love affair, you're willing to take innocent people with you. I've spoken with Joanna and with Walt and they concur with my assessment."

"Screw them," I shouted. Then, more calmly, I said, "Ben, Joanna left because she disagreed with ramming the ship. Every other crew member is free to leave also. Walt left. I'm not forcing anybody to do anything they don't wish to do. This is what we do. We ram ships. We sink ships. I'm being consistent with the policy and practice of this organization, and I founded Sea Shepherd for the express purpose of enforcement, not protest."

"So, throw that founder crap into my face," Ben retaliated. "Well, buddy, this organization is more than you and what you want."

"Perhaps," I said, "it's now about you and what you want."

Ben ignored me again, "Scott Trimingham and I both agree, and Peter Wallerstein will back us up, which means that we have the majority on the board of directors. We will denounce you publicly and we will remove you from the organization if you ram this ship."

"It's my ship, Ben. I own her and I'm the master."

"But you don't own Sea Shepherd," he retorted.

I was shattered; the possibility of having all of my work, the years of effort and sacrifice, taken away from me was sobering.

I turned quietly to Peter Brown, "Where do you stand?"

He smiled. "With you, of course. I was just concerned that you would do something without me around to shoot it."

Ben interrupted, "It's still three against two. You lose. Unless of course you look on the board of directors as a charade."

Resigned, I said to Ben, "You told me the tuna seiner was here. We're here now. Perhaps you can suggest a course of action."

He smiled. "I will in the morning, after I've met with the crew to hear what ideas they have."

Ben then booked into a hotel, leaving Peter, Rod and me on the beach.

I shook my head. "A meeting with the crew. That'll be fun — 20 people, 20 ideas, 20 strategies. We'll be here for days and the tuna boat will be long gone."

Rod agreed. "You can't run a ship on consensus."

Peter added, "I say we go out and ram her anyway, but after the sun rises so I can film it properly."

Feeling betrayed by Scott, Ben and Peter Wallerstein, I was in no mood to discuss it any further.

The next morning, Ben met with the crew and convinced most of them that we shouldn't be too aggressive. He painted a bleak picture of life in a Costa Rican prison, and pointed out that he was making progress with his talks in San José with the politicians.

Peter, Rod, Sue and I had breakfast at a beach café while Ben talked with the crew for more than two hours. We saw him leave the ship and approach the shore in the inflatable. He walked up the beach and approached us at the table and took a seat.

"Good morning." He smiled. "Rod, I don't think it was fair for you and Sue not to attend the crew meeting."

Sue answered, "The Sea Shepherd II does not have crew meetings."

"Well, it does now," Ben said with a wide smile. "This Society is going to be run democratically from now on."

I said nothing.

Ben turned to me. "The crew," he said, "have agreed with me that we should not damage the tuna ship. We've come up with the idea of handcuffing some of our crew to the anchor chain of the *Pan Pacific* to prevent them from leaving. This will focus media attention on the issue and it will send a message to the dolphin killers."

"Ben," I protested, "that's a goddamn Greenpeace tactic."

"I disagree. The key to success is we will use only female crew members. This will work against the macho mentality of Latin men."

We returned to the ship where Ben organized his crew of women. They motored over to the seiner and shackled themselves to the anchor chain. I pulled up our anchor and made ready to move, if needed.

They did anger the crew. One fisherman tossed a seal bomb close to the inflatable with the four women in it. Another threatened to drop a large iron bar on them. In response, I started the ship's engines and circled the tuna boat menacingly close.

The stand-off lasted most of the day. The Costa Rican Coast Guard came by, observed the protest for a few moments and left. Finally, in the early evening, Captain José Gavancho called me and asked what we wanted.

I told him that we would let him go if he allowed us to come on board to investigate the log books and if he would give us the working co-ordinates of the Venezuelan fleet. He agreed. I went on board with Ben, and Sue accompanied us as interpreter.

The log clearly showed a kill of 55 dolphins in the last 17 sets and the *Pan Pacific*'s charts gave us the working locations of both the Venezuelan and the Mexican fleets. In return, I thanked the captain and released his ship. An hour later, he was heading to sea.

The next morning, we were preparing to head to sea again. A few crew decided to leave. Walt Simpson came back to rejoin as radio operator, which seemed very suspicious. Joanna returned home to Seattle.

Ben took me aside on the beach and said that the crew demanded that I discharge Sue and Rod.

"What for?" I asked.

"They think, and I agree," said Ben, "that they influenced you to ram that ship and they are worried that they might talk you into further acts of violence."

"I'm sorry, Ben, if you believe that. I have not been influenced by anyone to ram a ship. I have been threatened by you and Scott into *not* ramming a ship. I will not discharge two of my best crew."

"If you don't," said Ben, "then the majority of the crew will leave here and the *Sea Shepherd II* will be stranded."

"I will not reward loyalty with dismissal. The crew can go screw themselves. I would rather have two real Sea Shepherd crew members than a pack of cowards. Besides, I would be very surprised if David Howitt and Myra Finkelstein would be party to such nonsense."

Sheepishly Ben said, "They were among the few who supported them."

"Well," I countered, "I have all the crew I need. Because in addition, I have Peter Brown, Marc Gaede and a couple more. Tell the others to bugger off, then."

Most of them stayed and we headed out into the Eastern Tropical Pacific to search for tuna seiners. To my relief, Ben decided against sailing with us and returned to San José to resume his pretense of being a diplomat.

Six days later, we located two Mexican tuna boats. We chased the first, the *Gloria H*, for seven hours and disrupted her fishing sets. She finally outran us and we lost her.

The next day we intercepted the *Norman Ivan* and I took a close run at her, passing at full speed within a couple of feet of her stern.

During this run, Walt Simpson came onto the bridge. "What the hell are you doing?"

"It's a tuna boat, Walt."

With a shocked look on his face, Walt said, "She's got the right of way."

"I know she has the right of way. It's a tuna boat. We are trying to intimidate her into leaving the area and we ain't going to do that by being polite."

Walt shook his head, "You're fucking crazy."

He left the wheelhouse in disgust. Marc Gaede said, "I don't trust that guy."

Peter Brown added, "Is that the guy who wants to 'kick ass'?"

"Yep, that's him," I replied.

Despite Ben's warning, I did attempt to ram the *Norman Ivan*. Unfortunately, I was forced to abort the run when the Mexican fishermen working on the ponga boat on the stern refused to move out of the way. The risk of causing an injury automatically negated the ramming.

After two weeks of searching for and chasing tuna boats, we berthed in Los Angeles. One lone figure stood on the pier waiting to take our lines.

"Who's that?" I asked Adrian.

He focused the binoculars. "I don't believe it," he said.

"Who is it?" I asked again.

Adrian looked at me surprised. "It's Dolphin Dave."

As he took our ropes, Dolphin Dave shouted up to me.

"Did you see my brothers and sisters?"

"No, should we have?" I answered.

"It's worse than I thought," he replied. "They've all been killed."

He looked devastated. I called down. "Oh, those brothers and sisters. Yeah, we saw quite a few."

A look of relief came over his face and then disappeared when I yelled down, "Hey, Dave, Catherine's pregnant."

Looking a little white, he said, "You're telling me that I'm going to be a father."

"Yeah," I answered, "just think: a little dolphin, swimming around, quoting the Bible and trying to call home."

Scott Trimingham arrived and was standing on the dock — all smiles.

"I've called a press conference at 11:00," he said.

At 12:00, after not a single journalist appeared, he said, "I can't understand it. I notified them all that you were arriving."

"Scott, let me tell you why they didn't come," I said. "Because we didn't do anything. You and Ben made it impossible for me to make this into an international media hit. So we chained a few women to an anchor line à la Greenpeace; so we pursued a few boats about on the high seas. The fact is that we blew it. We didn't do what we do best — in fact, we didn't do shit."

Scott looked hurt. "I dunno. Mayor Bradley was implicated in some scandal this morning. Maybe that's why they didn't show up. I mean, you did have people chained to a tuna boat. Ben said it was a great protest."

"I don't care what Ben's opinion is," said I. "That happened two weeks ago and it got a little air time in San José. It's old news. We had this problem in our hands and we could have made media hay over it, but I blew it because I listened to you and Ben. No, I was threatened by you and Ben, and I don't intend to have this bullshit happen again. The next campaign will be under my exclusive command or there won't be a campaign at all."

Scott said nothing. I knew, however, that I would have to deal with this power rift that was developing. If not, I would be overthrown by Scott and Ben. They wanted control and it was becoming obvious that they wanted me out of the picture.

15

The Seattle Saboteur

We have met the enemy and they are us

Walt Kelly

In September 1989, I moved the *Sea Shepherd II* to Seattle, Washington, to begin preparations for an expedition to intercept the Japanese North Pacific drift-net fleet. The Society set June 15, 1990, as the departure date for the expedition, which gave us nine months to prepare. The ship was hauled out and her hull cleaned and zinc anoids replaced at the Lake Union Dry Dock. Hobie Stebbins, who everybody called Hobie III to distinguish him from his father and grandfather, had graciously allowed us to berth at his family company dock to complete the work. This gave us a very convenient location in the centre of Seattle and made it easy for us to recruit volunteers.

First mate Cliff Rogers took charge of preparations, which meant organizing dozens of volunteers, most of whom were not very dependable. Volunteers usually come on board eager and willing to do almost anything to save marine wildlife. After a day or two, however, doing anything seemed no longer to include painting cleaning, diesel mechanics, electrical wiring, plumbing, carpentry or driving about scrounging materials and food. One in every hundred or so shore volunteers has what it takes to be a Sea Shepherd crew member. The ones who stick it out, work without complaint and keep a good attitude about them will form the crew of the next expedition. By May 1990, we were beginning to forge the crew we needed to take on the Japanese. The ship was painted a sinister-looking black and the kill flags had been proudly painted on the sides of the bridge. We touched up Berke Breathed's Opus motif and purchased flags representing the nationalities of the crew. We had Canada, the U.S., Great Britain, the Philippines and Peru. On the port and starboard funnel, a volunteer artist had painted the Earth.

I brought in an engineer, Nicandro Bastido from the Philippines, and paid him $1,200 a month to sign on for a year. Myra Finkelstein returned and signed on as an apprentice engineer. I hired a second engineer who, because of libel laws, I'll call G. He had sent me a respectable résumé from England, although he said that he could not afford to volunteer. Being desperate for engineers, I wrote back and agreed to hire him for $1,500 a month. G. flew over and signed on as chief and Nicki from the Philippines became the second engineer.

With the arrival of Jim Heddenshau, a Native Indian, I had an excellent third engineer and volunteer diesel mechanic. A six-foot-four former marine, he was ideal, except for one small detail: he had a tendency to become mean when he drank, which fortunately was not often. On the ship, he did the work of five men, although he intimidated many of the crew with his strength and straightforward attitudes. The day he joined after busing up from Los Angeles, he walked on board and reported directly to me.

"So, what'd ya want me to do? I'm Injin Jim."

I looked him over. Man, he was big.

"What skills do you have?"

"I'm a damn good mechanic, ship-fitter, carpenter, plumber and I'm a crack shot with a rifle, good with a knife and I'll beat the shit out of anybody you want me to."

"Good to know that. I don't think I need any strong-arming at the moment but I can use your more technical skills. I'll put you in the engine room. Report to G."

"Aye, Captain."

He picked up his duffel bag, tossed it on his shoulder and went below.

Lisa Weber collided with Jim as he entered the companionway. Both of them fell on their ass.

Jim was immediately apologetic. "Did I hurt you?"

"No you didn't, ya big ape. Why don't you watch where the hell you're going, eh? Who in hell are you?"

"New member of the crew, in the engine room. Hey, I'm sorry for knocking you down."

"Thank God you're in the engine room."

"Why?"

"Why, because I'm on the deck crew, that's why, and you ain't."

Lisa walked away, leaving Jim staring in admiration after her.

"Now that's a woman."

Lisa Weber was our bosun. A tough, strong, blonde Amazon, she was a former Alaskan fishing woman. Reynal Chaves arrived from Los Angeles to take the position of second officer. Gary Neilsen was appointed third officer.

By June 10, the ship and crew were ready for departure. I contacted the media people who wished to join us and told them to arrive before the fifteenth. Good old Bob Hunter arrived with Jamie Tumelty, his cameraman from City TV in Toronto. I put them in the pit to share a cabin with Chuck Bowden, a friend of the late Edward Abbey, who had joined us as a freelance writer. Chuck was a desert rat from Arizona. I was curious to see how he would take to the water. He had never been to sea before.

An arrogant, loudmouth dude sporting a *Rolling Stone* magazine T-shirt and black leather pants arrived at dockside and yelled up to where I was standing on the deck.

"Hey, is this rusty tub the *Sea Shepherd*?"

"It is," said I. "Can I help you?"

"Yeah. The name's Trip Gabriel. I'm the reporter from *Rolling Stone.*"

I looked him over, thinking to myself that this guy reeked of trouble. "Welcome aboard."

He walked up the gangplank and I met him at the rail. He looked at me scornfully and said, "You don't really expect me to sail on this piece of shit, do you?"

"I don't expect you to do anything you don't want. If you don't feel safe on this ship, then I don't expect you to make the trip."

"Where's my cabin?"

I motioned to Myra to come over.

"Myra, this is Trip Gabriel, heap big-shit reporter from *Rolling Stone.* Would you show him to his cabin in the pit."

Hunter walked over and joined me at the rail. "Bad news, Paul. You've got yourself a troublemaker with that one."

"It appears so," I answered. "Let's do lunch."

Bob and I were sitting in the mess room a few minutes later when Gabriel stormed in. "You don't really expect me to sleep in that dungeon down there, do you?"

I smiled. "Trip, this is Bob from City TV in Toronto. He's in the pit also, which, by the way, is the driest, warmest place on the boat."

Bob laughed. "It works for me."

Trip ignored Bob. "I'm afraid it's not suitable."

"Sorry, Trip, it's the best we got. If you don't like it, then you can leave."

"You don't seem to understand, asshole. I'm with *Rolling Stone*. What I write can make or break you. If you treat me like a common deck hand, then I'll deal with you accordingly in print. Do you understand that?"

Bob looked at me knowingly. "I told you so."

I stood up slowly and looked hard at Gabriel.

"Get the hell off my ship, you prissy little prick. Nobody calls me an asshole on this ship. I'm the captain, you son of bitch, and you're nothing but a goddamn literary mercenary. Get your bags and piss off. I couldn't give a sweet goddamn what bloody *Rolling Stone* magazine writes about me. I'm not selling any records. If you want to take a cruise, then bus up to Vancouver and hop on board the *Pacific Princess*. I'm not your whore."

Gabriel stammered, "I'll crucify you, you bastard."

"Like I care. Myra, escort this fancy pants down the gangplank and tell him to hustle his ass back to New York."

"Smart move, Paul," said Bob, "Remember the first rule of eco-activism and the media: control your propaganda. Never let the enemy's media on board."

"I thought *Rolling Stone* was on our side," I responded naïvely.

"Rule number two," said Bob, "once a media outlet has become mainstream, it ain't on our side any longer. *Rolling Stone* sells music and entertainment and advertising. It's status quo. Hell, to be radical is status quo now. The mothers have co-opted radicalism, for Christ sakes. They sell it for circulation."

"If that's so, Bob, then why should I trust City TV and you?"

"Rule number three, Paul: sometimes the mainstream is controlled by us. It's a complicated situation, which boils down to knowing who your friends are and what side you're on."

"What about Bowden?"

Bob chuckled, "Passes with honours. The man is a freelancer, a friend of our dear departed Edward Abbey and, most important, he drinks like a fish. Rule number four: you can always trust a reporter who drinks — like me, like Chuck."

Thus we had three "objective" reporters along with Marc Gaede, our crew photographer, and Peter Brown, the crew cameraman. Everything was ready for departure the next day.

I was standing on the deck talking with Cliff Rogers early the next morning when I heard G. preparing to fire up the engines. The crew were all on board. Finally, after months of work, the ship was ready to go. A loud thump and a blast of white smoke indicated that the main engine had started. I could hear the growing rhythm of the pistons when suddenly, a loud whine could be heard from the engine room, a whine that grew in intensity and that I immediately identified as the tearing and ripping of metal.

Cliff and I raced for the engine room. Big Jim had pushed G. up against the bulkhead and was screaming wildly at Nicki. The Filipino hesitated, looked at G. and then back at Jim, unsure of what to do. I ran down and screamed in Nicki's ear, "Shut it down!"

He pulled back the throttle and stopped the engine. What sounded like tinkling glass followed the eerie quiet and then it to stopped.

"What in hell is going on?"

G. yelled, "This bastard attacked me."

Jim tightened his grip on G.'s shirt. Through clenched teeth he hissed, "Tell him what you've done!"

"I haven't done anything, just warming up the engine," G. responded meekly.

"Bullshit, you just destroyed the turbo-charger."

G. turned pale. "That's ridiculous. Let me go."

"Let him go," I said. "G., was that the turbo-charger?"

"Yes, I'm afraid it was. An unfortunate accident really."

"Bullshit," Jim bellowed.

Ignoring Jim, I asked G. what this meant.

"Well, it looks like we're not going anywhere for a while."

I questioned each crew member in the engine room and had the damage investigated. From the various engine-room crew, the story emerged.

When the big eight-cylinder Mirlees diesel was started up, Jim had heard a small noise in the turbo-charger. He brought it to the attention of G. the chief. G. ignored the warning and instead increased the revs on the engine. At this point, Jim recognized the unmistakable sound of an object impacting on the internal blades of the turbo-charger. He ran to the control panel and began to shut down the engine. The chief intervened and ordered Heddenshau out of the engine room.

Jim was about to leave to notify me when he heard G. increase the power. The turbo-charger screamed louder. Jim turned and physically lifted G. off the deck and away from the controls.

Nicki told me that he had seen G. opening up the inspection plates on the exhaust manifolds the day before. He said that this was the only way a foreign object could have reached the turbo-charger.

Meanwhile, Jim had organized a crew to dismantle the turbo-charger. G. refused to help with the excuse that he could not work with Jim because he feared for his life. Without rest, the crew laboured for 20 hours to remove the 660-pound (300-kg) piece and wrestle it up three decks to the dock. Peter Brown and I then drove it north to Vancouver to a shop that specialized in turbo-chargers.

Two days later, we got an answer. The turbo-charger was totally destroyed. Every single internal blade had been smashed. The inside was coated with a fine coating of powered glass. We had been sabotaged. Marbles had been placed, with difficulty, into the manifold intake. Revolving at 16,000 rpm, the 74 precision blades had been mangled beyond any possibility of repair.

I called Jim to my cabin and requested him to inspect the engine room for other possible damage. He and the crew found a nut strategically placed so as to shatter the camshaft. They found wires reversed on some of the electric motors and ground glass in the engine lube oil lines. Oil filters had been removed.

Peter Brown and I were standing on the main deck discussing the problems when G. approached us. He was smiling as he calmly asked, "I hear rumours going around that you suspect somebody sabotaged the engine."

Peter answered, "It was sabotaged."

G. hesitated, then asked, "Any suspects?"

I looked G. in the eye, "We have one suspect — you."

He looked back at me without emotion. "All you can prove is incompetence, and that isn't a crime."

He was right. What could I prove? I called the police and laid a complaint. G. caught a flight to England. I called a friend with the Port Police in London and was referred to an inspector at Scotland Yard. They said they would investigate my complaint and called the Seattle police for details. Months later, I was informed by Scotland Yard that they could do very little because the crime was committed in the United States, despite the fact that it was a British-registered ship. As consolation, they did tell me that G.m worked with Greenpeace in the U.K. and they could find no connection to the Japanese or the Icelanders. G. had said nothing about being connected with Greenpeace. He had even represented that he disapproved of Greenpeace. I made a note in the log that the Sea Shepherd Conservation Society would no longer allow former Greenpeace directors or any person known to have worked for Greenpeace to come on board any of our ships or to join our crew.

Meanwhile, we had a major problem: we could go nowhere without a turbocharger. Some of the crew were becoming angry that the voyage was delayed. The media guys had to leave. The campaign was falling apart.

I promoted Nicki to chief, and Jim to second engineer. Cliff Rogers and Gary Neilsen did not like Indian Jim and told me that I had to fire him or they would leave. They had been on real friendly terms with G. and insisted that he did nothing to the engine. I suspected that Jim intimidated them with his size and brashness. I told them that after what Jim had done, I could not and would not fire him. As a result, my first and third mates left. I promoted Reynal to first and made deck hand Nigel Crane second. Nigel, another Brit, had sailing experience and could navigate.

We put out an all-points computer bulletin to every ship salvager in the world to locate a replacement turbo-charger. To have one built would take two months and cost $75,000. Luck was with us. We located a junked turbo-charger in Scotland that needed only a few modifications. I borrowed $15,000 to purchase it and another $2,000 to have it flown to Seattle. Once again, Jim came through for us and manhandled the half-ton piece down to the bottom deck and had it installed. A month later, we were finally ready to go again.

And then, after all the frustration, sweat, blood and stress, we lost big Indian Jim. He had disobeyed my orders about becoming drunk on board and had threatened some of the crew. Sam the cook had called the Seattle police. They came on board to remove him. The first cop entered the galley and found Jim sitting at the table drinking with Lisa, with whom he had developed a romantic relationship.

"C'mon big guy, let's go."

"Who's going to make me?"

The cop swung his baton and slammed Jim across the chest.

Unfazed, Jim began to rise, "Was that supposed to hurt?"

It took six officers to subdue and arrest him. They hauled Lisa away also for trying to protect him. She had jumped one of the officers, who promptly backhanded her. They let her go when they reached the jail.

I saw Jim in court the next day, testified on his behalf and told the judge that I did not have a complaint. After he was released, I reluctantly told him he would have to leave. He had broken a direct primary order by drinking and acting aggressively against the crew. He had pushed Nicki down and threatened to hit Sam the cook with an iron bar. My policy was never to give a second chance on a primary order. He didn't argue, just shook my hand and quietly left.

Bob, James and Chuck returned. The crew that had become disheartened and left were replaced by new volunteers. In addition three of my nephews arrived from Ontario to join the crew. Fifteen-year-old Trevor was returning as a veteran along with 14-year-old Sean and 16-year-old Ronnie.

We had a small send-off party on board the ship on July the fourth. A holy man from the Beaver tribe came down to bless the ship. With him came a Tibetan Buddhist monk. He gave me a small statue of a horse-headed demon he called Hayagriva.

"I've been instructed to give this to you. It is symbolic of what you do."
"What is it?" said I.
"The symbol of the compassion of Buddhist wrath."

A year later, on an occasion when I was invited to attend a luncheon in Washington, D.C., with the Dalai Lama, I had the opportunity to ask His Holiness to explain why Hayagriva was symbolic of our actions.

The Dalai Lama shook my hand and said, "Hayagriva is the compassionate aspect of Buddhist wrath. In other words, you do not wish to cause injury but sometimes when people refuse to become enlightened, you must frighten them into seeing the light. Intimidation without hurting. It is sometimes the only way."

I was very honoured. His Holiness had understood precisely what the strategy of the Sea Shepherd Conservation Society was. It had always been my way not to injure or kill, but aggression was still the only motivating force sometimes. Aggression without violence to sentience.

I was impressed that the Tibetan Buddhist monk in Seattle had understood what we were attempting. Hayagriva was a perfect spiritual embodiment of our strategy. I had the small statue fastened to the top of the foremast, the highest point of our ship.

Reynal had organized a painting party of local artists to decorate our funnel. I told them to display what they thought would be appropriate. They gave me a painted blue, white and green sphere. We made ready to sail under the most important symbol of our planet — a portrait of the Earth herself.

The pilot took the ship to Port Angeles, where we anchored for the night. The next morning, David Howitt came on board to see us off. He was living in Port Angeles with his wife, Linda May. Myra asked David to join the crew and come along. He hesitated for only a moment before sending a message back to his wife that he wouldn't be returning home for dinner and to notify his boss that he was quitting his job. Without a toothbrush, a passport, a change of clothing or a sleeping bag, he was all smiles as he descended into the depths of his beloved engine room, where he took over as second engineer.

With David on board, I gave the order to weigh anchor and we headed out the doorway of the Strait of Juan de Fuca and west southwest towards the open Pacific Ocean.

Some two thousand miles (3,200 km) ahead, the Japanese were setting their curtains of death. We intended to invoke the spirit of Hayagriva with a high-seas attack on a Japanese drift-net fleet.

16
Tora! Tora! Tora!

I am overcome by an immense feeling of relief whenever the bow of my ship points seaward. The beginning of an expedition is a welcome rest from the labours of preparing for the voyage. But most satisfying of all is the joy and the freedom — free of the trivialities of the land, joy for the anticipation of the adventure. The ship comes alive as she eagerly lowers her head into the oncoming swells. She heaves, bucks, plunges, rolls and shakes briny wisps of intoxicating spray about her. Excitement ripples along the deck plates and reverberates along the rails as a prevailing sense of aliveness, of belonging, infects the entire crew, or at least those who are not falling victim to sea-sickness.

The vast horizon, the miles and miles of azure blue water and pale blue skies interwoven with the satins of clouds that change to fiery reds at sunset and tangerine orange and tobacco yellow at sunrise — together they form a tapestry of time and distance, depth and vastness, never experienced on land. The sea surpasses the shore in enchanting the senses, provoking the imagination and resting the soul. The ship becomes a cradle gently massaging rainbows and symphonies into vibrant, vivid dreamscapes. By contrast, sleeping on *terra firma* is dull and uneventful.

No words can describe the personal liberation that heading seaward bestows upon me. In this aquatic realm no man or woman is subject to the petty decrees of social bureaucracy. No traffic cops lie in wait. Neither television nor newspapers distract you from the joy of living. There are no appointments to keep, schedules to meet or egos to stroke — just the peace, serenity and beauty of mother ocean. This joy, this personal freedom, is something I have never tired of. In fact, the more time at sea I have put in, the greater the intensity of the rapture. A love of the sea is my link to my own past, the bond of memory and emotion that enables me to remember where I have been, to realize where I am and to know where I am bound.

As the *Sea Shepherd II* headed westward under the stars into the gentle undulating swells, I realized again what satisfaction the ocean has given me. As I often do, I climbed the foremast and straddled the cross tree. I thought to myself just how wonderful my life has been. Amid and despite the cruelties of humanity, I was finding peace, peace with myself. I was growing more and more each day in my realization of who I was and what I could do. I let my thoughts sway with the roll of the mast.

My thoughts drifted back two decades to when I lay on my back on the dark green steel deck hatches of the *Bris*, the Norwegian freighter on which I served on as a deckboy in 1968. Cruising through the Sulu Sea on a balmy night, the fragrance of the nearby Philippines wafting over me, sky clear and blazing with the pinpoints of infinity. It was like yesterday, that memory, fresh and alive.

My recollections flashed forward a few months from the Sulu Sea to the South China Sea. I was on the deck of the *Bris* in a November typhoon. I saw the onrushing wall of water surge over me as I struggled to secure a turn-buckle brace on some deck cargo of lumber. Diving between the hatches, a wave swept pass me and plucked away the tons of dressed timber like matchsticks. I had not been frightened; I felt blessed and overjoyed to be alive.

In truth, I loved both the serenity and the violence of the ocean, the still nights and the raging storms, the bitter cold winds and the warming breezes. As deckboy, jungman, ordinary seaman, fireman, able seaman and mate, I had enjoyed it all. But to be captain was the essence of freedom and fulfillment. For more than a decade I had been master of my own course, free to decide where to go and what to do, how to do it and when.

It was my decision that had launched this voyage. It was my course that this ship and her 25 crew were following. The choice of targets was mine; the tactics, the strategies, the decisions and the responsibility were mine. There can be no position more fulfilling than this — to be a captain of your own ship, to chart your own course and to decide your own destiny.

At the same time, I took my responsibilities very seriously. I had a crew to protect, including three young nephews. I also had the responsibility to confront the drift-netters, expose and dramatize their activities and to do so without hurting or, worse, killing anybody.

The drift-net fleets were out there, setting their monstrous nets and cutting a path of death across the North Pacific. Out of sight and out of mind, they were secure in their belief that they could take what they might without interference. After all, who was there to oppose them in international waters?

Just us.

But this night, our first night out from shore, with the outline of the Olympic range fading to our stern, this was the time during each campaign that I relished the most — returning to the realm that I love so much and escaping the "civilized" social tyranny of the land that I so violently detest.

Bob Hunter joined me on the foremast.

"It's great to be back at sea again, eh, Paul."

"That it is, Bob, that it is."

We said nothing else, content to sit between the deck and the stars, in the centre of the sacred circle between the sea and the heavens.

The next morning, as the sun rose to our stern, Nigel asked me when and where we intended to find the drift-netters.

"We will find them when and where we find them. They are ahead of us, straight ahead of us — a week, possibly two weeks ahead."

"It's a big ocean, Paul," replied Nigel. "We can't be sure we will find them. I figure the chances of finding these vessels in an area this large are very remote."

"That it is. It's a big ocean. But it's becoming smaller. As they suck the life out of her, she becomes smaller. We will find them because it is necessary that we find them."

"Isn't that putting too much faith in spirituality?" he asked. "It sounds a little New Agey to me."

I looked at him, "I don't believe in putting faith in spirituality. That's just a crutch for those who don't belong. I can assure you, I'm no advocate of New Age philosophies."

"Belong where?"

"On this Earth, in these waters. If you have to ask why and if you need to demand answers to impossible questions, well then you don't belong. That's what it's all about — belonging, being a part of something unfathomable and letting that which you seek come to you."

Days drifted by as we sighted neither ship nor whale, nor seal, and only a few solitary birds charting their lonely way over this forsaken realm. It was only a few years ago that there were many more birds out here. They were disappearing, of this I was certain, but to convey this dire message to a world of uncaring hominid souls was a burden fit for Hercules. How do you educate a world that hears but does not listen, that observes but does not see?

Six days later, at dawn, my watch saw a great plume of thick black smoke on the horizon and we altered course a few points to the southwest to investigate. We were now about twelve hundred miles (1,920 km) west of the northern coast of Oregon. We had two targets on our radar at 16 miles (26 km). As we approached to six miles (10 km), it appeared that one of the ships was burning. The other vessel had changed course and was rapidly approaching us. It quickly became evident that the ship was military. I radioed her but there was no answer. The other ship continued to belch smoke. Apparently they were conducting some sort of naval exercise.

Minutes later, a trim frigate with extraordinarily beautiful lines passed and circled us. It was a Soviet frigate, displaying a large *770* on her dagger-sharp bow. There were numerous uniformed military personnel on her decks.

Marc Gaede rushed into the wheelhouse with his cameras. "It's a goddamn Russkie! Man, what a beautiful ship," he said as he expertly changed to a telephoto lens. "What do you think's going on?"

"Just exercises would be my guess," answered Hunter.

The VHF crackled. "*Sea Shepherd, Sea Shepherd*, this is the Soviet warship *770*. Do you copy?"

I responded immediately, "Soviet warship *770*, this is the *Sea Shepherd*."

"Good morning. Excuse us, but could you tell us please what the symbol on your smokestack means?" The Russian officer's English was very good.

I answered slowly, "Good morning. Thank you. The symbol is the Earth. We have the planet painted on our stack."

"That is what we thought. It looks like that, but why do you have this?"

"We are an ecology ship, a conservation ship. This is the *Sea Shepherd II*, a vessel operated by the Sea Shepherd Conservation Society. We are out here looking for illegal drift-net activities."

There was a brief silence.

Marc spoke, "Maybe they remember Siberia?"

"Let's hope not," I answered.

The Russian voice returned. "We think that this is admirable. You have a good cause, a noble cause, and we wish you all the luck in the world in your . . . your . . . your voyage. We are with you in spirit."

"Thank you." I answered. "Perhaps you can help us. Have you seen any drift-net ships to the west?"

"We believe that you may find some of these boats, possibly four days to the west. Good luck."

Incredible! Eco-glasnost! It had been nine years since we belled the Russian cat off Siberia to bring attention to their illegal whaling activities. Before that, in 1975, Bob Hunter and I had survived a near-miss from a Soviet harpoon fired over our heads by an angry Russian harpooner when we had attempted to block his shot with our bodies. Now, we were being hailed by the Soviet Navy with a statement of support. It was evident that we were making some progress.

In fact, the Soviets were allies in more than just words. On May 19, 1990, a couple of months before, the Russians had seized a fleet of North Korean fishing boats that were caught red-handed with drift nets set in Soviet territorial waters. Japan was diplomatically embarrassed when it was discovered that the 140 supposedly North Korean fishermen in custody were, in fact, Japanese.

We left our newfound allies and continued westward. On the eighth day out from Seattle, I continued on a westward course but decided not to correct for drift. I would allow the natural drift in our course, with the hope that it would lead us to the drift-netters. Bob thought this was reminiscent of our old Greenpeace days when we sometimes steered by rainbows and full moons.

"I thought you didn't approve of those ways of navigating," he said.

"Usually I don't. However, in situations such as this, when you're looking for the classic needle in the haystack, it's as good a method as any. Besides, I concede that the moonbeams found the Russians for us in '75 and the turtles definitely led us to the *Sierra* in '79."

Bob smiled. "So you concede some credit to woo-woo faith."

I laughed. "Nothing that I would admit."

"But," said Bob, "you are putting faith in your intuition about the drift taking us to the drift-netters."

"No, Bob, there's nothing spiritual about my intuition, which has never failed me yet, and besides, I look on intuition as a normal biological function. The secret is to not complicate your mind with trivialities."

Slowly, we began to drift north of the original course line. Forty-eight hours later and 38 miles (63 km) north of the aforementioned line, my intuition came through for us again. The sea herself had taken us on the right path. Six blips on the radar, and in this remote section of the North Pacific, considering that the water temperature was ideal for squid, chances were better than 95 per cent that the blips were drift-netters.

At 2030 hours, on the evening of Sunday, August 12, we barged into the midst of a fleet of six Japanese-registered drift-net ships. They were just completing the laying of their nets for the evening. Between them, there was nearly 200 miles (320 km) of monofilament drift net in the ocean.

The Japanese ships were each about 200 feet (60 m) in length, equal in size to the *Sea Shepherd II*. The hulls were dirty white, encrusted with scaly rust. Behind each ship shot streams of brine to allow the continuous net to be laid with greater ease. They looked eerie, almost surreal in the darkening dusk. The one we were following, the *Shunyo Maru #8*, resembled a large aquatic spider, spreading her deadly webbing from her anus. Indeed, her treacherous webs were already set, her victims struggling hopelessly beneath the waves. More victims were being ensnared as we watched. The Japanese spider would let them thrash and tear their flesh, from squid to birds, to turtles to sharks, to dolphins and perhaps a whale — all of them at the mercy of these invisible curtains of death.

Having set the remainder of her net, the drift-netter began to return to where she had first laid the net earlier, some 40 miles (64 km) off. She set off eagerly, in anticipation of the dawn when she would begin to haul in her prey. As we approached the *Shunyo Maru #8*, the Japanese skipper came on the radio to warn us off, angrily telling us to avoid their nets.

I brought the *Sea Shepherd II* close alongside, our cameras rolling as we filmed the crew and their ship.

The skipper could speak little English. Nigel handled the radio.

"*Shunyo Maru #8*, this is the *Sea Shepherd II*. We don't understand you. We're just passing by to take some pictures."

The radio sputtered. "What you want? What you want?" His voice sounded frantic, and it was not surprising. I was aiming my bow straight at his ship, coming on at full speed.

At the last possible moment, I swung the wheel to starboard and passed close behind his stern, so close that the stream of brine squirting out from the anus-like net dispenser sprayed across our decks.

I picked up the transmitter. "I want you to stop drift-net fishing."

Not understanding me, the skipper returned, "Why you cross my ship."

"Because," I said, "you're killing too many dolphins, whales, birds and turtles, and you're taking too many fish."

This was followed by an outburst of angry and shrill Japanese.

"What the hell is he saying?"

Reynal offered, "I don't think he likes you."

Marc rushed in to the wheelhouse. "Well, are we going to ram them?"

"We sure as hell will, Marc. However, I won't do it until we have enough light for the cameras. We'll wait for the dawn."

With darkness fallen over the ocean, we found ourselves waiting in the middle of the fleet. Their lights were all around us. They had no idea of who we were or what we wanted. Most likely they thought we were a Greenpeace ship, and if so, they would be thinking they would only be inconvenienced by our protests.

Around midnight, the ships began moving off. We stuck with the *Shunyo Maru #8*. An hour later, she hooked her net and began to haul it in. I was surprised at how fast she moved as she retrieved it, close to eight knots. The net was illuminated by the deck lights on the drift-netter as we followed alongside, our cameras rolling.

For three hours, we moved with them as they hauled in that massive net. The nets were ghostly in appearance and more deadly than ghosts in action. The power blocks pulled the nets in at a rapid pace, the bodies of squid, fish and birds catapulted from the nets to the deck, many bodies falling out before being boarded, tumbling back dead and wasted to the sea. The catch of average two-foot (60-cm) squids was not great. There appeared to be a squid every 100 yards (100 m) or so. As each squid was landed, the fishermen gave the net a flick and whipped the animal onto the deck. Occasionally a bird would be hauled in, whipped to the deck and tossed back into the sea. We saw a few sharks, two Dall's porpoise and an unidentified dolphin brought on board and kept.

I had previously given an order to Reynal to log the incidental kills observed. Turning to him I said, "Reynal, make a notation: the hauling in of the sea birds observed is a blatant violation of the Convention for the Protection of Migratory Birds, a treaty signed between the United States and Japan on March 4, 1972. The nets impact on 22 species of birds, 13 of which are protected by treaty. I believe that one of those birds landed is a pink-footed shearwater and I identified another as a black-footed albatross. Both are on the list. I think we've found our violation and our justification."

We had the evidence we needed. We had seen the bodies of protected species in the net. However, before I could ram, I needed more light. It was painful to continue watching, but it was imperative that we wait for the dawn and the arrival of the morning light, which we needed to film events.

Finally, at 0540 hours, there was enough light for us to make our move. We had the deck and the engine room cleared and prepared for confrontation. We positioned our cameras and photographers. Jamie Tulmety of Toronto's City TV covered from the starboard monkey deck above the wheelhouse. His expensive Betacam was ready. The central position on the monkey deck was taken by Peter Brown and his 16-millimetre film camera. He was ready. Marc Gaede had his still cameras on the port side of the monkey deck. He signalled that he was ready. On the main deck, David Howitt signalled that he was ready with his still camera. And finally, on the starboard bridge wing, Bob Hunter had his handycam. Documentation stations were all go.

I took the wheel. Reynal manned the radio and Nigel took lookout with the binoculars. The signal came up from the engine room that Nicki, Myra and Trevor were prepared. I telegraphed down to them that I wanted full power and our 700-ton ship charged like an avenger across the swells towards the *Shunyo Maru #8*. I was approaching from behind at a close angle to their port side. Our objective was to destroy the power block, the net retrieval gear. To do so properly, I had to take a steady aim on an angle to crush the targeted equipment without risking sinking of the ship.

The distance was closing, Nigel sounded three loud blasts on the air horn to warn the fishermen that we were coming in. At the same time, he radioed the ship and said, "*Shunyo Maru, Shunyo Maru #8*, we are going to ram you. Repeat, we are going to ram you."

I couldn't resist the temptation to take the radio and yell, "*Tora! Tora! Tora!*"

"What's that mean?" asked Nigel.

Laughing, I said, "It means 'Attack! Attack! Attack!' It was the battle cry of Yamamoto's bombers as they swooped in for the kill at Pearl Harbor."

Our bow rose on the swells. I could see some of the fishermen looking up, wide-eyed, as they retreated from the port side, abandoning the net. Our bow wave came on before us, colliding with the wake of the drift-netter. A collision of spray erupted between the two ships and like a hammer we struck, the power block exploding in a shower of sparks, the gunnels of the Japanese vessel collapsing as the steel plates buckled and ripped. The ships ground their hulls together amidst a cacophony of tortured steel. The net was severed and the power block crushed.

I was overjoyed. "Boy, we took out that machinery," I yelled to Reynal and Nigel.

Not one person had been knocked down by the impact on either ship. We had pushed the Japanese ship over and her bell rang as she came back on her keel. The blow had slowed us down, and our starboard side scraped along her forward port side as we slid by and in front of her.

One of the fishermen hurled a flensing knife through the air and it passed over Jamie's shoulder. The same fisherman grabbed a second knife as his comrades stood speechless. He threw it directly at the monkey deck. Through his camera lens, Jamie saw and recorded it coming at him. The knife landed at Bob Hunter's feet.

Reaching down, Bob picked up the knife and said, "Hey, they threw this at us. Got a souvenir, ha, ha."

The Japanese captain called immediately. "*Sea Shepherd*, Greenpeace ship?"

Snatching the transmitter from Nigel I answered, "Negative. Not Greenpeace. Sea Shepherd. Repeat, Sea Shepherd."

"Why did you hit my ship?"

"Because you're killing dolphins, birds and fish, and you insulted us by calling us Greenpeace."

I switched the radio to deck intercom.

"Stand by for number two. Stay at your stations."

A quick glance in the radar gave me the position of the next target, the *Ryoun Maru #6*, some two miles (3 km) away.

Setting the course, I turned the wheel over to Reynal and ran down to the main deck and forward to the forepeak to inspect the damage. Jim Knapp was already on site, his welding and cutting gear in hand. A gaping jagged hole about two feet (60 cm) long had been ripped in the hull about three feet (1 m) above the main deck, well above the water.

"Jim, stand off. We have another target coming up. This is minor damage, and we'll have plenty of time to repair it on the way home."

As I returned to the main deck, Bob met me with his camera.

"Paul, have you got time for a brief interview?"

"Sure, Bob, but brief. We have another ramming coming up in a few minutes."

"Got ya," said Bob. "OK, what did we do?"

"We took their power block and retired them from any more fishing. They'll have to return home to Japan for repairs."

"How about damage to our ship?"

"We have a hole in the bow. Looks like a cannon ball ripped through to hull."

"So," said Bob, "we got them, but they got us also."

"Not exactly. Our damage is a simple welding job. We just took out a $20,000 power block. I think we came out on top."

I had to break off the interview to run up to the wheelhouse. We were fast approaching the second Japanese ship and, strangely, she was behaving like nothing had happened to make them alarmed. Surely, the others had radioed ahead about what we had just done to their ship?

As we approached, we could see the fishermen attempting to haul in a huge shark, entangled in the net. Our horn blasted. The fishermen suddenly became aware that we were coming in fast on a certain collision course. They dropped the net and the shark and raced towards the opposite side of the deck.

We struck where intended. Again to the roaring crescendo of ruptured steel, the power block and the gear was crushed and the deck and rails severely buckled and bent. The net was severed.

We broke off immediately and set out for the third ship. By now the other Japanese ships in the area were aware that they were under attack. The first and second ships had been successfully damaged. The third ship was not to be surprised. As we approached, she dropped her net and fled. We pursued, passing over her abandoned net and giving chase. She was too fast for us.

We turned and targeted a fourth ship, She also fled, dropping her net in a panic. We stopped and pulled up alongside the radio beacon marking the abandoned net. We confiscated the beacon. We then grappled the net, secured a ton of scrap metal from our hold to the net and dropped it, sending the deadly net to the bottom, some two miles (3 km) beneath us. It was with great satisfaction that we watched the cork line drop beneath the surface, the floats disappearing in a line radiating out from our ship to the horizon.

Some months before, I had met with one of our members, a theoretical physicist employed by the Jet Propulsion Lab in Pasadena. She had investigated the physics of sinking a drift net for us. I asked her for the best method of destroying a 40-mile (64-km) long net in two miles (3 km) of water. The net panels were 26 feet (8 m) wide with styrofoam floats on the top and lead weights on the bottom. Could it be sunk? I was worried that sinking it would simply anchor two miles of the net to the bottom, leaving 38 miles (60 km) of floating net to terrorize marine life on the surface. She had assured me that the entire net would sink if only one part of it were weighted down. The reason for this was that as the net was pulled down to a depth of 60 fathoms, the styrofoam floats would be crushed by the water pressure, thus increasing the weight on the net more and more with every metre dragged down. This would result in the entire net being taken to the bottom. And as the net descended, it would tangle itself with the weights and non-buoyant floats, resulting in a monofilament, ropelike bundle falling to the ocean floor to be quickly buried in the benthic mud below.

We cleaned up the remaining nets and sank them with weights as well. We estimated that we had probably sunk a million dollars' worth of net that morning. We had also succeeded in chasing the entire fleet of six ships out of the area completely, two of which would be forced to return to Japan for repairs.

Our attack had been effective. Two ships disabled from further fishing, vastly expensive nets destroyed and all six ships prevented from fishing in the area and running scared. Most important, we had delivered a very strong message to the Japanese fishing conglomerates. Our tactics had been both effective and educational. Effective in that we had directly saved marine wildlife by shutting down a fleet, and educational in that we had successfully informed the drift-netters that they no longer had a free hand to rape and pillage the seas.

Our ship sustained only minor damage and there had been no injuries on any of the ships involved, including our own. With great satisfaction, I turned the bow of the *Sea Shepherd II* southward to Honolulu to deliver the documentation to the media. The infamous drift-net fishing fleets and their curtains of death were no longer out of sight and out of mind.

Two days after the confrontation, we were approached by a Japanese government vessel, probably a fishery patrol vessel. They followed us for half a day but did not attempt to contact us. We in turn ignored them.

It was six days southward to Hawaii. We stopped frequently along the way to retrieve ghost nets, remnants of drift net lost by the fleets. In one we found 54 rotting fish. In another, a large dead mahi-mahi, or dolphin fish, and in another a dead albatross. These ghost nets represent an additional deadly plague for sea life. Each day the fleets of Taiwan, Japan and Korea lose an average of six miles (10 km) of net. By 1990, it was estimated by the U.S. Department of National Marine Fisheries that 10,000 miles (67,000 km) of these remnants were drifting in the North Pacific alone. These non-biodegradable nets kill millions of fish and sea-creatures. Decaying fish attract more fish and birds, a vicious cycle of death and destruction and incredible needless waste.

We arrived in Honolulu and berthed at the Aloha Tower dock downtown. Ironically, two fishery patrol vessels, one from Japan and the other from Taiwan, were berthed just ahead of us. The crew of each scowled at us as we passed.

We were prepared for the Japanese to attempt to lay charges against us for our high-seas attack, or failing that, to publicly denounce us. Instead, surprisingly, they refused even to recognize that an incident had taken place. We contacted the Japanese consulate and declared that we had attacked their ships and that we had destroyed and damaged Japanese property. We informed the consulate that we were ready to contest charges, be they in the International Court at The Hague or in Tokyo itself. The consulate told us that he had no idea what we were talking about.

We sent the video footage to Japan, where it aired on Japanese news programs. Still, the official Japanese response was to disclaim all knowledge of the incident. It seemed obvious to me that Japan wanted to keep the controversy of drift-net fishing as quiet as possible. They realized that they would gain nothing by taking us to court and that, in fact, any publicity would only serve to illuminate their questionable activities before the eyes of the public.

I called a press conference on the dock.

One Japanese reporter asked me if I was concerned about Japanese public opinion.

I answered, "I'm not that concerned about Japanese public opinion or American public opinion. I'm only concerned that unless we do something to protect endangered species of marine mammals, sea birds and fish today, then future generations will be robbed of these species. Therefore, it is in the interest of future generations of Japanese, Americans and people all over the world that we act. So no, I am not that concerned about Japanese public opinion."

A Hawaiian reporter asked me how I justified vigilante activities.

"Well, somebody has to do something. Canada and the United States do not seem to have the courage to act as nation-states, so we are acting as citizens. We're here to say that we don't do anything covertly. We're here to answer for our actions, and if Japan wants to take us to court, then we will welcome the courtroom as a forum to present our case for conservation and for a heritage for tomorrow."

A day later, the U.S. Coast Guard raided the ship to look for safety violations. Most of the men complimented us on a job well done and a couple apologized for the harassment and said that it came from "up top."

We had fired our first shots to open the drift-net wars. Our film footage of the ramming made the international news. The confrontation successfully exposed Japanese drift-net fishing and its destruction to the public. We had demonstrated again that confrontation and drama were the keys to attracting media attention.

17

Buccaneers, **P**irates and the **D**efence of **T**reasure **I**sland

There is one God that is Lord over the Earth,
and one Captain that is lord over the *Pequod* — On deck!

Herman Melville (*Moby Dick*)

The *Sea Shepherd II* journeyed to San Diego in preparation for a return voyage to the Caribbean. One of our members, Sid Johnson of the Trinidad and Tobago Game Fishing Association, had sent us documentation of Taiwanese drift-netters using Port of Spain as a base. I felt that a confrontation in the Caribbean would expose drift-net operations in the area.

We left California on February 5, 1991. The first leg of our trip would serve as a patrol for tuna seining activities.

My daughter Lilliolani, who was now ten years old, had taken a month off school to sail with me to Key West. Because of my continuing campaigns, I still didn't have many opportunities to spend time with her. This trip would give her an idea of what I did. I hoped she would understand that my work was important for her future. I wanted her to know that I was not neglecting her. As my link to the future, she was very important to me. Conservation work is really nothing other than being a custodian for future interests. We are sometimes criticized for opposing the will of the majority — those who support development and progress at all cost, or who simply don't care. In reality, I know that we represent the real majority of humanity, because we represent the interests of those countless unborn whose heritage is being ruthlessly exploited by the greedy generations of the twentieth century. If nothing else, the work that we as conservationists do today will be appreciated by our children's children's children. We may be a pain in the ass to the establishment today but we will make great ancestors.

It was a pleasant voyage down the Pacific coast of Mexico. On the evening of February 14, I had just retired to my bunk. It was shortly after midnight when there was a knock on my cabin door and then a voice telling me I should come to the bridge. It was urgent. Throwing on a pair of jeans, I ran up to the bridge.

Raynel Chaves, my first officer, had the watch. "Check this out," he said.

A hundred yards (100 m) off, a tuna seiner drifted motionless, her engines stopped and deck lights ablaze. She had a helicopter and a bank of dolphin-chasing speedboats.

"Raynel," I asked, "what's our position?"

"One hundred and four miles [166 km] west of Guatemala."

"What's her nationality?"

"Don't know."

I turned to him and said, "Wake the crew. Let's circle her. We need an identification."

As the crew prepared for action, I was able to identify the vessel as the *Tungui*. Her home port was Ensenada, Mexico. She had no lawful authority to be fishing inside the 200-mile (320-km) territorial fishing zone of Guatemala.

Reynal spoke Spanish. I handed him the radio transmitter. "Ask them how many dolphins they've killed?"

On the other end, a chuckle, then a voice responded in Spanish.

"What did he say?"

Raynel frowned and said, "He said 'he's killed a thousand this year. So what, and who wants to know?' "

"Identify our ship and tell him we intend to hit him."

The Mexican did not reply. On the deck of the *Tungui*, some crew members were arc-welding. They seemed to be making repairs.

I quickly went below to tell my daughter to stay away from the portholes and not to go on deck. Our thick steel plating would protect her if the Mexican decided to shoot at us. She was not happy with being left out of the excitement. Returning to the bridge, I took the wheel, came round behind the tuna vessel, and set my sights on damaging their aluminum ponga boat, the small craft they use to set the one-mile (1.6-km) long purse seine net. The boat hung off the stern at an angle, the prow jutting towards the stars, the big black pile of nylon bunched up in front of it on the aft deck of the seiner. It was a tricky operation, I had to hit it slowly. Too hard and I could pop it over the net and onto the fishermen. Bearing down on the stern, I used the intercom to advise the crew to take precautions in case the Mexicans fired on us.

A couple of the crew drew my attention to hundreds of dolphins in the water around us. Seeing this made us more determined to chase this bandit out of the area. If not, many of these dolphins could die in the morning, entangled in the purse seine trap.

As we moved forward, we throttled down to half speed, then to slow . . . still too damn fast. I stopped the engine. Our bow was already obscuring our view of their stern from our bridge. We were looming high above them and closing in.

Unfortunately, with the engines stopped, we began to drift slightly to port. We struck the seiner a glancing blow to her stern, missing the ponga boat. We scraped down her port side. The Mexicans stood stunned with mouths agape on her decks as we passed. The ugly shriek of steel scraping on steel was accompanied by the sickly smell of paint burnt by friction. As our bridge passed by their wheelhouse, our monkey deck lined up evenly with their helicopter deck. Three of my crew, with fire hose in hand, opened the nozzle full throttle and blasted the chopper with seawater, guaranteeing a serious and time-consuming overhaul.

As we cleared the seiner's bow, I pulled the wheel hard to starboard and came round for a second run. Slowly we came about and struck them on their starboard side, scraping them again and giving us a second opportunity to douse the helicopter.

Circling a third time, I put our sights on the ponga boat again. This time I decided to take it from the starboard side. Closer . . . closer — we were almost upon them when we saw the water churning to the seiner's stern. The funnel belched thick black smoke. The *Tungui* was running.

The *Sea Shepherd II* pursued.

A crackle of Spanish erupted on the bridge.

"What did he say?"

Raynel laughed. "He said he will deal with us if he sees us in port."

I asked Reynal to relay to him that if he wanted a showdown, the time was now and the place was here. He didn't answer and continued to run. We chased her for three hours before we lost her over the horizon. She was faster than we were.

Satisfied that we had chased the Mexicans from the area, we turned and resumed our course to Panama. We had ruined his day. The damage to the helicopter would seriously ruin his week. What is more important, we had prevented them from setting on the dolphins we had spotted nearby.

"That was fun," I heard my daughter say as she entered the bridge. "Did you see the doggie on the deck? I was worried we would hurt him."

"Lani," I scolded, "I told you to keep out of sight."

"Why?" she retorted. "I thought this voyage was going to be educational. How am I supposed to be educated by not being allowed to see what's going on?"

Heading southward some six hours later, I was notified that a military ship was bearing down on us. She was four miles (6 km) behind us and closing fast. Suspecting that it was a Mexican Navy vessel, I gave instructions for the crew to defend the ship from boarding.

Our position was 140 miles (220 km) off the western coast of El Salvador. The approaching ship was a frigate. I could see the nervous looks on the faces of my crew. The situation was tense. The prospect of fighting the Mexican Navy was a frightening one.

With great relief, we saw that the ship was not Mexican; it was a U.S. Navy vessel.

An American officer radioed us and began to ask questions. I asked them what they were doing. They replied that they were on a routine patrol of the sea-lanes. They were a long way from the United States. They had no business making traffic-cop inquiries of a British ship. I told them so and said that I saw no need to answer their queries. They responded by telling me they would make life difficult for me in Panama if I didn't co-operate.

I picked up the radio, smiled and said, "Hey, are you guys operating out of El Salvador?"

This question was followed by a long pause, then, "Have a good trip to Panama, Captain."

Obviously they were operating from El Salvador, but politically they were not officially there and did not wish to risk any publicity concerning their activities.

So we carried on. We did manage to reach Guatemalan officials by radio. They confirmed our suspicions that the Mexicans were illegally setting on dolphins in Guatemalan waters. They did not have the facilities to patrol their waters adequately. We received a note of support from the Guatemalan government for our efforts in escorting the illegal Mexican fishing boat from their territorial waters. The Mexican government was not so friendly. The incident was reported widely in Mexico and reached the U.S. courtesy of Reuters news agency. The Mexican Navy was given orders to search us out and bring us back for prosecution in Mexico.

However, we reached Panama without seeing a single Mexican Navy vessel. We waited two days for permission to transit to the Atlantic and that gave me the opportunity to show my daughter the aftermath of Operation Just Cause, the so-called U.S. liberation of Panama from Manuel Noriega. The buildings near the Balboa yacht club were riddled with bullet holes. Parts of statues had been shot away and burnt hulks of cars and trucks lay about the streets.

We made the transit and reached Key West without incident. Pridim Singh again provided us with free berthage to allow us to prepare an expedition to investigate drift-net activity in the Caribbean.

From Key West, I flew back to Los Angeles and met with Martin Torres, who represented the Mexican consulate in California. I told him to inform the Mexican government that we would co-operate with any charges they might wish to pursue against us. A few days later, Señor Torres met with me again and said that the Mexican government no longer had a complaint against the Sea Shepherd Conservation Society because it was obvious that the *Tungui* was fishing illegally. He requested that in future we document infractions and report violations of Mexican vessels directly to the Mexican government.

Scott Trimingham was upset by the ramming. I was becoming increasing concerned about Scott's attitude about confrontation. He was administrating the Society for us, collecting the mail, helping to raise funds and issuing press releases. He did not have an appreciation of the task we had to perform in the field. The nature of our game was confrontation.

Now that we were involved with outlaw drift-netters, I was concerned for the safety of my crew. At our spring 1991 board meeting, which took place at Ben's place in Virginia, I had moved that the *Sea Shepherd II* take on two semi-automatic rifles and a shotgun so that we wouldn't be entirely defenceless in the event that we came under attack by firearms. The Taiwanese had already publicly threatened to shoot us.

Both Scott and Ben White were infuriated by this idea. They voted against the motion. Peter Wallerstein was not at the meeting in Virginia, which meant that Peter Brown's vote in favour tied the vote. Peter Brown pointed out that it was interesting that the votes in favour were cast by the two directors who sailed on every voyage. It was easy, he said, for Ben and Scott to be opposed to carrying firearms. They were never in a position to be shot at. Scott insisted that our rules forbade firearms.

I answered him. "Scott, rules can be changed. If our opposition is government, then I agree. These drift-netters are pirates and they carry guns, and if they start shooting at us hundreds of miles out at sea then it won't do us much good to call the police."

Scott argued, "The strength of our group is maintaining the moral high ground. I don't like guns."

"The moral high ground ain't going to do us much good if we're dead," interjected Peter Brown.

Scott held his ground. "If you carry guns, you will use them."

"I don't think so," I answered. "We carried guns unofficially on past campaigns and we never have used them. It's my responsibility to protect my crew and I will not stand by helplessly and watch them massacred."

Scott was shocked. "What do you mean you've carried guns in the past?"

"That's what I said."

Angrily, Scott shouted at me, "Our rules have always stated that our crew do not use firearms."

"Precisely, Scott. We have never used firearms and we have no intention of using firearms. I'm asking for a backup plan for self-defence only."

After the meeting, Peter Brown asked what we were going to do.

"It's a tie vote," I said. "They don't want guns. We do. I suggest we maintain the status quo — and that means we carry guns."

"Scott and Ben won't like that," said Peter.

"Scott and Ben are not going to be shot at," I responded. "Now that we have this tactical disagreement on hold, at least for the moment, we can concentrate on our primary objective for this summer."

Sid Johnson was the man who got the ball rolling. His photos of Taiwanese drift-net vessels refueling in Port of Spain in Trinidad had caught our attention. The pictures, published a year before in the August 14, 1990, issue of the *New York Times*, clearly contradicted the Taiwanese government's insistence that their ships were not operating in the Atlantic or the Caribbean.

Sid was convinced that the drift-netters were to blame for the greatly reduced populations of fish in Caribbean waters. The decline in billfish and other game fish was a fact. The game fishermen's association had made considerable efforts to educate their members to utilize catch-and-release methods and unbarbed hooks. They were becoming increasingly frustrated over the unregulated commercial strip-mining approach of the Taiwanese. And to add insult to injury, the governments of Trinidad and Tobago and other Caribbean nations were courting and subsidizing Taiwanese incursions.

I had contacted Sid Johnson and he eagerly provided information. The Trinidad and Tobago government included a Ministry of Agriculture and Marine Exploitation. This branch of the government owned a company called National Fisheries, which was built with financing from the Taiwanese fishing industry. In return, another government-owned corporation, National Petroleum, was providing millions of dollars in fuel subsidies to Taiwanese fishing vessels. This, of course, was an open invitation for Taiwan to send hundreds of their drift-net vessels to the Caribbean. With the exhaustion of other bodies of water, the fish-rich Caribbean sea was ripe for a rapacious onslaught of the 40-mile- long (64-km) curtains of death.

I asked Sid if he felt there was anything to be gained from provoking a confrontational incident. He said we would be very welcome. He had been in touch with Greenpeace and the Environmental Investigation Agency, both of which had contacted him from London.

"They warned me not to get mixed up with you. They said you were pirates and an embarrassment to the movement. They wanted me to send them film and information but said they could not come to Trinidad themselves. Besides, the only group that has sent me money for phone calls and postage has been yours. As far as I'm concerned, I'll take pirates over rhetoric any day. If you're an embarrassment to the movement, I guess it's because you're *moving* in a movement that doesn't move."

On May 28, 1991, the *Sea Shepherd II* departed from Key West, Florida, for a long-range patrol in search of Taiwanese drift-netters. As my crew of 22 volunteers and I passed Cuba, Haiti and the Virgin Islands, I felt an eerie sensation, like something was out of place. By the time we reached the waters off Barbados, just what felt wrong hit me like a thunderbolt: there were no birds.

Years before when I had passed through these waters, the ocean was alive with feathered friends. I remembered the albatross majestically gliding with the tips of their wings softly fanning, but never quite touching, the ocean surface. Gone also were the boobies, whose habit had been to hitchhike a ride on our mast, waiting for us to scare up breakfast with a fright of flying fish. We had good-humouredly cursed them in years past for fouling our decks with faeces. Now we missed them terribly. The absence of birds was a sure sign that the killing nets were being used in the area.

Reynal entered the bridge as I searched the horizon for a sign of a flying bird. "It's a lonely sea out here, isn't it?" he asked.

"It is," I replied. "They're near. I can almost smell them."

"What do you intend to do when we find them?"

I laughed. "The usual," I said. "We'll ram them and seize the nets."

The next morning, just before dawn, we spotted a white vessel, her deck lights ablaze. She had the lines of a drift-netter with large Chinese characters on her stern and bow — definitely a Taiwanese ship, heading northeastward from Barbados. I changed course to intercept her and came alongside some hundred yards (100 m) off her port side. She was the *Jin Yi Shiang* out of Kaoshiung, Taiwan. I closed to within 50 yards (50 m) to examine and film her fishing gear. As we moved closer, I gave the order to slide out the "can-opener." This was a long steel I-beam girder that had been cut to a sharp, spear-like point. This point extended out nine feet from the side of the ship. Eighteen feet (6 m) of the beam ran inward across our deck, where it was bolted securely to the base of the winch. It was an intimidating sight, all the more so because the tip, painted bright red, stood out vividly against the complete blackness of the *Sea Shepherd II*. If any ship came alongside, this new deterrent device would cause some serious damage to its hull.

On our bow, we raised the Sea Shepherd Jolly Roger, a black flag with a skull above two crossed monkey wrenches with the Sea Shepherd name below.

As the two ships raced alongside each other, the Taiwanese skipper quickly realized that he would not be able to outrun us. Our cameras angered him, for he could plainly see our cameramen focusing on the piles of drift net on his stern. He knew who we were. Our rammings of the two Japanese drift-netters in the Pacific the year before had been a big news story in Taiwan.

The master of the *Jin Yi Shiang* decided to intimidate us. He closed to within six yards (6 m). With the seas rough and choppy, the two large ships bucked and plunged like two race horses, hearts straining to reach the finish line first. Our bow waves crashed together sending showers of swirling spray high into the air.

Suddenly the *Jin Yi Shiang* lurched violently to port. Her bow came crashing down on our mid starboard rail, a blow that crushed and buckled the thick steel plates, bending the thick steel beam supports like cardboard. Both collided with a bang, and a wall of water erupted between the slamming hulls. I saw the Taiwanese bow rise again then plunge down a second time with a shriek of ruptured steel. The entire port side hull of the drift-netter slammed with a bang along our starboard side. The "can-opener" sliced a small jagged tear in the upper hull of the Taiwanese ship and then with a pop, the two-ton beam bent and sheared off its bolts. The two hulls slammed together a third time, with our ship taking most of the beating.

I swung the wheel hard over to port. The *Sea Shepherd II* pulled away slowly, disengaged and fell back. They had drawn first blood. Our investigation of their fishing gear had elicited a violent response. Peter Brown's cameras had documented both their aggression and the damage we had just received. I smiled. We were now in a position to retaliate.

The *Sea Shepherd II* approached again on the starboard side of the *Jin Yi Shiang*. I anticipated that the Taiwanese captain would manoeuvre his ship to intimidate us again. As we closed the gap, I looked across a space of 30 feet (10 m) to see the Taiwanese skipper scowling at me. I gave the order to put the wheel hard to starboard. Within seconds, the Taiwanese ship lurched and pivoted starboard with us. They had hoped to crush our port-side rails. Our timing was perfect. The move to starboard on our part slowed us down. As the Taiwanese moved rapidly towards us, we fell back and he missed our vulnerable port-side midship section. Quickly, I gave the order to bring the ship hard to port.

The Taiwanese were trapped. As they continued to come towards us, our bow connected with their midship section. We rode up on their bow wave and then hammered downward with our flared bow, striking their rails and deck. The deck plates were crushed and buckled and our bow crashed across the deck into the bulwarks of their galley. I saw the cook stick his head out the side deck door and then trip backward, wide-eyed, as our port anchor followed him into the entrance-way. On our upper deck, some of my crew hurled vials of butyric acid onto the drift-netter's deck.

The *Jin Yi Shiang* was sorely damaged and she stank with the rancid-butter stench of our butyric-acid stink bombs. We fell back, watching as they fled. We did not pursue. The smell alone, wafting back off her fleeing stern, dissuaded us from chasing her. Instead, I set course for Trinidad.

The story of our skirmish with the Taiwanese preceded us to Port of Spain. The Taiwanese were furious and were demanding that the Trinidad and Tobago Coast Guard take action against us.

After clearing Customs, we were visited by Commander Iain Cross. Instead of investigating the Taiwanese complaint, he invited us to dock at the Coast Guard facilities and invited me to brief his officers on pelagic drift nets. It was readily apparent that the Coast Guard was one branch of the government that did not feel any affection for the drift-net vessels. Commander Cross told me of the number of ghost nets that had been found, many of them washed onto the beaches full of the rotting corpses of fish and birds. Because he could not publicly condemn the drift nets without political reprisals, he welcomed our taking a stand. I received a great deal of inside information and called a press conference to accuse National Fisheries of corruption, including bribes and kickbacks. I then demanded that if National Petroleum could subsidize the Taiwanese to assault the seas with drift nets, then they should subsidize us for our efforts to rid the seas of the deadly monofilament traps.

To our surprise, National Petroleum responded by agreeing to provide fuel to us for the same price paid by the Taiwanese. A Coast Guard contact said they were doing this to encourage us to leave as soon as possible. In addition, the Coast Guard provided engineers to undertake repairs on our engine. Sid Johnson, who had been our most helpful supporter since our arrival, recruited his brother's engineering firm to overhaul our exhaust cooling system.

While we were actively pursuing our campaign in the Caribbean, we were contacted by Alston Chase, a syndicated newspaper columnist. He had been contacted by Scott Trimingham and told that the *Sea Shepherd II* was now carrying guns. Apparently, Scott had his spies on the crew. At the same time, Scott sent me a wire that he was resigning as president because we had rifles on board, although he intended to continue to serve as our only paid administrator.

I was furious. He had absolutely no right to jeopardize our lives by announcing that we carried weapons. I called him from Trinidad.

"Scott," I asked straight out, "what the hell are you doing telling Alston Chase that we have rifles on board?"

Defensively, he countered, "I do not want to be responsible for anybody getting shot. You know how I feel about guns."

"Look, Scott," I retorted, "because of you shooting off your mouth, we could now get shot. If the drift-netters think we have firearms, they will shoot at us first. If they don't know, then they will not be provoked into a first-strike state of mind."

Scott continued with the confidence of the morally superior. "I will not abide guns, not for self-defence, not for any reason."

"That's easy for you to say, sitting comfortably at home in Redondo Beach, while we slug it out with the Taiwanese. How would you feel if they shot and killed some of the crew and we had no way of defending ourselves. A rifle can be a tool that saves lives. That's why I've got two AK-47s. Just looking at them can be intimidating, and the more intimidating, the less chance there will be of using them."

Scott was adamant. I could sympathize with his philosophical adherence to pacifism, but he had deliberately placed my life and the lives of my crew in jeopardy by painting, through the media, the equivalent of a bull's-eye on our ship.

In an effort to repair the damage, I donated the rifles to the Trinidad and Tobago Coast Guard and made a public announcement that the *Sea Shepherd II* was unarmed. It was too late, though. Scott's story was gleefully and widely reported. The risks we faced were henceforth greatly increased by his betrayal. Although I had publicly disarmed the vessel, I was now forced to rearm secretly. I maintained the policy that I had initiated with the voyage against the *Sierra*. If our opposition was outlaws and pirates, the ship would carry defensive arms. If the opposition was government, the ship would be unarmed. If we encountered an unplanned government encounter while engaged in a campaign against outlaws, the policy would be to deep-six any firearms immediately.

Within a week, we bade adieu to all our newfound friends in Trinidad and headed south to patrol for drift nets. We covered over 3,000 miles (4,800 km) from Trinidad to the equator in the area off the mouth of the Amazon. It was a long, tedious patrol in the hot doldrums. Although we found and retrieved numerous remnants of ghost nets, most of the drift-net vessels eluded us. The few we found quickly outran us.

We returned to Trinidad on July 15 to discover that the government had announced an investigation into allegations of corruption in National Fisheries. We then returned north to restore our energies in Norfolk, Virginia.

Our entrance into Norfolk was amusing. By mistake, Ben White had given us the wrong bay to enter for moorage. The pilot took us into a U.S. naval base and we tied up alongside the dock. We were surprised to find ourselves inside a restricted dock, but since we had entered so matter-of-factly we were accepted without comment. Our unique all-black paint-job with the British red ensign seemed to convey the mistaken notion that we were a visiting British Royal Navy vessel. They hooked us up to the water supply and issued base passes for the crew.

Three days later, two high-ranking officers boarded and demanded to know what were about. We told them that the ship was involved in conservation research work. They left and returned a few hours later to tell us that we had no authority to be in the naval base. In fact, they informed us that by entering the base we had committed a serious crime involving questions of espionage and violations of national security laws. They politely requested that we leave, and when we told them we had no place to go, they made some phone calls and instructed us to tie up to the City dock in downtown Norfolk. I think the only reason they did not arrest us was because it would have been a little embarrassing for them to explain how we had entered and stayed for three days before being discovered.

With the *Sea Shepherd II* safely moored in Norfolk, I took a skeleton crew down to Charleston, South Carolina, to pick up a small ship we had purchased a few months before. It was a former U.S. Coast Guard patrol boat called the *Cape Knox*. We bought her for $100,000 plus a $150,000 tax write-off to the company we purchased her from. We receipted them for their contribution to our charity. I decided to name the ship *Edward Abbey* after my friend and literary hero, who had died in 1989. Ed Abbey had featured Sea Shepherd in his last fictional work. In the novel *Hayduke Lives!*, which is the sequel to *The Monkey-wrench Gang*, the *Sea Shepherd* under my command rescues the hero, George Washington Hayduke, from the Sea of Cortez.

The *Edward Abbey* was a fine vessel, built in 1955, with brand-new engines installed in 1979 and, as typical with the government, a $300,000 overhaul just two months before being sold as surplus by the Coast Guard. She was 95 feet (30 m) in length and her real asset was her speed, which topped out at 28 knots. Finally we had a ship that could catch the bandits.

We moved her without any navigational equipment other than a hand compass. I hugged the coast northward, calculated the distance out to avoid the shoals of Cape Hatteras and brought her in to Norfolk to tie up alongside the *Sea Shepherd II*. Our volunteers worked on both ships for four months, then we moved the *Sea Shepherd II* south to Nassau in the Bahamas, leaving a caretaker crew on the *Edward Abbey*.

In December 1991, I made the *Sea Shepherd II* available to the Gitksan and Wet'suwet'en nations of British Columbia. She was temporarily renamed the *Aligat*, the Gitksan word for warrior. Taking my instructions from the Indians, we intercepted, boarded and seized the *Santa Maria* near Puerto Rico. The Spanish caravel *Santa Maria* was part of a re-enactment voyage to celebrate the five-hundredth anniversary of the rape, pillage and slaughter of the New World.

After that campaign, I had only a few volunteers left. We departed San Juan and plotted a course north back to Key West.

In January 1992, I moved the *Edward Abbey* down from Norfolk to Savannah through the intercoastal waterway and then headed out the Savannah River to the ocean and south to Key West to reunite with the *Sea Shepherd II*. In February, I passed command of the *Sea Shepherd II* to Jon Huntemer and took the helm of the *Edward Abbey*. We headed for Panama.

We made use of our wait in Cristobal by raiding a derelict Moroccan freighter that had gone aground. It was a good training exercise. Under cover of darkness, some of the crew and I dropped overboard from our moving inflatable, swam to the wreck and then climbed a rope hanging from the side. We were able to salvage hundreds of charts and a few tools.

The transit of the canal was not without incident. Our two ships entered the Gatun locks at different times — the *Sea Shepherd II* first, followed by the *Edward Abbey* an hour later. On the Pacific side, however, the locomotives were down, but they allowed the *Sea Shepherd II* to proceed using only hand lines. As they waited to enter the lock, I caught up with them and we entered the lock together, the *Edward Abbey* rafted up on the port side of the *Sea Shepherd II*. The lock doors opened to the second lock and the pilots instructed the *Sea Shepherd II* to proceed first. She started her engines and began to move rapidly backwards at an angle that would crush the *Edward Abbey* against the stone lock walls. It was obvious that David Howitt had neglected to ensure the engine was geared forward before starting up.

I didn't have much time to react. I pulled the throttle back full on both my engines and the patrol boat rocketed backwards. I could see the lock gates to my stern approaching fast but the trawler was moving in and closing the gap. We just squeezed by without even scraping paint. I swung the wheel hard to starboard and throttled full ahead. She stopped only inches from the gate. The engines whined and shuddered and the *Edward Abbey* pounced forward and sped by the *Sea Shepherd II* on their starboard side.

I couldn't help thinking just how embarrassing it would have been to have had one of my ships rammed and sunk in the Panama locks by the other.

We picked up a couple of journalists in Balboa — a writer for *Playboy* and a crew from a program called "Eco Spies." Both ships headed northward to Treasure Island.

This island, some three hundred miles (480 km) off the coast of Costa Rica, is actually called Cocos Island. It was, however, the island that inspired Robert Louis Stevenson's classic *Treasure Island*. Centuries before, in the days of classical piracy, so legend had it, this island was where Captain Henry Morgan had buried a king's ransom of treasure.

Approaching it, I marvelled. It was indeed a treasured island. Morgan's gold was never found, though, heaven knows, many tried and some died, their lives wasted in the fruitless search. The moilers for gold had missed the real treasure — the island itself.

I have spent a score of years at sea and I have voyaged on the waters of all four of our Earth's fair oceans and most of her seas. I have seen thousands of islands and, except for those scarred and devastated by human greed, they have all been jewels, scattered emeralds in an aquamarine and sapphire setting. This island, with her three spired peaks, however, must rank as the crown jewel in our Earth Mother's diadem. She is simply the most enchanting bit of paradise I have ever laid eyes upon.

Isolated and lonely, she rises from the oceanic depths like a majestic verdant kraken, her peaks cloaked in thick green robes of fern and tropical lushness. Silvery springs cascade down the steep peaks from hundreds of well-fed ponds. The island looks like a giant's bonsai, more a calculated work of art than an island wilderness. Unpeopled, unspoiled, practically untouched, definitely unpolluted, Cocos is the essence of the desert island paradise of a million imaginations.

I opened a copy of Stevenson's book. There could be no doubt. He had written: ". . . we saw two low hills, about a couple of miles apart, and rising behind one of them a third and higher hill, whose peak was still buried in fog. All three seemed sharp and conical in figure." But we had not come here for the scenery. I called up the *Sea Shepherd II* and told them to be on the lookout for small fishing boats.

Cocos is a Costa Rican National Park. It is illegal to fish within 32 miles (53 km) of the island. Unfortunately, the government of Costa Rica is unable to finance conservation enforcement around the island. It is also one of the best diving locations in the world. A few dive boats have developed a small trade in transporting divers to the island from the coast. An operator of one of these boats had sent a letter to us in 1991. He had reported that Costa Rican and Panamanian fishermen were engaged in unlawfully harpooning dolphins in the vicinity of the island and using the dolphin meat as bait for sharks. The sharks in turn were being exploited only for their fins. Shark fins brought a high price in the markets of Taiwan and Japan.

We had approached Cocos in the early-morning hours before sunrise. The dawn brought sighting of dozens of active fishing vessels. We circled the island, leaving the *Sea Shepherd II* on one side.

I pulled into Wafer Cove and saw a few sailing yachts and a couple of dive boats. I hailed the larger of the dive boats and they asked who we were. I answered that we had received a report about dolphins and sharks being killed near the island.

The voice on the other end of the marine telephone replied in surprise, "That was *me*. I wrote you. I didn't think anyone would actually do anything."

"Are these the boats you witnessed killing dolphins?" I asked.

"Yes."

I radioed the *Sea Shepherd II*. "Jon, we have these guys on three violations. One, fishing illegally in an exclusion zone, as defined by Costa Rican law; two, killing dolphins; three, killing sharks, all within the exclusion zone. Let's send them home."

With that, we moved in. The *Sea Shepherd II* intimidated three of them immediately. We sent four additional boats packing from our side of the island. Two more boats decided to be stubborn and refused to pick up their lines. I ran down their lines, severing their gear. Turning towards them we put our bow only feet behind their stern. The fishermen began to swear and threaten us. I stepped out of the pilot house armed with a semi-automatic CO_2-powered paintball rifle and proceeded to rake their boat with about 200 rounds of red paint splats. They dove for cover, then rose with their hands up, obviously relieved that I hadn't used real bullets.

"Where are you going?" I asked.

"Putarenas. We are going home, back to the mainland," they replied.

We turned on the second boat. I pulled the tarp off our new toy, a replica of a Civil War field cannon. It was loaded with eight ounces (226 g) of black powder and primed to fire. I aimed the gun at their small wheelhouse. The fishermen dove for cover when they saw it. They didn't know that the cannon had no projectile. The cannon thundered with an explosion of flame and thick white smoke, which effectively conveyed our message. They also headed home.

A third vessel came round the point with a crew member waving a dirty white undershirt. We acknowledged them and waved them homeward to the mainland. Our two ships then escorted the flotilla of pirate fishing boats some 20 miles (32 km) out to sea to ensure that they were indeed heading home.

When they arrived in Costa Rica, two days later, the fishermen filed a complaint against us. They said we attacked them without provocation some 40 miles (64 km) from the island. They did not know who we were and described us as American pirates armed with cannons, swords and machine guns. They said we attempted to sink them and that they were not even fishing at the time.

The Costa Rican government did not have a problem identifying us. I had sent them a full report and informed them that video tape would follow. Our film established the facts and proved that the boats were engaged in illegal fishing activities only a quarter to half a nautical mile from the shores of Cocos Island. In response, the Costa Rican government brought charges against the fishing boats involved and identified in our video tape.

Our ships then spent two weeks harassing a few Mexican tuna seiners before docking in Los Angeles to begin preparations for another drift-net campaign and the final voyage of the *Sea Shepherd II*.

The first thing I did upon returning was call a board of directors' meeting. We accepted Scott Trimingham's resignation. Ben White also resigned shortly thereafter when I refused to support his civil-disobedience campaigns inside U.S. territory. He had been arrested for attempting to release captive dolphins in Florida. He knew that our policy was to intervene only outside of U.S. waters. He went ahead anyway, and Peter Brown and I would not support him. Also, I would no longer allow myself to be put into a position where my hands were tied, where I could not take action and where I had to fear denunciation by my own directors and crew.

I had pretended that the Sea Shepherd Conservation Society could be run by a group and I had welcomed Ben's and Scott's input. The truth was that Ben White was right. The Sea Shepherd Conservation Society was my organization. I created it, built it, struggled for years to raise the funding, and I had suffered financially and personally while others put Sea Shepherd second and their own businesses and careers first. I did not think that equality after the fact was fair. From here on, I expected people to join Sea Shepherd because they believed in my philosophy and my approach. I would no longer allow other agendas to overshadow the primary objective of investigation and enforcement of international laws and regulations. Ben White wanted to focus on captive dolphins. Scott Trimingham wanted to focus on direct-mail fund-raising, and was preparing to institute a permanent paid position for himself as administrator. Ben and Scott had even talked of deposing me and taking over themselves. I would never allow it, and thus I chose dictatorship over consensus. I had a vision in 1977 when I created the Sea Shepherd Conservation Society. I had absolutely no intention of having that vision diluted.

Our new board of directors included veterans Myra Finkelstein and Susana Maria Rodriguez Pastor, Rosemary Waldron, Peter Brown and former chief engineer Carroll Vogel. All of them were veterans of past active campaigns and I could count on them not to lose sight of what was important — the action out there, beyond territorial waters, where pirate whalers, outlaw drift-netters and bandit dolphin slayers continued to rule the waves. It was our job to stamp them out, not to picket aquariums and call for tourist boycotts and gather petitions. The days of being manipulated by the moderates was over. The Sea Shepherd Conservation Society was a proudly maverick organization. We made no excuses. We sank ships, we rammed ships, we made waves, rocked the boat and stood up to proclaim that we were mad as hell and we definitely did not intend to take it any more.

18
O.R.C.A.FORCE!

I am not what you call a civilized man! I have done with society
entirely, for reasons which I alone have the right of appreciating.
I do not therefore obey its laws, and I desire you never to
allude to them, before me again!

Captain Nemo

For some time I had been contemplating the need for a less costly
and more effective approach to illegal whaling activities. The raid
on Reykjavik in 1986 had demonstrated that maximum damage
could be caused at minimal expense. In addition, such an action provided more publicity bang for the buck. The ship-centred expedi-
tions were extremely expensive and limited us to only one or two campaigns per
year. We needed more field actions utilizing a few effective saboteurs. The United
States Navy has its marines and its Navy Seals. Sea Shepherd could develop an
equivalent. In early 1992, I decided to establish a specific organized body within
the Sea Shepherd Conservation Society to undertake deep-penetration campaigns
using agents instead of ships. We called the new group Oceanic Research and
Conservation Action Force, or O.R.C.A.FORCE.

I had a dynamic person in mind for the job, a woman named Lisa Ann Distefano. She had expressed interest for some time in working on something like
this. She was employed by Dun and Bradstreet as a sales executive. However,

despite her Fortune 500 employment status, she had been a longtime activist, going back to her native North Carolina. She was also a very beautiful brunette of Cherokee, Cajun and Sicilian ancestry and a trained actress. In other words, she offered good media presence. And she confessed that I had been her hero since she was a teenager.

I was flattered of course, but more than that, I was intrigued. She was the perfect leader for the undercover unit I wanted her to put together and command. Conservative good looks, a conservative résumé and all the trappings of an establishment child. Inside, however, she was a fiery, angry, determined and committed defender of the Earth and wilderness. Here was a woman after my own heart, who understood the passion to conserve, to protect and to fight for the future. She also shared my passion for history and had graduated with a degree in history from East Carolina State. I made her director of O.R.C.A.FORCE and gave her a few months to prepare for the unpaid and taxing position.

Lisa would soon be responsible for recruiting and running security checks on both O.R.C.A.FORCE and Sea Shepherd personnel. This would relieve me of the responsibility that I most detested within Sea Shepherd — dealing with crew problems.

In May, the first O.R.C.A.FORCE action took place in Kao-hsiung, Taiwan. One of our newly recruited crew, an Indiana man named Dwight Worker, travelled to Asia and sank a Taiwanese drift-netter in Kao-hsiung harbour. He was successful in finding one unoccupied vessel that he was able to board and then scuttle. The *Jiang Hai* (which means building co-operation) settled into the filthy mud on the harbour bottom. Before returning, Dwight photographed huge piles of new monofilament drift net being loaded onto ships despite the United Nations ban on deployment of new equipment.

Dwight was one of the first O.R.C.A.FORCE recruits and a prime example of the type of person we were looking for. We needed people who had experience getting into and out of tight situations, people who could make decisions in the field and could operate without guidance, depending on their own skills and resources. Most important, we needed people who did not feel that it was unusual to risk life, limb and freedom in an effort to protect non-human lives.

Dwight had presented a book and a television movie video as his résumé. Both were entitled *Escape*. He had been the first man since Pancho Villa to escape from Mexico's notorious Lecumberri prison. He had served hard time — the hardest. Life was not easy or pleasant for a gringo in a hell-hole like Lecumberri. He had suffered bloody, bone-breaking thrashings, soul-numbing bouts of enforced solitude, severe illness and the contempt of his Latino cellmates. Despite the hardships and the overwhelming odds against escape, he succeeded. After five years in Mexico's worst shit-hole, he escaped. He had known that death was the punishment for apprehended escapees. He had not been deterred. As a self-freed man, he returned to the United States with a flawless grasp of Spanish and a new-found realization that time was short, life was precious and there were many things of more importance than the petty trivialities of human self-centredness.

What impressed me most about Dwight was that he had actually returned to Mexico a few years after his highly publicized escape.

"I had to," he told me. "I had looked out every day and saw Mount Popocaté-petl. That mountain was my only connection with the other universe that existed outside those formidable walls. I had to climb that mountain and look down on that shit-pit of a prison in the midst of that stink-hole of a city. When I reached that summit, I pulled down my pants and I purged one mother of a turd. It fell on the snow, steamed and slowly hardened. And there it sits to this day. When the greasers had beaten me, I kept my sanity by vowing that I would shit on Mexico. It was a fantasy that kept me alive. All of my frustrations, disgust and anger for the Mexicans was expelled on that mountain top, locked into a fos-silized monument to my hate. After realizing my fantasy, I was able to forgive the Mexicans and to get on with my life."

Dwight's successful venture into Taiwan was a great boost to the morale of the crew as they struggled to ready the *Sea Shepherd II* and the *Edward Abbey* for a summer's campaign against drift nets in the North Pacific. Months of hard work had already been invested in preparing both ships. We suffered a major setback when I was reluctantly forced to fire David Howitt as chief engineer. We had scheduled June 20 for departure. David, however, wanted to go later and refused to have the engines ready on schedule. He told me he had some other projects that he had to attend to. When I told him that we had to leave on time, he responded by telling me that I wasn't going anywhere until he was ready. Despite his years of service, and despite his heroic achievements, I had to reluc-tantly replace him. A captain cannot be compromised by a prima donna attitude in his chief engineer.

I promoted Glynn Collard to chief, only to have Glenn break his leg a week later while partying on shore. I promoted David Cole to chief and made Myra Finkelstein second engineer. My nephew, only 18, became third engineer. Pro-motion sometimes comes swiftly in Neptune's Navy. It was not the most expe-rienced engine crew I ever had, but all three had been familiar with the engines for a few years and I was confident that they could do the job. They took over completing preparations as I flew to Rio de Janeiro to attend the Earth Summit meeting called by the United Nations. The international forum would provide us with an excellent opportunity to toss the gauntlet down before the Norwegians before they went any further with their plans to resume commercial whaling activities. I had attended the U.N. Conference on the Environment held in Stockholm in 1972 and I was curious to see the differences 20 years later.

It was depressing. Whereas the Stockholm Conference vibrated with confidence, energy and optimism, the Rio Conference was an exercise in cynicism, marketing and censorship. The issue of population was not even on the agenda, despite its being the primary concern of the '72 meeting. Chief Paolo Paiukan of the Kaiyapo was effectively closed out of the conference by a timely accusation of rape brought against him by a teenage white girl. Everyone seemed ready to condemn him without the benefit of the facts. I had met him in the Amazon in 1989 when I had travelled to Brazil with Dr. David Suzuki to support the Kaiyapo's opposition to a World Bank–proposed hydro project. I could not see him risking his people to rape a white girl. It made little sense. Months after the conference, the investigation was dropped because of lack of evidence. The victimized girl, it turned out, was the daughter of major white landowner in Amazonia who was involved in a land dispute with the Kaiyapo. It had been a bogus charge but an effective strategy to undermine the credibility of a great leader. Perhaps in hindsight, it was for the best. His attendance would have only lent dignity to a sordid orgy of corporate and government green-washing.

The Stockholm Conference had been a major influence in my life. I was 21 years old then. World leaders had raised the call to action. They made promises and commitments and talked of aggressively addressing overpopulation, nuclear and toxic waste and the conservation of wilderness. They told us that we could make a difference by dedicating ourselves to taking aggressive and determined action to protect the future of Planet Earth.

Over the following 20 years, I watched as the promises failed to materialize. I watched as the Earth was violated more and more every year. And, most irritating of all, I have had to suffer accusations of being a fanatic, a militant, an extremist, a criminal and a terrorist from the very same leaders who told me and other young people that it was our responsibility to take action. I had listened to my teachers sincerely. Only years later did I come to realize that my teachers were hypocrites spreading false encouragement. It was perfectly fine to talk about shutting down polluters, whalers, overfishing and clear-cutting, but they never actually expected us physically to do something about the problems.

Originally, the conference in Rio was called the United Nations Conference on the Environment and Restoration. Maurice Strong, the Secretary General of the conference, had it changed to the United Nations Conference on the Environment and Development. This was the same Maurice Strong, former president of Petro-Canada, who was quoted in 1991 in the *Financial Times* as saying that there must be no environmental legislative barriers to world trade. It is this theme that was at the core of negotiations in Rio, negotiations protected from non-governmental and non-industrial organizations by a phalanx of the Brazilian Army. How could we be anything but cynical when a conference to discuss environmental problems was restricted to those responsible for the problems.

The Earth Summit was the largest T-shirt bazaar I had ever seen, and the display of hypocrisy, profiteering and hype was sickening to witness. I spent most of my time simply observing the charades, the games, the posing and the politics.

One experience at the Earth Summit epitomizes for me the incredible hypocrisy that defined the very foundations of the conference.

The Greenpeace Foundation's ship the *Rainbow Warrior* was moored near the site of the Summit. It was open to visitors. I was invited to go on board by a peace delegation the same evening that the Dalai Lama would be visiting the ship to bestow blessings of peace. Because I had met with His Holiness and because we proudly carried the symbol of Hayagriva on our masthead, I joined his delegation to visit the *Rainbow Warrior*.

I was hoping that after so many years of bitter feelings between the original founders and those who had co-opted the organization, this might be a perfect opportunity to heal the wounds between us. The Dalai Lama was a messenger of peace and I felt that at long last here was an opportunity to bring peace between our two camps. After all, that is half of what Greenpeace, as a peace organization, was set up to be, and how could they ever hope to influence peace between nations if they could not find peace within their own family. For better or for worse, I was a part of that family, a founding father, and sincerely interested in Sea Shepherd and Greenpeace joining forces.

I had reason to believe that the long rift that separated us had been healed. A few months before, Steve Sawyer, the International Director of Greenpeace, had responded to my overtures for peace by sending me a letter that welcomed mutual co-operation. I hoped that it would be so. Greenpeace with its awesome war chest and Sea Shepherd with our knack for devising tactics and the crew with the guts to risk implementing those tactics — together we could make a daunting team.

Thousands of people were lining up to see the Dalai Lama board the Greenpeace ship. Greenpeace was taking full advantage of the opportunity to sell Greenpeace shirts, baseball caps, posters and plastic corpogrammed water bottles. Hundreds of Brazilian soldiers, armed with rifles and riot batons, were on hand to control the crowd.

The Dalai Lama arrived, and at the invitation of the Tibetan delegation I fell in behind the Tibetan entourage and began to walk up the gangway. I saw His Holiness step on board to be greeted by the official Greenpeace dignitaries and I couldn't help speculating how surprised they would be to see me step on board in a few moments. I intended to renew our peace greetings and I wished to accentuate our willingness to co-operate on campaigns and actions.

I never got the chance. I felt a thud in my side and I was violently pushed out of the line and off to the side by a Brazilian soldier. Suddenly I was surrounded by soldiers, all heavily armed.

"Get this man out of here. He is a terrorist," I heard, and then saw this small, balding man with a thick Portuguese accent, who identified himself as the captain of the *Rainbow Warrior*.

I attempted to explain to him, "I'm a guest of the Dalai Lama's delegation."

He retorted angrily, "You are an insult to the Dalai Lama."

"Maybe," I answered, "His Holiness would be a better judge of that. Besides, Steve Sawyer and I have agreed that our two groups should co-operate."

He ignored me and turned to the soldiers, addressing them in Portuguese. "Get this man out of here. He is a terrorist."

I turned on him, pushing the barrel of one of the rifles aside.

"How dare you risk my life by accusing me of being a terrorist in front of a bunch of Third World, trigger-happy buffoons. This is really something. You have the Dalai Lama blessing your peace ship at the same time you force a Greenpeace founding father off your ship at the point of a gun. You hypocrite. It was I who first put a rainbow on a Greenpeace ship, the *James Bay*. And this is my reward, to be treated with contempt by you . . . ."

He shouted at the soldiers and three of them pushed me away. I shouted back over my shoulder. "This is really what it's all about and Greenpeace symbolizes it perfectly. You have the illusion of peace and harmony and goodwill with this show of Tibetan Buddhist blessing. The reality is very different. Greenpeace and this conference go well together. Both are illusions."

As the soldiers led me away, I shook my head in disgust. Greenpeace accuses Sea Shepherd of being violent, yet Sea Shepherd has never threatened, injured

.illed any person. Greenpeace can willingly endanger my life by doing the equivalent of yelling "Fire!" in a crowded theatre. Sea Shepherd has never had a crew member injured, yet Greenpeace has had numerous injuries and one death. Sea Shepherd has never had a crew member convicted of a crime while Greenpeace has tallied a healthy criminal record of convictions for trespass, slander, obstruction and disorderly conduct. The real difference is that Sea Shepherd does not hesitate to destroy material objects to protect life whereas Greenpeace has watched whales and seals and other species die without taking action to neutralize the killing machines. Underlying it all is the very real threat that Sea Shepherd poses for Greenpeace. Our actions reveal their relative inaction. Our integrity as a volunteer organization exposes their corporate mentality today. Our ability to act quickly exposes their bureaucratic inertia, and our dedication to action over rhetoric exposes their hypocrisy.

Sadly, I realized that I would never be able to co-operate peacefully with Greenpeace. The Foundation that I and Hunter, Marining, Spong, Garrick, Johnson and the others had built had been co-opted. We are now modern-day Dr. Frankensteins, having created a green corporate monster beyond our control, a mindless monster motivated by eco-buck profits, a logo on the move and a dynamic threat to the integrity of the green movement overall.

I left before the Earth Summit was over. I was nauseated by the thought of continuing to be a part of it. Before leaving I called a small press conference at the Gloria Hotel and invited the Scandinavian media. I told them that the Sea Shepherd Conservation Society would not tolerate Norway's planned withdrawal from the International Whaling Commission, and we were prepared to send our O.R.C.A.FORCE agents to sink Norwegian whaling ships if Norway made any move to return to whaling outside the authority of the International Whaling Commission.

Returning to Los Angeles, I made a quick trip to Las Vegas to meet with Steve Wynn, who had become a strong supporter of our activities — despite Ben White's attempt to attack him publicly for holding captive dolphins. I had visited him to investigate the situation for myself and discovered a man with an intense love for dolphins and the other citizens of the sea. He had set up a superb facility at the Mirage Hotel Casino to house dolphins rescued from inferior captive facilities where they had suffered neglect and abuse. He also recognized the danger of the drift-netters and I returned to Los Angeles with the means to fuel my ships.

Jon Huntemer moved the *Sea Shepherd II* north to Santa Cruz and I joined him a few days later with the *Edward Abbey*. We picked up a film crew from

Britain's Yorkshire Television and made ready to depart westward. I radioed over to Jon to weigh anchor when we were notified to remain where we were and prepare to be boarded.

Within minutes, agents from U.S. Customs, the Federal Bureau of Investigation, the Coast Guard and the Alcohol, Tobacco and Firearms Agency boarded both ships. They checked out each crew member and searched the ships.

Although they told me that the search was routine, I knew they were looking for Rod Coronado, and fortunately he was not on board. He had wanted to crew on this trip but I told him he couldn't. He was an excellent crew member and the best damn activist I ever had. Unfortunately, he had been implicated in an investigation of Animal Liberation Front activities and was wanted for questioning.

One of the FBI agents asked me the nature of our voyage.

"We're off to enforce international law against illegal drift-net activities as defined by United Nations Resolution No. 46/215," I replied.

"What gives you the right to do that?" he inquired.

"The United Nations World Charter for Nature gives us the right, especially since no one else is doing anything about the problem other than talking."

The agent thought for a moment and then smiled and said, "You're right. Good luck."

Having failed to find Rod, the agents left, just as a storm was kicking up. I was eager to get to sea before the storm increased, and we headed seaward immediately on a three-week voyage in search of drift-netters.

The next morning found us heading peacefully westward, two small ships on a vast heaving ocean. This alone made these voyages so meaningful to me. I loved the days of seemingly endless horizons, starting each morning with the sun on our stern and ending each day with the sun settling straight before our bow. The immense aquamarine ocean under the big azure sky, surrounded by water, turtles, dolphins, whales and birds. Most important, a plane of immense distance devoid of people and their trivial anthropocentric attitudes and arrogance.

To save fuel, we hitched a line from the *Sea Shepherd II* back to the *Edward Abbey* to bring her under tow. This gave me, for the first time, the opportunity to rest and enjoy the ocean without spending much energy in running the ship. It also gave me the chance to savour my freedom.

What the sea meant to me was freedom. Total, complete, liberating freedom. Freedom from the oppressive laws of humanity, freedom from harassment and freedom to think without distraction. Most important, out here I had the freedom to protect the Earth, her seas and the life within, upon and above her waters.

Ten days out, I called the *Sea Shepherd II* and gave them an order to switch to salt-water cooling. This would give us the extra two knots I anticipated would be needed to keep up with a fleeing drift-netter.

Mark Heitchue, the officer on watch, said, "I don't know, Captain. The engineers won't like it. They say it'll be too hard on the engines."

"Mark," I replied, "this is her last voyage. Any damage caused will take months to occur. Do as I say and tell them to switch to brine cooling."

The next day, when I asked how the engines were running, Mark answered, "The consensus on this ship is that we should not use salt-water cooling, Captain."

Patiently I asked, "Are you telling me that the ship is still on fresh-water cooling?"

"That's right," Mark answered.

"Mark, I want that engine switched. Now. I don't want any excuses. I don't want any of this consensus shit. Switch to brine cooling. Do you understand?"

"Loud and clear, Captain."

"Good."

Twelve days out from Santa Cruz we spotted a Japanese drift-net fleet. I made a note in the log: "July 11, 1992: Position: 41.27" North, 160.58" West. Sighted: A Japanese drift-net fleet." It was 11 days since the U.N. resolution banning drift nets had taken effect. Yet here they were, setting drift nets under the red beach ball flag of Japan. To me they were nothing more than Japanese government–sanctioned privateers.

Upon sighting the drift-netters, we dropped our tow and the *Edward Abbey* sped forward to scout out the Japanese vessel.

We came alongside the *Gen 1 Maru #68* just as she began laying her net. I decided to follow and film her as she spewed the deadly web from her stern like a giant water spider. She shat drift net for five hours, laying down more than 35 miles (56 km) of it.

Behind us the *Sea Shepherd II* began to retrieve the net, hauling it on board as the Japanese laid it out miles ahead. Throughout the night, our flagship struggled to fill her hold with confiscated drift net, occasionally fouling her propeller on the nasty stuff. Our divers had to constantly plunge into the inky blackness of the sea to cut the monofilament lines away from the prop and rudder.

At 0500 hours, I called Jon on the *Sea Shepherd II* to request that he cease hauling in nets and join up with me to shut down the operations of a second Japanese ship, the *Gen 1 Maru #76.*

At 0530, I transferred over to our flagship and left Peter Brown in command of the smaller ship. Both of us followed closely behind the stern of the Japanese ship.

"*Gen 1 Maru #76*, this is the *Sea Shepherd II*. Please be advised that we intend to ram you to destroy your power block."

My voice on the radio was the signal for Peter to run the *Edward Abbey* up ahead of the drift-netter. He fired a cannonball across the bow of the Japanese ship from our antique civil war cannon. The ball sent up a fantail of water 100 yards (100 m) to starboard of the Japanese ship. Peter then fell back to take up a position to film the ramming.

The *Sea Shepherd II* moved quickly into a ramming position. As our bow swung into position and the gap began to close, I noticed the Japanese fishermen standing on the main deck. Seeing us, they ran to the starboard side of the deck to avoid our oncoming battering ram.

Unfortunately, one lone fisherman refused to move. Perhaps he was immobilized by shock. It must have been an awesome sight from his point of view, looking up to see our massive black flared bow rising up and about to crash down upon his ship — in fact, about to strike where he himself stood. I had no choice. I pulled the wheel hard to port to avoid striking the ship, aborting the ramming.

Our starboard side swept past the port side of the Japanese at full speed at a distance of two yards (2 m). Our bow struck the net, snapping the line and cutting it free from the drift-netter. At the same time, six Sea Shepherd crew members delivered a volley of butyric-acid vials onto the Japanese deck. The putrid-smelling acid drove the crew inside, giving me the opportunity to make a second ramming attempt.

Cut free from her net, the Japanese captain revved his engine and sped ahead of us. Confident that we could catch her, we pursued. The *Edward Abbey* attempted to slow the drift-netter down by crossing the bow and firing flares over her mast. But she still gained on us.

I turned to Jon. "I don't understand this. We should be getting an extra two knots with salt-water cooling."

Jon looked puzzled. "What do you mean, salt-water cooling?"

"I told Mark two days ago to switch," I said.

Jon answered, "He didn't relate that to me and as far as I know we're still on fresh water."

I ordered the chief engineer up to the bridge. Dave Cole arrived covered in oil and sweat, complaining the engine was overheating.

"It wouldn't be if you had followed orders," I reprimanded him.

"We felt it would be too hard on the engine," he said defensively.

"Oh, you did, did you?" I answered. "Well switch it now."

"It'll take at least 10 minutes."

"Goddamn you people and your infantile disrespect for authority anyway. You're not a crew, you're just a bunch of anarchists looking for a cause to undermine. You just lost that drift-netter for us. Get out of here."

I had to call off the chase. The Japanese fled the area, leaving us to confiscate miles and miles of floating drift net. As we hauled it in on the power block of the *Sea Shepherd II*, we recorded the number of bird, mammal and fish corpses entangled in the web. Fortunately, the kill was small. The net had not been left in the water for long.

At the end of the day, I returned to the *Edward Abbey* and gave the order to head back to the west coast — to Vancouver Island.

A few hours later, some of the crew asked why we were heading home.

"Because you can't follow orders," I answered.

It was not a total loss. We had a cargo hold full of drift net and a couple of Japanese ships on the run. The drift-netters would find it difficult to keep on fishing with the loss of so much net.

Three days later, on the threshold of a rising full moon, a U.S. Coast Guard C131A aircraft overflew us. That far out it had to have been there by intent and not accident.

The pilot informed us that the government of Japan had laid a complaint with the U.S. State Department over our actions against two Japanese-flagged vessels. I answered that we were fully prepared to co-operate with the State Department, the Coast Guard and the Japanese government. The pilot said he would convey that message and then headed north to Alaska to return to base.

Five days later, on July 19, we were 300 miles (480 km) off the west coast of Vancouver Island. Throughout the night, we had been trailed by a ship that refused to answer our radio calls. The morning light revealed the daunting outline of the U.S. Coast Guard cutter *Resolute* standing off the starboard beam of the *Edward Abbey*. The Coast Guard informed me by radio that they would be boarding the U.S.–registered *Edward Abbey*. The *Sea Shepherd II*, because of her British registry, had permission to proceed.

They approached us in heavy seas and boarded us with caution. I met them, shook hands and invited them below for coffee. More than a dozen officers came on deck and a few were turning slightly green. Our heaving deck takes a little getting used to after leaving a larger, more stable ship like their cutter.

In the galley, Peter and I informed the Coast Guard that we had indeed confiscated the net, although we were forced to abort the ramming. We signed statements, gave the Coast Guard copies of video and audio tape and told them that they could count on our complete co-operation in any investigation. They thanked us and left and we proceeded after the *Sea Shepherd II* towards Vancouver Island.

We must have disturbed a political hornet's nest. Upon reaching Ucluelet on Vancouver Island's verdant cedar- and pine-scented west coast, both ships were boarded by the Canadian Coast Guard, the Royal Canadian Mounted Police and Canadian Customs and Immigration along with two German shepherds. Again, we confessed our actions and stated our willingness to co-operate with any authorities.

I was planning on taking the *Sea Shepherd II* to Seattle until I could find a place to retire her. The Canadian government solved the problem of where to retire the ship by arresting her.

A government branch called Pacific Pilotage Authority had refused to give me a price quote for pilotage services entering Ucluelet. Because of this I had ordered Jon to take the ship to Seattle. Canada Customs countered by ordering the *Sea Shepherd II* into port despite the fact the ship was 25 miles (40 km) off shore. On arrival, they informed me that the pilotage bill for only 15 minutes of service would be $7,500. I was outraged. The transit of the Panama Canal cost under $2,000. They said that all ships, including mine, were required to pay a subsidy for pilotage of log transport ships into and out of Port Alberni. In other words, it was a subsidy to the logging industry.

I refused to pay. There was no way in hell I would ever pay a subsidy to the accursed logging industry, and I told them so. Pacific Pilotage chartered a seaplane to send over a representative from Vancouver to explain the situation.

"Captain Watson, you have no alternative but to pay this tariff," said the bureaucrat.

"I will not pay it," I answered.

"You don't seem to understand, sir. You either pay this fee or your ship will not sail."

"Then it will not sail," I answered.

"Captain Watson, you don't understand. Your ship will never be allowed to sail unless you pay this fee."

Smiling, I answered again. "Sir, *you* don't understand. I will not pay the fee today or at any time in the future. I will not pay a subsidy to the logging industry."

"Then you will not sail," he said firmly.

"Then we will not sail," I agreed.

The local people, most of whom were loggers, laughed at us when they found the ship had been arrested. They were puzzled by my response, which was, "It's fine with me. She can sit here until hell freezes over, for all I care. Ucluelet is just as good a place to retire her as anywhere."

I was eager to return to Los Angeles. Lisa's voice had beckoned to me across the waters and I was yearning to see her again. I took her out for dinner and presented her with an Italian naval diving watch for her birthday. A week later, in August, we motored out into Santa Monica Bay and swam together miles off shore. A week after that, we were in each other's arms constantly. We drove north to Canada and attended the Clayoquot Days celebrations on Clayoquot Island.

It was such a beautiful island, surrounded by temperate rain-forested mountains. We lay in a lovingly carved bed in a house surrounded by wild raccoons and chipmunks.

"You know," I said, looking into her lovely brown eyes, "I could happily marry you."

She threw her arms around me and we kissed passionately.

In September, we attended a Cree gathering near Jasper, Alberta. Wii Seeks had come, along with Bob Hunter, David Garrick and Rod Marining. Lisa and I rode horses along the banks of the Athabaskan River and I gave her an engagement ring that I had hastily hammered together in the stable, made from a horseshoe nail.

We left the Rockies behind and drove south, back to California. I loved her and she loved me, and together we had much to do. I had at long last found my warrior bride.

In July, the Norwegians had declared their intention to return to commercial whaling. Lisa and I decided to prepare a pre-emptive strike against Norway. We recruited only one other person, Dwight Worker, who had already proven himself capable of scuttling a ship. We decided to strike at Christmas. Lisa and I would conduct reconnaissance and surveillance. Dwight would be the mechanic of the operation.

On December 14, Lisa and I landed at Arlanda airport, near Stockholm. We rented a car and drove south to visit Sarah Hambley and Sten Borg, who were now married with four children and living in Sweden. Dwight arrived a few days later. He then took a train north to Kiruna, Sweden, while Lisa and I drove to Trondheim and scouted the Norwegian coast. Dwight rented a car in Kiruna and drove to the Lofotens to wait for us there. We kept in touch daily by calling in to a central number in Sweden.

Our first stop on the Norwegian coast was Bonnoysund, which is the home port for Steinnar Bastesen, who a year before had boasted he would have a whale-meat feast on July 4 and "show those Americans that we will eat whale meat until we puke all over the American flag."

Unfortunately, we were unable to locate Bastesen's ship. We drove north to Bodø. Again we could not locate any whalers, so we took the car ferry across the Vestfjorden to the Lofoten Islands. We were now some 170 miles (275 km) north of the Arctic Circle.

The Lofoten Islands are extraordinarily beautiful, although we had little opportunity to view the snowy mountain crags. There were only a few hours of twilight each day. Darkness defines the Arctic winter. The long days were dark, bitingly cold and deathly quiet.

Dwight had driven to Harstad and we based ourselves out of Svolvaer, where we reconned Henningsvaer, Stamsund, Steine and the island of Skrova. We discovered two ships on Skrova, but it would be too difficult to reach, take action and escape. There was only one daily ferry. We checked out the two-mile (3-km) crossing, but the vicious sea currents, the coldness of the water and the constant stormy conditions ruled out a kayak crossing.

The Skrova ferry operator pointed us in the direction of two whalers in Steine. The vessels were the *Nybraena* and the *Brandsholm Boen*, both owned by the Olavsen family, a notorious whale-killing clan.

Lisa, utilizing her drama training, pretended to be an American tourist looking for her Norwegian roots. The skipper of the ferry was very friendly and when she asked if there were any Olavsens around he told her to go to Steine. She said her father had told her that the Olavsens used to be whalers, that her grandfather had been a whaler and she wanted to take a picture of a whaling ship for her father. The ferry skipper told her that would not be a problem — the Olavsens had a couple of whaling vessels in Steine, where they lived.

With the target whalers located, we contacted Dwight where he was staying in Andennes. On Christmas Day, he arrived in Stamsund to execute the operation. He boarded the *Nybraena* in the early-morning hours of December 27 under the cover of an incoming snowstorm. Monkey wrench and bolt-cutters in hand, he struck. The whaler's intake seawater pipe was opened. The ship began to sink.

Lisa and I drove to Narvik, crossed the Swedish border and headed east and then south to Stockholm. It was a risky 930-mile (1,500-km) drive over icy roads where we ran a gauntlet of reindeer. We had numerous near-encounters and although we passed some 18 road-killed reindeer, we were relieved that we did not contribute to the casualties.

Dwight returned by train from Kiruna to Stockholm and then flew back to the States. Lisa and I took a train from Stockholm to Amsterdam, where I telephoned Inspector Elisabeth Kaas of the Lofoten and Vesteralen police. I told the police that we were responsible for the sinking of the *Nybraena*, and that we would return to answer charges should they decide to bring any against us. Inspector Kaas said that there had been no decision on laying charges. I gave her our address and telephone number and requested that she inform us when a decision was made.

Of course, the usual host of critics paraded themselves before the media to condemn our methods as violent, extremist, criminal and terroristic. The truth, when all was said and done, however, was that we had inflicted some heavy damage on a whale killer and the Norwegian government was reluctant to act against us. A Norwegian reporter who had attended my press conference in Rio said to me, "Of all the promises made in Rio, your promise to sink a Norwegian whaling ship is the only one that has been kept."

In April 1993, after much prodding and goading by us in the Norwegian media, the police finally agreed to travel to the United States to question us. We met them in the offices of the Federal Bureau of Investigation. It was a thoroughly enjoyable session. Lisa and I both admitted our involvement with the action and invited charges. Instead of charges, the Norwegian police thanked us for our co-operation and returned home.

Using the sinking as a threat of more actions to come, we announced a plan to voyage to Norway to confront the whalers directly.

⚞19⚟
The Great Canadian Cod War Caper

**It seems to be a law, inflexible and inexorable,
that he who will not risk cannot win.**

John Paul Jones

The beefy loggers jeering at us from the government wharf dove fearfully for cover. Our cannon shot reverberated across the harbour and echoed back to us, reflected from the forested slopes of Clayoquot Sound. The *Edward Abbey* moved alongside the pier as the embarrassed loggers got to their feet before the small battalion of media cameras. It was all smoke and noise, a salute to the spirit of the besieged ancient forests.

Premier Michael Harcourt had just announced the intention of his government to allow the clear-cut devastation of some 85 per cent of this wilderness paradise. Lisa and I had first made love within the boundaries of this mysteriously noble wilderness. We did not want to see it destroyed.

We were here because Michael Harcourt had betrayed us. He had personally told me that he would be a strong defender of the wilderness and a staunch advocate of the old-growth forests of the province. But, like most politicians, he was an opportunist. Instead of advocating for the forests, he had purchased for the

ne 2 million shares of the McMillan Bloedel Logging Company with
rs of the people of British Columbia. By giving the forest-raper the
go-ahead to clear-cut, he manipulated the increase in the price of those shares.
Anybody else would have been hauled off for insider trading, but not Mikey. He
was the big enchilada in Victoria now and had discovered that life was sweeter
after deciding to shine the corporate boot with his tongue.

He was not alone in selling out. My old Greenpeace shipmate and the former
president of Greenpeace, Patrick Moore, had joined the payroll of the forest
industry. As a consultant, he was now touting the virtues of clear-cutting and
preaching about how the "spirit of the ancient forests remains even after the trees
have been removed." Both Patrick and Mike had become what the Kaiyapo of
Amazonia refer to as the "termite people." In the name of profit, they would
gobble their way through the forests until nothing was left.

We had been active in the Clayoquot area for some time. Arriving in Tofino
allowed me the opportunity to announce the existence of a covert group I had
formed years before called the Couer du Bois. I calmly informed the press that
this group had spiked more than 20,000 trees over the last few years.

Tree-spiking was an idea that I came up with after hearing about a Vancouver sawmill on Vancouver Island that had been shut down for a few days in the
late 1970s after one of its saws struck a cannonball. The ball had been fired two
centuries before by Captain James Cook and had lain within the guts of an
ancient cedar until discovered by the probing obscenity of the saw, which had
shattered on impact.

A little research revealed that accidents caused by hitting stones and metal-
lic objects in trees were not uncommon and each occurrence was very costly to
the logging industry. Further research revealed that the possibility of injuries to
loggers and sawmill workers was minimal due to the safety equipment, including shields and chain guards, utilized by the industry. They were already prepared for a tactic that became known as tree-spiking, which I initially described
as the "inoculation of a tree against the disease called clear-cutting."

In 1982, a small band of my crew spiked more than 2,000 trees on the southern slope of Grouse Mountain overlooking the city of Vancouver. We had called
ourselves the North Vancouver Garden and Arbor Club and spoke through our
fictional leader, Wally Cedarleaf. In response to our week-end activities on the
slopes, the sawmills cancelled their agreement to purchase the trees, and the
forested slopes survive to this day as direct evidence that tree-spiking as a tactic
does save trees.

As expected, the media, the government, the public and most of the other environmental groups were outraged, and the predictable condemnations followed. The Western Canada Wilderness Society responded by announcing a $1,000 reward for the arrest of any tree-spiker. The media ran a series of eco-terrorist editorials. Vicki Husband of the Sierra Club told me I had no business in the forests and to mind my own business and stick to the oceans. The oceans and the forests, however, are interdependent and the destruction of forests has a direct link to the diminishment of salmon and the pollution of coastal marine habitats. For a defender of the oceans, the protection of the forests is essential and falls within the overall activities of marine conservation.

It was all very amusing. Despite the whining, moaning and moral indignation, our objective was achieved. We succeeded with just one cannon blast and a few sound bites in laying the foundation for a summer of controversy over the Clayoquot issue. I had simply moved in our shock troops briefly and then sailed away. With the ball rolling, the moderates and the right-wing extremists could battle it out. They could both call me names for all I cared. The important thing was that we had set them at each other's throats and the seeds of a summer of confrontation had been sown.

Having ignited the controversy on the West Coast of Canada, Sea Shepherd set out to inspire another controversy on the East Coast. It was our contribution to *A Mari Usqve ad Mare*. I felt we could act as a catalyst to connect the most sensitive ecological issue on the Pacific side with the most sensitive ecological issue on the Atlantic side. What did ancient cedars and cod have in common? The answer was that both were serious indications of the rapaciousness of human greed and spoke loudly to the fact that ecological problems were not localized but becoming globally epidemic and increasingly interdependent.

We made the decision to tackle the dragger gangsters in April 1993. It was an opportune target en route to Norway and her pirate whaling operations. The Nose and the Tail of the Grand Banks of Newfoundland was an area only a few days from Halifax, where we had just purchased another second-hand ship. I had been thinking of doing something about the problem for some time. However, I had felt that the Newfoundland fishermen, having a vested economic interest in cod, would take action themselves.

Despite the fact that the Canadian commercial cod fishery was closed and thousands of fishermen were out of work, nothing in the way of serious protest has occurred. The Fishermen's Union staged a ridiculous protest by taking a Canadian dragger out to the Grand Banks and making a big whoop-de-do of tossing a traditional dory into the storm-tossed waters. The foreign draggers missed the point of the protest, although it was extensively covered by a Canadian media desperate to cover any aspect of the much-talked-about but very inactive Canadian cod wars.

An en-route confrontation with foreign draggers on the Grand Banks was within our range and finances as a practical strategy. Our objective would be to create an international incident concerning the continued exploitation of diminishing populations of northern cod.

Our overall summer strategy was to create an illusion of voyaging to the coast of Norway to confront the outlaw Norwegian whalers, with the objective of increasing Norwegian security costs. It was obvious to me that we were not yet ready for a face-to-face confrontation with the Norwegian Navy. Whales are also a sexier issue than cod, and this helped to generate the greater part of the funds for our two-issue campaign.

Both of these strategies were subservient to the real priority objective, and this was a plan known only to Lisa Distefano and myself. An O.R.C.A.FORCE agent had returned from Iceland just before we left Halifax with a video and photos of the Icelandic fleet in Reykjavik harbour. The crew was unaware that our target was not the Norwegian whalers at all but the unsuspecting Icelandic whaling fleet.

To carry off all three levels of strategy, we needed a large, expendable, ice-class vessel of Canadian registration. For the Norwegians, we needed an intimidating vessel. For Canada, we needed a Canadian flag so that we could provoke the Canadian authorities outside the 200-mile (320-km) territorial limit. For Iceland, we needed a ship with the capability of ramming and crushing the four Icelandic whalers as they lay rafted together against a concrete pier in Reykjavik harbour. The plan would include being arrested in Iceland, and the loss of our ship. I figured, however, that one ship in exchange for the entire Icelandic fleet would be an acceptable exchange.

In May, at the eleventh hour, I found the perfect ship for our purposes for sale in Halifax. It was the former Canadian Coast Guard buoy tender the *Thomas Carleton*. We purchased her for $85,000 and made a deal with the owners, a company called North East Dynamics, to put in a couple of used generators and prepare the ship for sea. This would cost another $90,000. If we had had more time, we would have been more cautious. The two sellers of the ship, Jens Trygstad and Cliff Hodder, were engineers for a reputable Halifax shipping company called Secunda Marine. Unfortunately, we quickly discovered that we could not rely on them. They promised us a completion date and then delivered the ship a month later with the work uncompleted. To make things worse, they arrested the ship when we refused to pay additional charges that had not been agreed to. We were forced to put up a $30,000 bond to release the ship until we could challenge them in court. Jens Trygstad was also an expatriate Norwegian. Once the Norwegian media and police discovered that, he became a steady source of information for them.

Lisa recruited a good crew. Oh, we had a few whiners and malcontents but far fewer than usual for us. Lisa had done a good job. The 23 crew members were mainly Americans with a couple of Brits and Canadians. A film crew from *Der Spiegel* TV joined us as the only independent media crew. A local Halifax reporter, Malcolm Dunlop, wrote a flowery article about us, then pestered Lisa to join the crew. Based on his complimentary article, we agreed to take him on.

Despite the delays caused by the previous owners, the usual Coast Guard harassment and the additional expenses, the ship was ready to put to sea in late July. I renamed her the *Cleveland Amory* in honour of our first patron and a man I respected immensely.

The Coast Guard almost stopped us from sailing. Fortunately, Lisa had sweet-talked the bureaucrats in Ottawa and Halifax into giving us a temporary registration as a yacht. This removed most of the Coast Guard's authority over us. Proof of this harassment came when a small posse of Coast Guard officials appeared on the dock one morning. I was not on board, but Lisa challenged them quite sternly.

She met them halfway down the gangway. "Can I help you?" she asked.

"Yes, we would like to see your commercial registration," one of them said.

Lisa responded, "This is a registered yacht."

The bureaucrat smiled and patiently repeated his request. "We would like to see your registration as a lighthouse supply and buoy tender ship."

Lisa handed them the blue registration book. They opened it up, their smiles disappearing.

"This is a yacht," one of them said.

"That's what I told you," Lisa responded.

"When did you have her re-registered?" they asked.

"Yesterday. Is there a problem?" Lisa asked sweetly.

One of the Coast Guard men, flustered by the revelation and forgetting himself, turned to the other and said, "Maybe we can get them on tonnage?"

"Aha," said Lisa. "This isn't routine, is it? The name of the game is to *get* us, is it?"

"We'll be back," one of them said as they walked to their car.

"I'm sure you will," Lisa shouted after them.

The next fed tactic was to send Captain McDavit from the Canadian Steamship Inspection branch of the Coast Guard. He proceeded to crawl over our safety and fire equipment with a fine-tooth comb. This was acceptable. I have no argument with safety regulations. However, he decided that I was not acceptable to command my ship.

Looking at me sternly, he said, "I find it very disturbing that this ship is under the command of a man without the required Canadian papers."

"Sir," I responded, "this ship is a registered yacht. I do not require Canadian papers to command a Canadian-registered yacht."

"On the contrary," he smiled. "According to the regulations, you must have the proper papers. This is a yacht in excess of 100 tons."

"Your regulations are not valid. The parliamentary statute that is the Canadian Shipping Act describes a yacht without reference to tonnage. The stature takes precedence over the regulations passed outside of Parliament."

McDavit looked troubled. "There is some dispute about that," he said.

"I see no dispute. Besides, my record of experience more than qualifies me to command this vessel. I have never written for papers for the simple reason that if I had spent the money and the time to do so, it would have been fruitless. Any papers that I obtained would have long since been taken away from me for political reasons. I believe my record of experience is sufficient."

"Mr. Watson, you have no papers — at least you do not have Canadian papers — and because of this I cannot support your command of this ship. It is very disturbing to me that a person such as yourself would be entrusted with the lives of others."

I returned the insult by addressing him as he had done me. "Mr. McDavit, papers don't mean squat. Captain Hazelwood had papers and he still ran the *Exxon Valdez* aground. The captain of the *Titanic* had papers. You've got a few Navy captains in this port who run their ships aground as a matter of routine. I won't mention any names, but a certain Canadian Coast Guard captain just cost the taxpayers a hefty sum with some irresponsible antics in that ice-breaker just down the way. I have taken my ships through storms, through ice and into dozens of confrontations. In over 20 years I have never injured a crew member and I have never had an accident. So what's the big deal over papers, other than to exercise control from some bureaucratic paper-pushing office of swivel servants with nothing better to do than to harass real captains."

They tried a few more tricks but we had hired a marine lawyer and they soon lifted the restrictions to our departure. We finally left Halifax with a crew of 27. This was our first seagoing campaign to protect a species of fish. We had worked on opposition to fish-farm projects in British Columbia because of the serious negative environmental consequences of that industry. We had also confronted the Japanese and Taiwanese drift-netters. Although our efforts against drift-netters had saved fish and squid, our primary concern had been the large incidental kills of marine mammals and sea birds. This was our first attempt to fight exclusively for the fish.

Politically, the timing was right. The Canadian government had been promising action to protect the cod for years. The action never materialized. Instead, we were fed a constant stream of rhetorical double-talk and newspeak. The Canadian dragger operations had been shut down a year before and only after they had voluntarily quit fishing because they could find few fish to catch. The government then declared a moratorium on cod fishing that had the effect of punishing the inshore fishermen, the very people who had been warning the government about dragger overfishing for the previous 10 years. Despite this, the foreign draggers of the fleets from Spain, Cuba, Portugal, Sierra Leone, Norway and elsewhere continued to ravage the cod on the Grand Banks, operating just outside the Canadian territorial limit.

The massive bottom draggers were continuing to plow every square foot of the Nose and Tail of the Grand Banks. I decided in May that the Sea Shepherd Conservation Society could spice up the controversy over ongoing drag-net operations by launching a dragnet of our own. Our objective would be to create an international incident on the Grand Banks.

On the second day out from Halifax, with Sable Island in view to our starboard, a thunderous explosion tore through the engine room. It was a crank case explosion in the port-side engine. Our speed dropped from 12 knots to between six and seven. Frantically, the engineers pulled off the inspection plates. The inside of the engine was a shambles of metal fragments. There was no possibility of repairs. The engineers had no explanations for me. I suspected sabotage, but we could prove nothing.

Both the chief engineer and my first mate, Richard Eurich, demanded that we return immediately to Halifax. I refused.

"You're being irresponsible, Paul. We have to return to Halifax," said Eurich.

"You don't understand, Richard," I replied. "This ship goes forward or she goes down. Sea Shepherd ships do not turn around until the situation is desperate. We have one engine left and many ships only have one engine. We are making headway and we are continuing to the Grand Banks."

Below decks, Lisa briefed her O.R.C.A.FORCE agents in preparation for our arrival on the Tail of the Banks. It would be her crew that would initiate any confrontation with the draggers completely independent of myself. As a Canadian captain on a Canadian-registered ship, I had to be very careful to avoid any direct involvement with a confrontation.

My task was simply to put the ship into position for Lisa and her agents to launch an inflatable attack with stink bombs designed to drive any foreign draggers out of the area.

In the early morning hours of July 28, the *Cleveland Amory* entered the Tail of the Bank. We found ships immediately, although not the ones we were hunting for. These vessels were waiting for our arrival — a reception party organized by the Canadian government. The Canadian Coast Guard ship *Sir Wilfred Grenfell*, the Canadian Fisheries Patrol vessel *Cape Rogers* and the European Community fishing patrol vessel *Ernst Haeckel* silently moved into position behind us. They refused to respond to us on the radio.

Sunrise brought overflights of planes from the Canadian Coast Guard, the Royal Canadian Air Force, the Department of Fisheries and the Royal Canadian Mounted Police. Three ships and four aircraft followed us throughout the morning, the government ships keeping pace with our slower speed, turning when we did, like silent, sinister shadows.

Lisa expressed surprise. "What's with the show of force? They can't be out here protecting the foreign draggers from us, can they?"

"That's exactly why they are out here," I answered. "You don't know my government. They will think nothing of spending millions to prevent one of their own citizens from doing something they haven't got the guts to do themselves."

Mid-morning, our radar gave us a target and we headed for it, leading our flotilla of *federales* with us. It had to be a dragger. The only other possibility was another government ship arriving late to join the posse.

As we approached, the target was positively identified as a dragger — specifically, the Cuban-registered vessel *Rio Las Casas*. She was preparing to lower her drag nets.

I contacted them by VHF.

"*Rio Las Casas, Rio Las Casas*, this is the conservation ship *Cleveland Amory*. Under the authority of the World Charter for Nature, we are requesting that you cease fishing and return to Havana. Do you understand?"

The Cubans did not argue. All they could see was a large black ship leading a squadron of government vessels with government air support overhead. They agreed to leave without argument.

The feds then ruined the day.

The radio squawked, "*Rio Las Casa*, this is the Canadian Fisheries patrol vessel *Cape Rogers*. You have every right to continue fishing in this area. That black ship is under the command of an environmental terrorist. You do not have to do what they say."

The Cubans were obviously confused. They requested clarification. The *Cape Rogers* again gave them assurance that they should continue fishing. They began to lower their net.

On the *Cleveland Amory*, I again requested the Cubans to cease and desist and then crossed their stern, which forced the Cubans to hurriedly retrieve their gear. The Cuban trawler stopped and I manoeuvred alongside to allow the documentary crew to shoot footage of the ship. To avoid physical contact with the dragger, I ordered the working starboard engine to go astern, pulling us back behind the Cubans. This brought the two ships close together, which presented an opportunity for Lisa to order her crew into action.

Two O.R.C.A.FORCE commandos, Brad Ryan and Lee Watts, hurled litre bottles of butyric acid from the monkey deck. Lee's bottle fell short but Brad scored a direct hit on the aft gear deck. The Cubans recoiled in disgust from the foul aroma of the stink-bomb hit. They picked up their nets and headed southward out of the Banks.

As we backed away from the Cubans, the Coast Guard ship *Sir Wilfred Grenfell* radioed the Cubans. The voice identified them as the Royal Canadian Mounted Police, which greatly surprised me. This radio exchange was the first indication to us that a detachment of Mounted Police had been placed on the Coast Guard ship. What the hell were the Mounties doing out here protecting Cuban fishing operations from a Canadian ship in international waters. It dawned on me that we had been set up and entrapped by the Mounties.

At first, Cuban captain Bernardo Pelaez wanted nothing to do with the authorities, he just wanted out of the area. However, after two hours of negotiations, with telephone exchanges between the RCMP and the Cuban Embassy, the Cuban captain gave in and allowed the RCMP to board.

Helmsman Paul Whalen reported to me that Halifax *Chronicle Herald* reporter Malcolm Dunlop was bragging to him that he had stolen a receipt from our office and that he would expose the name of the large donor on the receipt.

Whalen also reported that Dunlop was smoking marijuana in his cabin and talking about how he was going to get the "goods" on us.

"Why would he be telling you all this?" I asked Whalen.

"He thinks that because I'm in the Army Reserve I'm a trustworthy person to confide in. I share his cabin and he likes to talk."

"Do you think you can get him to talk about it again?" I asked.

"Sure," he said.

Peter Brown put a wire on Whalen and we sent him back into his cabin to engage Dunlop in conversation. Peter listened as Dunlop offered Whalen a toke and a drink. When Paul asked to see the receipt again, Dunlop took it out of his pocket and waved it in the air. This was our signal. Lisa and I stormed into the cabin with Peter following like a *60 Minutes* cameraman.

Lisa snatched the receipt from his hand and said, "We'll take back our property, thank you Malcolm."

"Consider yourself under arrest and confined to your cabin, Malcolm." I said.

Malcolm made a wild dash and attempted to jump over the side of the ship. Lee Watts tackled him on the outside deck to prevent him from the suicidal attempt. In response, I requested the RCMP to send an inflatable to arrest Malcolm and transfer him to the Coast Guard ship.

A few hours later, we approached a Spanish dragging fleet. I ordered them off the fishing grounds, citing the World Charter for Nature. The RCMP contacted me immediately to inform me that I was under arrest and that they intended to board the *Cleveland Amory*.

If it were not for the crippled port engine I would have ignored them and carried on. I was concerned that the starboard engine would not be sufficient to allow us to make the transatlantic crossing to Iceland. That body of water between Labrador and Iceland was not the place to take such risks.

I called Inspector Roney on board the *Sir Wilfred Grenfell*. "Inspector Roney, this is Paul Watson. Please be advised that you have my permission to send a boarding party. You will receive no trouble from us, sir."

We watched as the Coast Guard ship dispatched three inflatables carrying boarding parties of Mounted Police. At a point halfway to us, the small boats turned and headed back to the *Grenfell*. A few minutes later, they raced back towards us. I found out later from talking with some of the Coast Guard crew that the Mounties had returned because they had forgotten to take ammunition for their weapons.

Despite being prepared for a small gun battle, the officers boarded my ship without incident and placed me under arrest. I turned over command to the RCMP, after which I was transported to the Coast Guard vessel and placed under guard and confined to a cabin for the two-day voyage back to Newfoundland.

My only regret was the fact that we were now prevented from continuing on to Iceland. Our plans to moby dick the Icelandic whaling fleet had to be abandoned. All in all, I would have preferred an Icelandic jail to a Canadian hoosegow. The Icelanders were friendlier, the food was better and the cells cleaner.

The *Cleveland Amory* was taken under tow to St. John's harbour. Lisa remained on board to watch the activities of the Mounties. She and the crew were not placed under arrest, although the Mounties treated them as if they were prisoners.

Eager to determine the legal status of the crew, Lisa entered the bridge to speak with the officers. Their attitude was extremely hostile. One officer shouted at her to leave the bridge immediately.

Lisa stood her ground. "Am I under arrest?" she demanded.

"No, you are not under arrest," an officer responded.

"Then," said Lisa, "I have no intention of leaving the bridge of my ship."

Another officer responded angrily, "Please leave the bridge, miss."

"I will not."

The officer gave her a hard shove against the bulkhead. "I said, please leave the bridge, miss."

"If I am not under arrest, then I refuse to leave the bridge," Lisa shouted.

The Mountie looked her up and down. "You should learn to act like a Canadian woman."

"What the hell is that supposed to mean?" Lisa demanded.

"You should be nice and do what you're told," he said.

"I'm an American citizen," said Lisa. "I have every right to go where I like on this ship unless you place me under arrest."

The Mountie bodily pushed her off the bridge.

She, the crew and the ship were searched without a search warrant. Although they were repeatedly told that they were not under arrest, the crew were restricted from moving about the ship. Lisa was expelled from our cabin, which was commandeered by the Mounties for their own use.

As the ships approached St. John's, I was taken from confinement to prepare for a helicopter transfer to land. Apparently, our actions had been received with a great deal of sympathy on the island. Fishermen were gathering to give us a hero's welcome. Constable Peter Stevens informed me that the helicopter would ensure that I would avoid the reception.

"We can't have you being welcomed as a hero now, can we?" he said.

Waiting on the windy deck for the helicopter to land, I asked Constable Stevens if Malcolm Dunlop would be taken to the same jail.

"He's not under arrest," said Stevens.

"Why not?" I asked surprised. "I caught the man stealing documents and I filed a complaint against him. I am a captain on a Canadian ship and I duly turned him over to you with a request that he be charged with committing a crime on my vessel."

Stevens shrugged. "There ain't much we can do about it. The incident took place outside of our jurisdiction."

"Then how can you arrest me outside of your jurisdiction?" I challenged.

"It's not for me to say," responded Stevens. "You'll have to ask the politicians about that."

The helicopter lifted off into and above the fog. I saw the stone fortress and surrounding cannons on the top of the mist-shrouded Signal Hill. We descended into the milky haze and landed at the airport. I was handcuffed, hustled into a car and taken to the RCMP headquarters to be photographed and fingerprinted. After being properly identified and booked by the feds, they hustled me out the door and into a car for a drive downtown.

"What have we here?" the Newfoundland constable said as the Mounties escorted me through the archaic stone entrance of the St. John's lockup.

One of the Mounties handcuffed to me replied, "Watson will be staying over the weekend."

The jailer said, "Ya think ye b'yes would be chasin' some real criminals. He was only tryin' to protect our fish."

"He broke the law," the Mountie replied sternly.

"That's a matter of opinion," I interrupted.

"That's certainly true," added the jailer. "It appears, however, that you feds are more enthusiastic over some law-breakers than others. What are you going to do about the bandits stealing our fish?"

"That's not up to us," the Mountie answered. "But you can't have citizens taking the law into their own hands."

"I can see why," I said. "The public might begin to think they can do a better job than you."

The Mounties scowled at me.

I was ushered into my weekend retreat. It was a small, primitive rectangular concrete room with a steel bunk *sans* mattress and an odd sink and toilet combination unit. The walls were a dirty yellowish-green vomit colour, decorated with soot-smudged cryptic script — the artistic representations of the uneducated, proclaiming gutter-minded trivialities. The sewer art had been applied with burnt matches. The floor was red — good for masking bloodstains, I thought to myself. The ceiling contained a black plastic half-sphere housing a monitoring camera. Inset in the ceiling were fluorescent lights that remained on continuously.

"Oh well," I thought to myself. "Consider it a monastic retreat for the weekend."

I needed the rest. The grand thing about incarceration is that it slows down time. In fact, the last time I was given an opportunity to rest and take time to contemplate the nature of time itself was nine days of enforced leave in 1983 while waiting for an appeal release on my conviction for interfering with the seal hunt.

On Monday, I was escorted into the courtroom to be booked on multiple charges of mischief. This is the charge the government uses to harass people when they can't find any evidence of a real crime. Usually it is coupled with the other typical harassment charges like conspiracy or obstruction. Three of the counts of mischief had maximum penalties of life in prison, and the fourth charge carried the maximum of 10 years. Three life terms plus 10 for ordering foreign draggers away from the endangered cod fishery. I couldn't help thinking about the absurdity of it. The government of Canada had just spent more than $3.5 million to arrest one Canadian for protecting fish from fishing operations that the government itself referred to as pirate fishing.

After years of protecting seals and battling Newfoundland sealers, I was astounded to see some 200 fishermen, many of whom were former sealers, protesting in front of the courtroom.

"Save Paul Watson. Ban the draggers. Save Paul Watson," they shouted.

Until a few days ago, I was hated and reviled by these same men for my part in ending the commercial seal hunt in the years prior to 1983. Now these very same men were lauding me as a hero and saviour. This time they seemed to be of the opinion that we were acting in their interests.

One of them came up to me and quickly said, "Thank God, you're helping to save our fishery."

I didn't argue. My concern was for the fish, not the fishermen. They were good allies, however, and it would not do to discourage them. With a little encouragement, perhaps they could be persuaded to take action themselves against the draggers.

Inside the courtroom, I was ordered to reappear in six months for a preliminary hearing and released on $10,000 bail. Farley Mowat immediately put up half the bail money and Lisa covered the balance.

It was out of the legal frying pan and into the bureaucratic fire when I was released. The Mounties had tied up the *Cleveland Amory* at the Department of Fisheries dock. Fisheries was charging me the extortionate rate of $300 a day, which I refused to pay on principle. When I refused to pay, Fisheries demanded that I move the ship from the dock. I agreed, only to have the Mounties tell me that the ship could not leave the harbour. The Coast Guard also told me that the ship could not be moved. I told them all to talk to each other and when they agreed on what the ship *could* do, then perhaps they could let me know.

Lisa and I arrived back at the ship to find a Coast Guard bureaucrat waiting for us. He stepped out of his car as we stepped from our rental vehicle.

"Mr. Watson, I'm Captain Robert Turner with the Coast Guard and I'm here to tell you that we will not be allowing you to depart with this ship. You will . . ."

"Look," I interrupted. "I don't have time for this bureaucratic bullshit. Do me a favour and take a walk."

He was shocked. "You can't talk to me that way. I'm . . ."

"I know what you are," I interrupted again. "You're a goddamn insignificant petty bureaucrat. The cod are being destroyed off shore, the environment is being raped and pillaged and all you have time for is to harass people trying to do something about it. Frankly, I couldn't give a sweet goddamn who the hell you are or what your job is."

His face turned bright red. He was obviously not used to being addressed in anything but an ass-kissing manner.

As I walked up the gangway, he shouted after me. "You'll never sail from this port. You'll never . . ."

"Yeah, yeah, I've heard it all before." I turned my back and waved him away.

I heard him yelling at me as I walked away, "You have an attitude problem, mister. I'll have your ass. Count on it."

Lisa asked, "Do you think that was wise?"

"I'm sick of his type. Once the politicians in this country jump you, the harassment goes on forever. They're like lamprey eels. They clamp their filthy suckers on your flesh and they don't let you go until they suck all the blood from your body. The Minister is the eel and each of these scumbag bureaucrats, men like that bozo, are the suckers. He is right about one thing: I do have an attitude. I don't like his kind. I detest bureaucrats."

Lisa was worried that my outburst would prevent us from departing from Newfoundland with our ship.

"The answer to that is that we will not even attempt to fight the bureaucrats. We'll put the ship up for sale immediately and use the money to purchase another ship."

Our plan to attack the whalers in Iceland was abandoned. The situation with the Norwegians fared better. In anticipation of our impending arrival, the Norwegian government had spent millions on security measures to protect their whalers. The cost of security exceeded the profits from the summer's whaling. Our tactics of intimidation had paid off. We had scored an economic victory over the whalers and the government that supported their illegal activities.

It didn't take long to locate a buyer for the vessel. We stripped the gear that we needed, loaded up a U-Haul van and left the bureaucrats in a state of extreme frustration.

We arranged to have the preliminary hearing put off until March 21, 1994. In the meantime, we set to work to raise additional funds towards the purchase of two vessels. We needed a replacement ice-strengthened vessel, something more powerful and larger than the *Cleveland Amory*. I also wanted to find a submarine.

A submarine would give us new tactical advantages, the most important being the media attention such a craft would generate. The plan would be to incorporate traditional submariner mythology. The boat would be painted yellow and named the *Nautilus*.

The funds received from the sale of the *Cleveland Amory* were placed in a war chest that would renovate our fleet. We sold the *Resolution* in Hawaii. Steve Wynn, the owner of the Mirage and Treasure Island Hotel and Casino complex, presented us with a healthy contribution towards the submarine. Thanks to a large contribution from Europäisches Tierhilfswerk in Germany, we had the needed funding raised by the end of 1993.

On the action side of things, we had not been idle. Immediately upon returning from Newfoundland, O.R.C.A.FORCE began preparations for a second assault on Norway's pirate whalers. On January 24, 1994, a three-person O.R.C.A.FORCE team boarded the outlaw whaler *Senet* in a small port community south of Fredrikstad in southern Norway. Our crew opened up the sea valves and scuttled the whaler.

The Norwegians were predictably furious. The *Senet* had been warned that they might be targeted, and the ship was being closely watched at the time. Our crew had been able to penetrate the security cordon and scuttle the vessel literally under the noses of the whalers and the police.

The advantage of scuttling the *Senet* was that it focused attention on whaling operations in the south of Norway. Most Norwegians were unaware of these southern-based whaling operations. The attack also reminded the Norwegians that the first sinking a year before was not an isolated incident. We had proven their security measures to be ineffective.

The usual, predictable reactions were trotted out. Outraged Norwegian whalers protested their inability to make car payments on their BMWs because of our militant activities. Greenpeace made their routine denunciation, calling us "cowardly terrorists." The Norwegian government deplored the action. The Norwegian police, however, did not contact us or announce charges.

In February 1994, Alexi Yablokov, a scientific adviser to President Boris Yeltsin, announced that the former Soviet Union had deliberately falsified kill quotas for their whaling activities for 30 years. I had met Professor Yablokov years before at the Marine Mammal Conference held in Bergen, Norway, in 1976. He was a dedicated anti-whaler then and his persistence had paid off. I admired his courage in revealing information so obviously embarrassing to the Russians.

The revelation justified our actions over the years. I was sure that the Japanese and the Norwegians had been lying about their kill numbers. Evidence from the processing plant in Iceland obtained by Rod Coronado and David Howitt had proven that the Icelanders had been deliberately manipulating data to support their determination to continue to kill whales and to increase their quotas.

We had little time to argue the rights and wrongs of our actions with the Norwegians. Simply put, they could issue charges or they could shut up. I had little interest in debating the morality of our actions against their illegal whaling ships. You don't engage in ethical debates with jackals, and to me the Norwegians, with their overfishing, ruthless whale-killing and cruel sealing operations, are nothing more than oceanic jackals.

In mid-March, Lisa and I took a small crew to the Gulf of St. Lawrence to brush molting hairs from three-week-old seal pups. With the government of Canada seeking to create a market for harp seal penis parts in Asia, I wanted to research the possibility of introducing a non-lethal sealing industry. We found that the shedding pups yielded a large quantity of material per seal and enjoyed the physical removal of the itchy hairs. We packed up 70 bags of cruelty-free fur and shipped it to Prince Edward Island to be cleaned, carded and spun into two-ply yarn.

Then off by helicopter from the snow-shrouded shores of the Îles de Madeleines to Newfoundland for my scheduled appearance in the Newfoundland courts.

The preliminary hearing in St. John's, Newfoundland, lasted three days. The crown prosecutor, Colin Flynn, paraded some 20 witnesses before the court at considerable taxpayer expense. The captain of the Cuban vessel was flown in. Peter Brown came up on a first-class ticket from Los Angeles — the Mounties gave him $2,000 for his time. They also flew in Malcolm Dunlop from Halifax; the Halifax Registrar of Shipping, Jens Trygstad, who sold us the ship; and an RCMP chemical expert to identify our stink bombs as containing butyric acid. A posse of Mounties and a handful of Coast Guard "experts" and Fisheries officers rounded out the strategy of the Crown.

I marvelled at the expense the government was going to in their attempt to prosecute me for trying to protect the cod. The entire affair was ludicrous. Our film evidence demonstrated no contact between my ship and the Cuban dragger. There was no property damage and no injuries. Still, the government of Canada was taking no chances. We had embarrassed the politicians by doing something that they had only talked about doing. While they were talking tough, we had actually acted. Those who only talk usually detest those who actually do. By the end of the preliminary hearing, it was obvious that the motivation behind the charges was purely political. Despite this, the judge ordered the charges to proceed to trial at a future date to be decided.

If they hoped to keep me quiet and out of trouble by proceeding with the trial, they were wrong. I immediately called a media conference at the Hotel Newfoundland and announced that the Sea Shepherd Conservation Society would give Prime Minister Jean Chrétien until July 1, 1994, to fulfill his campaign promise to stop foreign overfishing off the Grand Banks. If he did not, we would return and we would intentionally cut the trawl lines on every dragger we encountered.

I was not about to have the government of Canada control our actions with threats and harassment. That which does not kill can only serve to strengthen resolve.

The day after the media conference, I appeared in court to answer to the six charges under the Canada Shipping Act. Again, the government ferried in a slew of expert witnesses from Halifax, including many of the top brass from the Coast Guard. Two of the charges were against me directly and the other four were against the *Cleveland Amory*. The charges were summary, and therefore I had no choice but to throw myself before the mercy of a provincial judge.

The swivel-servant bureaucrats acted like they were testifying at a major murder trial. Most of them carried the rank of captain and seemed outraged that I had sullied our mutual rank by my actions the summer before. In their eyes, I was a pirate, a flagrant violator of rules and a dangerous fanatic. They expressed their outrage about my acting on my beliefs outside of any established authority. In demonstrating my willingness to act, I was lower than a drug trafficker or a child-molester in their opinion. When citizens empower themselves, bureaucrats are rendered impotent. This lot testifying against me acted like their very manhood had been put at risk because of what I had done.

Charge number one was certainly dastardly: I was accused of failure to have the proper charts and publications on board. This was Captain Robert Turner's particularly petty piece of revenge. It was easily countered. I did in fact have the proper charts and books and I presented receipts bearing the chart numbers and titles. Evidence was also presented that the RCMP had removed a great amount of materials, including some charts and books. Despite Captain Turner's threat that he would have my ass, I was acquitted.

Charge number two was ultra-serious in the opinion of the Coast Guard: I had failed to abide by Canadian Coast Guard regulations by taking a Canadian-registered ship to sea without the necessary Coast Guard paperwork authorizing me to sail as master of my own ship.

The prosecutor addressed me on the stand. "Captain Watson. Did Captain McDavit of the Coast Guard in Halifax present you with copies of the regulations concerning the required qualifications for a Canadian-flagged vessel?"

"He did," I answered.

"But you left Halifax despite this, did you not?"

"I did," I answered.

"So, you admit that you saw the regulations and you admit to sailing despite the fact that you were aware of the regulations saying that you could not."

"I admit to doing so."

The prosecutor smiled. "So, Captain Watson, how do you justify your actions in deliberately ignoring regulations presented to you by the Canadian Coast Guard?"

"My ship was registered as a yacht; therefore I was fully qualified to take command according to the Canada Shipping Act."

"Captain Watson, you have admitted to seeing the regulations, and the regulations state that a yacht over 100 tons must comply with compulsory Canadian master mariner's certification."

"Yes, that's correct." I answered. "The regulations do in fact state such to be the case. However, the Canadian Shipping Act is a statute and thus an Act of Parliament. The statute does not impose limitations of size on a yacht. According to the statute, the regulations are not enforceable. The Canadian Coast Guard does not have the power to pass regulations that contradict an Act of Parliament. I did disobey the regulations but not the statute, therefore I believe that I am not guilty of violating the Canada Shipping Act in this respect."

The judge agreed that I was correct in my interpretation of the statute taking precedence over the law. However, he said, we were involved in a protest, and protest was not an activity engaged in by a yacht. He ordered a fine against me of $5,000.

On the four charges concerning the ship, all of which concerned close manoeuvres against the Cuban dragger, one charge was dropped and the verdict of the judge on the other four was guilty. A fine of $10,000 on each count was imposed.

I immediately filed for an appeal on the conviction against me. The judge had no right to determine the registered status of a ship based on the activity of a ship. The ship was registered as a yacht; therefore it was a yacht. Besides, my crew and I were not paid and it could be properly argued that the activity engaged in was for pleasure, since it was our pleasure to do so. It was certainly my pleasure to have harassed the Cubans.

The $30,000 fine was not of any real concern. It was a fine against the *Cleveland Amory* and the ship was responsible, not her former owners. Having sold off the ship in anticipation of just this outcome, I had no disappointments. The fines were simply an indication to me of the political nature of the events of last summer. My ship had not touched the Cubans, no property was damaged and there were no injuries. How this justified a $30,000 fine was a mystery to me. It was, however, academic and a shallow victory for the government against us.

The media in Canada did not see the fine as remarkable. In fact, there was little comment concerning the case. This was something that I had become used to with the Canadian media. However, a phone call on the day of the verdict, April 11, 1994, concerned me. Glenn Bohn, the environment reporter for the *Vancouver Sun*, contacted me for a response to the latest Canadian Department of Fisheries and Oceans propaganda blitz against me — conveniently well-timed, I might add, to distract attention from the Newfoundland case. Not content to let the *Sea Shepherd II* rest, they accused me of transporting rare Mediterranean mussels to Vancouver Island. The exotic mollusks had entered Ucluelet harbour attached to the bottom of my ship, they said, and now the west coast of Vancouver Island was being devastated by a plague of the foreign critters.

Glenn obviously believed the government's story, despite the fact that the accusation came two years after I had retired my ship and despite the fact that the *Sea Shepherd II* had never been in the Med and had been in the waters of the North Pacific and the west coast of North America for two years prior to our entry, in August 1992, into the waters of Vancouver Island. In that time, thousands of vessels had entered the same waters. Nonetheless, we were responsible, said Bohn's government contacts.

I told Glenn that if people condemned me for such nonsense then so be it. We could not be distressed at every ludicrous accusation that the government dreamt up and the media repeated in their never-ending quest for filth and intrigue. I did have our attorney Kim Roberts contact the *Vancouver Sun* to let them know that we believed the story was false and that if they printed it without confirmation of the facts, I would sue.

A few days later it was revealed that the mussels in question were indeed an exotic species but had been on the west coast of the island for decades. It was also revealed that a government scientist quoted in the article had made no statement to the *Sun* supporting the allegations fabricated by the Department of Fisheries and Oceans. With great reluctance, the *Sun* was forced to publish a retraction of the accusations a year later.

In the summer of 1994, we acquired two new vessels, the 236-foot (70 m) *Whales Forever* and a two-person submarine we named *Mirage*. We set forth to challenge the pirate whalers of Norway and found ourselves in a face-off with Norway's largest warship, the *Andenes*. Despite being rammed, shot at and depth charged, I managed to outmaneuver the Norwegians. In addition to humiliating their navy, we ensured, once again, that their security costs exceeded their profits from illegal whaling.

Bruised, battered and scarred, the *Whales Forever* limped into Lerwick harbour in the Shetland Islands. We had stood alone against the Norwegian navy. We had won.

By the summer of 1995, I was finally given a trial day of September 12. Ironically, on March 7, 1995, the Canadian minister of fisheries and oceans, Brian Tobin, was being lauded as a hero and patriot for arresting a Spanish trawler outside the 200-mile limit. Adding insult to injury, some of the Canadian media, including the *Toronto Sun*, the *Calgary Herald* and the television commentator Mike Duffy, were denouncing me for not being there to rescue cod and turbot. In 1993 the government and media had called me a pirate. In 1995 some European Union members were calling Tobin a pirate, and Canadian editorials were demanding to know why I wasn't on the Grand Banks protecting fish stocks.

Unfortunately, I was prohibited by Canadian law from returning to the Banks.

September 1995 saw me in the prisoner's box of the Newfoundland Supreme Court at the beginning of what would be a four-week trial. I admitted to having interfered with Cuban and Spanish trawlers, and claimed justification as my defense. My attorney, Brian Casey, argued that my belief in the United Nations Charter for Nature justified my actions. Some two dozen Crown witnesses took three and a half weeks to present their case, then the defense side wrapped up in two days with testimony from me alone.

The jury accepted my defense and acquitted me of the two serious charges of mischief endangering life. They found me guilty on a minor mischief charge for aiding and abetting the tossing of a stink bomb onto the deck of the Cuban trawler.

Having spent $3.5 million on my arrest and another million on my trial, the government succeeded only in winning a conviction on a minor charge that carried a thirty-five dollar fine. The angry Crown prosecutor demanded I be given a year in prison. Judge Derek Green felt bound to make an example of me and attached a thirty-day jail sentence to the fine "to send a message that interference with over-fishing must not be tolerated."

I appealed both the conviction and the sentence. Crown prosecutor Colin Flynn appealed my acquittal on the two most serious charges. And the legal battle continues. Meanwhile, the Spanish owners of the *Estai* laid charges against Brian Tobin for piracy and malicious prosecution. My conviction on the minor charge set a precedent that the Spanish could use against the minister. To prove that what Canada had done to them was illegal under Canada's own laws, the Spanish pointed out that Canada had charged, prosecuted and convicted one of its own citizens for doing exactly what the government had done itself.

The federal government had weaved a tangled and costly web, and I was relieved, in October 1995, to find myself clear of any serious repercussions. Clear and ready to carry on with the fight on the high seas to protect everything from corals to the great whales.

We have whales to save in the North Atlantic from the Norwegians, Russians, Faeroese and Icelanders. There are cod fish to save on the Grand Banks of New-foundland. We must return soon to challenge the whalers in the North Pacific and then head south to intercept the Japanese Antarctic fleet at the bottom of the world. Along the way will be Caribbean turtle poachers, Costa Rican shark poach-ers, Mexican manta ray killers, outlawed pelagic drift-netters, renegade Ameri-can dolphin-killing tuna seiners and, of course, their various official protection agencies operating under the guise of navies, coast guard and policing agencies.

There is never any rest on planetary duty.

Epilogue

here are many people who say that what we do is futile, that there is no way to stop the rising tide of human-spawned destruction. There are many who condemn my crew and I for taking the law into our own hands and for taking on the barons of corporate profit. There are some who would like to see us jailed, or even dead, so blinded are they to the conceit and folly of their own anthropocentrism.

I don't care. I do what I do because it is the right thing to do. I have never worried about winning or losing.

I am a warrior and it is the way of the warrior to fight against superior odds even when victory is no more than a dream. I have no illusions. I know that the rate of extinction on this Earth increases daily. This knowledge makes me angry. As a warrior, I cherish my anger, because it is anger that gives me courage and strengthens my resolve. The spectre of extinction, the prospect of diminishment, the certainty of a biological holocaust make me strong.

And yet there is hope. Perhaps, just perhaps, our efforts will buy a little time and a little space. My friend Edward Abbey once said, "Life is cruel, but compared to what?" He was right. Life is what we must cling to; there is no alternative.

Happily, my small hope that life will triumph is not merely theoretical or imaginary. When I looked into the eye of a whale, I could no longer be bothered with the trivialities of a self-absorbed humanity. I have seen the black, teary eyes of harp seals and the tortured red eyes of an oil-covered cormorant that stood dying in a pool of black filth. What I saw there has given me the strength to overcome my own anthropocentrism. I have refused to side with humanity in her war against the Earth.

I fully expect to be killed one day by one of my own species. A whaler, sealer, shark poacher or member of the crew on a drift-netter or drag trawler will kill me. Or it may be a government agent acting as the hired thug of a corporation. But the only thing that matters to me is that I use my life to save lives, protect species and conserve habitat. By doing so, I know that I can make a difference, and perhaps inspire others who will also make a difference.

I am not competing in a popularity contest. On the contrary: it is my function as an ecological activist to say things that people don't want to hear and to do things that people don't want to see done. I am trying to be what I wish my ancestors had been. I wish that there had been someone around to defend the great auk, the Labrador duck and the Biscayan right whale — all long gone. I am here to defend the species that might otherwise go the way they have gone, for the sake of my children and my children's children.

My work may amount to no more than a ripple on the ocean's surface. But there have been others who have made ripples before me. Rachel Carson and John Muir, Jules Verne and Farley Mowat, Dian Fossey and Richard Leakey have all disturbed the waters in their time. My own ripple will join theirs, and together they will become wavelets and waves, and eventually, perhaps, thundering surf crashing upon the rocks of human ignorance and selfishness.

My belief that the ripples will grow and multiply gives me confidence. That, and the simple satisfaction that comes from seizing drift nets, sinking whalers, ramming mechanized fish factories and destroying other weapons that have been used in the assault on nature. The thrill of saving lives, of knowing that a whale will sire, a seal pup thrive and a species survive for another few years, gives me a reason to go on.

Above all, in spite of everything that has been said or done to me, since July 16, 1979, the day I rammed the *Sierra*, I have been a happy man.

Index